NO EXCUSE LEADERSHIP

NO EXCUSE
LEADERSHIP

lessons from the
U.S. Army's
Elite Rangers

BRACE E. BARBER

WILEY

JOHN WILEY & SONS, INC.

Portions of this book were previously published in *Ranger School, No Excuse Leadership* by Patrol Leader Press, April 2000.

Published by John Wiley & Sons, Inc., Hoboken, New Jersey.
Published simultaneously in Canada.

For general information on our other products and services please contact our Customer Care Department within the United States at (800) 762-2974, outside the United States at (317) 572-3993 or fax (317) 572-4002.

Wiley also publishes its books in a variety of electronic formats. Some content that appears in print may not be available in electronic books. For more information about Wiley products, visit our web site at www.wiley.com.

Library of Congress Cataloging-in-Publication Data:
No excuse leadership: lessons from the U.S. Army's elite Rangers/ [edited by] Brace E. Barber.
    p. cm.
Includes bibliographical reference and index.
    ISBN 0-471-48803-8 (CLOTH)
  1. Leadership. 2. Management. 3. United States. Army—Commando troops. I. Barber, Brace E.
   HD57.7.N6 2004
   658.4'092—dc21   2003014086

Printed in the United States of America.

10 9 8 7 6 5 4 3 2 1

To my daughter, Tess Jenevieve Barber,
whose death at birth on June 13, 1998,
inspired me to put my pent-up energy
of anticipated fatherhood into another dream.

Contents

Foreword

Rangers lead the way. Rangers have led the way throughout history and were anointed with the motto "Rangers lead the way" from their lead in getting the V corps GIs off the bloody beaches of Omaha during World War II on June 6, 1944, D-Day. Rangers have led and will continue to lead the way because of their mental and physical toughness developed during Ranger training. It is harsh, demanding, and relentless training, which produces a warrior-leader who sets the example for others, always leading the way. Proven throughout history, these training standards are still followed today. Roger's Rangers raids during the French and Indian War; Darby's Rangers up front in North Africa, Sicily, and Italy; Merrill's Marauders' exploits in Burma; the extraordinary feats of Ranger Battalions at Normandy and in the Philippines; Ranger companies always fighting out front and outnumbered during the Korean War; Ranger LRRP (Long Range Reconnaissance Patrol) teams operating throughout the jungles of Vietnam; and up through the present day, Ranger Battalions accomplishing daring objectives in Grenada, Panama, "Desert Storm," Somalia, Afghanistan, and "Iraqi Freedom" all were, and continue to be, successful because of the reliable and tough leadership base established during Ranger training. Ranger training makes a good soldier better. It is the finest leader training in the U.S. Army, providing a base of toughness, dependability, and resolve essential to combat leadership. Today, Ranger training is provided by the U.S. Army's Ranger School, which awards the coveted Ranger tab to those who make the cut.

Brace Barber captures the commitment required for this hard and painful challenge of becoming a U.S. Army Ranger and the leadership value the training provides our officers, NCOs, and finest enlisted soldiers. He covers the essence of Ranger training in his comprehensive book *No Excuse Leadership: Lessons from the U.S. Army's Elite Rangers*. Ranger training has never been easy, and Brace explains what it takes to become a Ranger in today's forces. He highlights the essential component—stress—in training a leader to survive and to ensure his troops survive in combat; and why lack of food and sleep, continuous mission requirements, physical exhaustion and mental anguish, peer pressure, and teamwork integrated throughout Ranger training provide everything a soldier needs for war. Ranger School provides it all, aside from maybe the true fear that one must deal with under fire.

Ranger Barber brought back memories of my experiences as a second lieutenant 33 years ago during my training to become a U.S. Army Ranger—an achievement and distinction I wanted more than any other during my 30 years of service. I remember my ups and downs throughout the training, the emotional stress from failing a patrol (and passing one), pulling up my bootstraps and surviving injuries, the camaraderie developed in my Ranger squad, friendships forged from shared hardships, the value of teamwork, understanding that a GI could never get the sleep one needs during operations, always being hungry, and the elation of receiving the coveted black and gold Ranger tab.

Ranger training is not only inculcated throughout the Army, but Ranger veterans in the private sector also manifest it. Business leaders who have experienced Ranger training and service adapt rapidly to stressful situations, ambiguity, and uncertain environments. They bring to the business entity people who are reliable, tough, and determined, with a work ethic and duty mind-set cherished in the market economy. The Ranger standard and example setting continue outside of the armed forces.

Ranger training provided me with a bedrock of leadership principles, toughness, and a can-do attitude I carried throughout my military service. It did not matter if I was serving with Airborne or Air Assault; Light, Heavy, or Ranger Infantry; with Special Forces or Delta Force, it *always* provided that base of discipline, dependability, and toughness required to fight on to the objective and win.

Ranger Barber provides what you need to know and what you need to do to wear the Ranger tab. Read his book—and win.

—Brigadier General David Grange, retired

Acknowledgments

For the desire to go beyond, I thank God.

For the time to pursue *No Excuse Leadership*, and her constant belief in me, I thank my very special wife Natasha.

For an experience worth writing about, I thank all of the Ranger Instructors, both past and present.

For their willingness to test themselves and then allow me to candidly tell their stories, I thank Eric Faulkner, Lance Bagley, Eric Werner, W. John Hutt, David Stockwell, Steve Adams, Mark Chandler, Scott Sharp, and Colonel Robert "Tex" Turner.

For editing, I thank Kele Smith, Trista Wickstrum, Arthur Rizer, Bill Gameros, and Natasha Barber. For additional edits to this edition, I thank Larry Olson at John Wiley & Sons. For postpublication editing, I thank Patrick Gargan, William Schwartz, and many others.

For support of this project while it was just an idea and in its early development I thank Paul Voorhees of Ranger Joe's in Columbus, Georgia (as large a part of Ranger School history as is Hollis Creek). Thanks to Ranger Jim Tully and everyone at Orion International (they guided me through the minefield of exiting the military). Thanks to Ellen Mohrman of the West Point Bookstore (a rare, gentle person who can keep this Ranger in check). Thanks to Ranger Pete Neves of Milspec Group, Inc. (a Web presence worthy of a loud "Hoo-ah!"). Finally, thanks to Ranger Bill "Peg Leg" Spies. If I had my choice of point man it would be Bill—a personal hero and founder of Worldwide Army Rangers (WAR).

About the Author

Brace E. Barber is cofounder of Tax Recovery Group, Inc. and The Tax Firm, Inc. He is a 1987 graduate of West Point and 1988 graduate of the U.S. Army Ranger School. Through 11 years of distinguished military service, he led three combat arms platoons and two companies. He performed various other leadership and staff functions in locations as diverse as South Korea, Thailand, Honduras, Alaska, and Hawaii. He is a charter member of Worldwide Army Rangers (WAR) and a lifetime member of the U.S. Army Ranger Association (USARA).

NO EXCUSE LEADERSHIP

Introduction

Use your time wisely! Watch the first 20 minutes of the movie so the rest of the plot makes sense. Yes, even if you miss the beginning, the explosions, car chases, and narrow escapes will still be entertaining, but you won't completely know why they are happening. Use your time wisely! Read the first 20 pages of this book and you will add enormously to your experience.

No Excuse Leadership illustrates for leaders in all fields how to lead and succeed in difficult circumstances by using the leadership principles that the U.S. Army Ranger School experience helps people develop and that anyone can strive to master. Through the true stories of Ranger School graduates the book highlights these principles and also provides a comprehensive, ground-level description of Ranger School.

No Excuse Leadership is about personal foundations for individual leaders, and it is about providing a surprising and enlightening perspective on proven leadership principles and giving leaders concrete examples of how they work. It is not about transferring the military culture to a business! There is no reason you would want to. The language isn't pretty, and people with fragile sensitivities don't last. However, what businesses need today are people who understand why organizations like the Army Rangers succeed magnificently at their missions. They need to know the characteristics that shape these individuals and organizations and how they breed success. *No Excuse Leadership* gives readers a foundation of principles, purposes, and attitudes that they can begin using immediately to impact the long-term success of themselves and their organizations.

No Excuse Leadership will prompt you to be better and encourage you and your organization to enter into a campaign of improvement. There is no opting out of the leadership decision. You either develop yourself and your leaders through purposeful, planned effort or you choose the alternative—suboptimum performance and profit. In today's elbow-throwing world, you need every advantage. Latent leadership potential is your gold mine and will provide your future margin of victory.

You live your professional life in competition. From the time you leave your driveway in the morning you are competing. You secretly race three cars on your way to work because for a moment in time, keeping them from changing lanes in front of you is all you can think about. You are competing with your coworkers for the recognition of your boss and the next promotion. Your department is competing with other departments for projects, attention, and money. You are competing with the other bidders for the next contract. You are competing with other businesses for customers' money. It is a tiring life and one that can wear you down if you are using trial and error to search for methods that create success. Leave chance to someone else as you adopt a No Excuse philosophy.

Truly, winning *is* the name of the game. It means a better lifestyle for you, financial security, status, and corporate and community power. To win you must change the way you approach day-to-day situations. You must have the courage to choose the harder right over the easier wrong. In the service, the easier wrong means that your son dies in the mud; in business it means at least the loss of long-term competitiveness, at the worst appearing before a congressional hearing. You must change the way you look at failure. Doing so is as simple as not accepting it for any reason.

In this Introduction I will run through four areas that are essential to understanding the full concept of the book: Rangers, patrolling, principles, and people. Even if you are familiar with all of these areas, you'll want to continue on because my M16 is zeroed a little differently than yours—it is important to note my settings.

Rangers

Recently Rangers have been portrayed in movies like *Black Hawk Down, Basic, Con Air*, and *Saving Private Ryan*. U.S. Army Rangers have such a reputation for steadfastness in the face of danger and dedication to pure American values that the makers of these movies used them to create an image and set the stage for the entire movie.

In *Con Air*, Nicholas Cage is the idealistic good guy who excelled in the "hero producing" opportunities that the Ranger Battalion gave him. He had more strength than intellect and an iron will set on doing what was right regardless of the circumstances.

In *Saving Private Ryan*, the bloody scenes are strung together by a group of Rangers with an almost robotic dedication to getting the job done. In battle there is never a doubt about the focus of the soldiers: take the objective. In between the action we see the real side of each person, the bravado, the stoicism, and the fear. Each person is a real person put into unreal circumstances, and they all perform their duty without question.

Which characterization, *Con* or *Ryan*, is closer to the truth? There is a mixture of both. The Ranger mind-set and beliefs are developed in an organizational culture that demands strict discipline and high standards in constant preparation for the day the soldier will stand in the gap, leading the way. Ranger School is the rite of passage into this world. Primarily those who accept the challenge of becoming a Ranger are soldiers and officers from the U.S. Army, but all of the services and many foreign countries have sent representatives to the training. The constitution of a common Ranger School class is a mixture ranging from young second lieutenants fresh from Infantry Officer Basic Course (IOBC), PFCs and specialists from the Ranger Battalions, and sergeants and staff sergeants from various infantry units across the Army. Today there are real people with traits of all of these movie characters in the Ranger Regiment, throughout the armed services, in the corporate sector, and in your neighborhood.

The Rangers have lived high standards of selfless service, integrity, and hard work without waver since their inception. They are Americans who do not tolerate self-serving individuals, and they treasure America's freedom beyond their lives. These are the people you will get to know in this book.

Well, what are these Rangers going to do for you? One of the most powerful ways to develop a specific habit or skill is by associating with people who have that habit or skill. In this book you will associate with Ranger School students. If you want to develop the habit of perseverance, the trait of personal mental strength, the ability to work and succeed under difficult circumstances, it is important to know what they look like in practice, and these people will show you. They set an example that is unrivaled, short of combat; and even then, minus the fear factor, these guys take personal achievement to the limit. When you read their stories, you will change your expectations of yourself and your organization. You are capable of so much more.

It is imperative that each of us discovers that we are capable of achieving more. Our perception of difficult comes as a result of our frame of reference. The current struggle is put into perspective compared to all the other struggles of our lives. We were all normal people going through Ranger School. In the process we each have given ourselves a new standard for difficult, one to which we can now refer all of our future challenges. Ranger School graduates are the type of people who get things done under all circumstances. They are set up to be great leaders because they know themselves and their limits and can help others push theirs.

As a leader, you will face those inevitable times in your organization when you must brace for turbulent weather, be ready for heavy workloads, and prepare for unforeseen troubles. You will have to rely on yourself, and, more importantly, your workforce to see you through. In this book, you will see the kind of person you have to be in those difficult times. You will discover the mind-set that made people successful in Ranger School and the difference between those who simply survived and those who thrived.

Patrolling

There are many different ways to illustrate leadership, from business to military to political examples and many more. I have selected one, the U.S. Army Ranger School, the premiere *leadership school* in the Army. I use Ranger School to draw these lessons from because the successful completion of Ranger School is extraordinary. It is a situation of duress over an extended period of time, 61 days, that exposes how to succeed as an individual and as a leader in times of stress to achieve high goals. Ranger School graduates succeed in difficult circumstances because they operate using the leadership principles that make high accomplishments possible.

In the same way I am using events from Ranger School to illustrate leadership principles, Ranger School itself uses patrolling as the facilitator to teach and evaluate. The school uses patrolling because it is the most common denominator of military operations: men with weapons and an objective. The majority of the situations you will read about take place in the framework of doing patrols.

To imagine a patrol, think of 11 men, one behind the other, walking down the road. Ten yards separate each of them, and they are dressed in military-issue battle dress uniforms (BDUs) with their faces camouflaged in green, brown, and black. Their BDUs are stripped of all insignia except their names and "U.S. Army" patches—nothing differentiates officer from enlisted. They each have a large rucksack—a backpack that matches the Ranger's uniform and is about half the size and weight of his body. Each person carries an M16 rifle at waist level, one finger near the trigger, and one or two have an M60 machine gun. On their heads are patrol caps, and on their feet are green and black jungle boots. Take that picture and put them in the middle of a forest, swamp, or desert. They walk methodically, each rotating a bit to either side to observe the landscape around them, looking for the enemy. With some variations, this is what a patrol looks like.

Now that you have a picture, consider also that they must have a mission, a reason for doing this. In brief terms, the objectives are a reconnaissance, an ambush, or a raid. The purpose of a reconnaissance mission is to bring back detailed information on a specific site or area without being detected by the enemy. Rangers find themselves crawling through the underbrush to good vantage points all around the site. This mission can take a long time because of the stealth involved.

The purpose of an ambush is to surprise and destroy a moving enemy. It is the setting up and springing of a trap. We would set up positions along a road or trail the enemy commonly uses, usually in an area he considers safe, behind his lines, then wait for him to move by. We would sometimes wait for hours, quietly hidden just a few meters off the road. When the enemy came into our sights, completely covered by our weapons, we would begin firing. We would then attack across the road to complete the job, secure the area, and gather intelligence from the enemy.

The raid is the opposite of an ambush, comprised of a moving attack force and a stationary target. A raid objective might be a command post or radio tower. We would move to that location, set up our forces, and attack across the objective in a rapid, deadly manner.

The planning of these missions is virtually identical except for the actions on the objective and the required equipment. So, as you picture the patrol, understand that the Rangers have a specific purpose for moving to where they are going. It is understood that they are behind enemy lines and must maintain constant vigilance, even while resting. There are leaders responsible for every aspect of the plan—preparation, execution, and sustainment of the mission. They are the ones being graded by the Ranger Instructors (RIs). Ranger School increases the difficulty of the missions as the course progresses by enlarging the patrols from 11 to 44 people and by using more difficult missions to plan, going from reconnaissance to raid patrols.

The school also varies the environment where these patrols take place. No terrain is necessarily more difficult than the other, but the change keeps life from getting too comfortable for the students in any aspect. The first phase is conducted at Fort Benning, Georgia, and consists of City Week and Camp Darby. City Week is the first five days, followed by a week or more in patrolling basics at Camp Darby. The second phase is the mountain phase, which is conducted outside of Dahlonega, Georgia. There has been some variation in the order of the final two phases, the swamp phase and desert phase. The swamp phase at Eglin AFB, Florida, is always present and has typically been the final location. At times, however, while it existed, the desert phase at Dugway Proving Grounds, Utah, could have been the next to last or final phase of the course. No matter the terrain or location, we were learning and being tested.

Using patrolling as its maneuver, Ranger School is able to train and evaluate leaders in positions of increasing difficulty and under conditions of extreme stress. What I have done is take the same situations and used them to help you discover leadership lessons and encourage self-analysis and improvement. We're getting down to the nitty-gritty now. The purpose of *No Excuse Leadership* is to help us *all* be better leaders. To put all of those lessons into an understandable framework, we organize them into principles and focus on two very important ways of doing business that will aid in your future success.

Principles

The *Ranger Handbook* is an essential reference for every Ranger School student, probably the only book all of us carried. It is primarily a set of checklists for missions and tasks. Mine is covered on the front and back with camouflaged duct tape and is bound at the top by a plastic lock-tight strip through the two binder holes. It stayed with me throughout the school, neatly stashed in the top flap of my rucksack for easy access. Chapter 1 starts out with leadership.

> Wars are fought and won by men, not machines. The primary function of tactical leaders is to induce soldiers to do difficult things in dangerous, stressful circumstances.

You are fighting a different war.

> Business is won by people, not machines. The primary function of business leaders is to induce people to do difficult things in pressure-filled, stressful circumstances.

To think that you are in anything less than a business war is to accept mediocrity, and ultimately this will lead to your enterprise's demise.

Through experience and study, the U.S. Army has established a set of Principles of Leadership. These are the principles that Rangers must master in order to survive on the violent and rapidly unfolding forward edge of combat. These are the same principles that apply to the entire army, but we are talking about the instruction and implementation of these principles under extreme conditions, where they truly shine as foundational precepts. When applied properly, they will easily differentiate you and your organization in a positive way, allowing you to survive and succeed on your chosen battlefields.

- Seek responsibility and take it for your actions.
- Know yourself and seek self-improvement.
- Make sound and timely decisions.
- Be technically and tactically proficient.
- Train your soldiers as a team.
- Set the example.
- Know your soldiers and look out for their well-being.
- Employ your unit in accordance with its capabilities.
- Develop a sense of responsibility in your subordinates.
- Keep your soldiers informed.
- Ensure that the task is understood, supervised, and accomplished.

No list of leadership or success principles should be considered comprehensive. Each person and team hunting for these principles will phrase the points differently, depending on the person's personality or the organization's culture and purpose. They will, however, cover the same ground and attempt to produce the same successful results.

The same way no list of leadership principles is comprehensive, no one experience or school will teach every principle equally well, and Ranger School is no exception. The principles taught and reinforced at Ranger School are the most important ones, and the ones that will help you clearly stand out from your peers in any situation. Here, I will focus on two: *Seek responsibility and take it for your actions* and *Know yourself and seek self-improvement.* These two principles are the common thread that binds all of the stories together. I don't hang a sign on every instance where someone took responsibility or learned something about themselves. I chose to let the subjects speak about their own insights instead of inserting my commentary; however, it is important to explore the two main principles in more detail.

The first principle is to seek responsibility and take it for your actions. It is easy to differentiate yourself from other people and your organization from other organizations. As the saying goes, "Watch what direction the majority is going, and go the opposite way." If even a good minority of the people would embrace and act in accordance with certain basic precepts, they would turn their life around as individuals; but more importantly, they would begin to remake the United States of America into a country with its priorities straight. One idea in particular will make a difference (it was a way of life at West Point and reinforced at Ranger School), the idea of absolute responsibility for yourself and the people you lead as expressed in the response, "No Excuse."

As a leader, you take responsibility for the success or failure of a job. You pass credit for accomplishment to the team and accept responsibility for a failure, regardless of the reason. You have to cut yourself off from excuses and focus on solutions. This idea of not giving excuses or reasons is perhaps the most misunderstood and difficult concept to grasp for most people. This is not a zero-defect mentality. The fact that you stop the reasons at your level and pass on to your boss the statement "There is a delay, but a solution is in hand" is continuing to maintain leadership of, and responsibility for, your team. If, however, a superior's support or guidance is needed, it should be sought.

The first time you stop yourself from giving a perfectly legitimate reason why the job did not get done will be tough; but do it, and then do it again. Emotionally, you have burned your bridges and must now succeed. You will see yourself start to succeed beyond your peers who allow themselves reasons to fail. Remember, "No Excuse."

Notice, as you read the following chapters, the self-determination and lack of excuses you hear from those who succeeded. Imagine the effect the philosophy of "No Excuse" will have on your life. What if you incorporated this into your life and job?

The second most important principle is knowledge of yourself and seeking self-improvement. If you have never pushed yourself, how can you know what you are capable of? How can you know what others are capable of? Many people in leadership positions are afraid to test the physical and mental limits of their organizations because they do not know if they themselves can handle the stress. If you are attempting to get more out of your subordinates, doesn't it make sense that you should know how to motivate them to do more? You should be able to draw on your past experiences to find what motivated you to substantially exceed the standard and translate that to your employees to get them to do substantially more than the standard.

You must learn your limits. Through the process of testing yourself you will also build self-esteem, which is essential in a leader. Self-esteem does not come from always succeeding. It comes from achieving a tough goal. It comes from the natural comparison a person makes between himself or herself and the person who did not succeed. This is not a judgment of the other person. It simply gives value to the achievement and to the person who achieved it.

We tend to minimize that type of experience as it relates to future accomplishments; however, it does have an impact because of perspective and expectancy. Someone without that level of experience may look at a challenge and say, "This might be the hardest thing I've ever had to do." There is a standpoint of doubt and possible failure, and a fear of learning where our limits lie. That is a decidedly different perspective on life than what a Ranger-qualified person has. "This is hard and this is tough, but, you know, I've been through something that is harder than this." It is a position of confidence and belief with an expectation of success.

In today's society the trend is to equalize everyone, to downplay the exceptional in order to protect the feelings of the vast average. Protecting the feelings of these people can be read as trying to protect their self-esteem. That philosophy is counter to human nature, considering that people don't have self-esteem until they earn it for themselves through struggling and succeeding. It doesn't come from a parent telling their children they are great or everyone passing the history exam with a score of 100 percent. What good is a competition if everyone wins, or if you win but your opponent was not trying or was designed to lose? My parents told me I was the best all the time, but I didn't believe it until I proved it to myself through a series of difficult accomplishments that not everyone was able to finish. What my parents did by the positive reinforcement was give me the motivation to try, and that is where they did a great job.

Ranger School has value because it is a challenge that only the minority of people achieve. It teaches a person about himself under conditions of stress augmented by the lack of food, sleep, information, and in the case of winter classes, warmth. When a person achieves the success of graduation, he knows he is a person of endurance and he knows his physical and mental limits since he has been much closer to them than most people will ever be. At Ranger School he was pushed by an outside force, the RI, and an internal goal to graduate. Because he, *himself*, went beyond *his* known limits, he knows people are able to do much more than they naturally push themselves to do. He is able to be the outside force that pushes, like the RI, and the help others need to develop internal goals. He can then work alongside them to accomplish those goals.

If you have never challenged yourself beyond your known limits, either physically or mentally, I suggest you find an area you desire to push yourself in and set a goal in that area that will stretch you for an extended period of time. Try something like a 10-kilometer run if you have never run before, or achieving the top grade in your graduate school class, or losing those extra pounds through exercise and discipline, or quitting smoking or some other nasty habit. You must learn about yourself.

Whatever goal you set, if it is high enough and hard enough, by definition, you must question yourself somewhere along the way: "Do I really want to do this? Is the reward that great?" You will rationalize how little you want the reward, and you must think about how much easier it would be if you were to rest, if only for a little while. If you do that, you are pushing yourself. If you quit, you quit; you lose for now. If you continue to try, you are among the minority. If you continue to quit, you are part of the majority. It does not matter what excuse you make. They all have the same result—failure. If you continue to try and you succeed, you are part of the elite, a winner.

These high goals give you the opportunity to develop the habit of making the right decisions in times of duress. The point you must remember is that in order to continue to be a winner you must continue to set higher and higher goals and accomplish them. Please do not ever rest on your laurels. Your competition is with yourself, not the person next to you. The person who displays persistence and consistence will win every time. Over time, dripping water wears down the rock.

The lack of perseverance is what causes most people to quit. Perseverance is not tested in good times; it is tested in times of stress. Ranger School tests each person's resolve to achieve graduation, but even more importantly, it tests each person's resolve to get up each and every day. As each day passes, more and more people forget about the goal, graduation, and see only the distractions of comfort, warmth, food, and sleep. They fail to persevere and so they quit. This book will give you the standard for mental toughness. When you think you have it bad, remember somewhere—at Fort Benning, Georgia; Dahlonega, Georgia; or Eglin Air Force Base, Florida—there are Ranger School students experiencing new tests today and succeeding.

To sum up these principles, remember to seek responsibility and take it for your actions (No Excuse), and know yourself and seek self-improvement (Persevere). It is almost self-evident that conscientiously incorporating these two principles into your life will set you apart and help you succeed in whatever your venture is: athletic, military, political, business, or life. The lack of incorporation of these principles is the reason the majority fail. Remember, "Watch what direction the majority is going, and go the opposite way."

It is essential that you hold yourself to this standard, but as a leader in a nondictatorial organization you cannot force your team members to embrace this philosophy. You can only teach it and use it yourself as an example of doing what is right. This truth brings to light arguably the most important leadership principle: *Set the example*. Trying to force this philosophy on others is a losing game; it is something each individual must accept responsibility for himself or herself.

Enjoy the following chapters. They will expand and illuminate the concepts already put forth. Some of the stories in here are funny, others are disturbing, and still others are thought provoking. *All of them are true*. You will, no doubt, be entertained and enlightened. You will start to appreciate the necessities of life like running water, a soft bed, and dry clothes. Those of you with a very good imagination and ability to visualize will be scared, and I encourage all of you to put yourself into the shoes of these Rangers. Above all, I challenge you to think as a leader and see yourself leading these people. How would you do it?

People

Here is a brief snapshot of each soldier highlighted in this book to give you a picture of each person as you begin their tales. The men in these accounts represent many different backgrounds. They are anything but cookie-cutter infantry soldiers and officers, as you might expect.

Brace Barber. The author is already described in too much detail. Though I claim to be six feet tall, I'm a genuine five foot seven (and a half) inches tall and a buck 55 dripping wet. Like I tell my business partner, "You may be bigger than me, but I'm a better shot."

Robert "Tex" Turner. After a West Point briefing I wrote, "He is a broad-built individual. From stage he did not look very big but he always talked loud and had a permanent flattop haircut. He was something of a legend at West Point partially because of his Ranger manner and partially because we knew almost instinctively that he had accomplished some great things in his career and was respected throughout the Army as an authority."

Eric Faulkner. Eric lives the "No Excuse" motto. He is a revved-up 500 horsepower engine in neutral. It takes only a small decision to get him working full bore toward a goal. Eric's concentration makes you notice his eyes and their intensity. With his high and tight haircut you can almost miss his red hair, but you can't overlook his solid six-foot frame and military posture.

Mark Chandler. Mark has a keen intellect and is always ready for a good discussion of the issues. He has dark hair atop the body of a runner. Mark is a philosopher in training and takes pride in accomplishing a wide range of goals not normally seen on one resume. He often comments on being the first Vassar College graduate to finish Ranger School.

David Stockwell. Immediately you notice Dave's white hair. The first time I saw him I thought, "His face doesn't look that old." He is a thin man of average height and with much more strength per pound than most men. Dave is a driven and compassionate leader who puts his soldiers first.

Lance Bagley. Lance is six feet tall and constantly wearing a smile. He is an optimist, encouraged by a belief that he can innovate and turn any negative situation into a positive. Lance is full of life and excites people through his excitement.

Eric Werner. Eric is six foot five inches tall and 250 pounds—a bear of a man who stands out wherever he goes. Eric's size makes it impossible for him to hide. As a result of living life as a point of interest, Eric has gone with the flow and had fun with the attention. Eric continually does the unexpected, not to gain attention, but because he knows it is there; he teases the onlookers with intentionally different behavior. No matter what he undertakes, Eric does it with confidence and positive anticipation.

W. John Hutt. John is easily the quietest of the bunch. He is just over six feet tall and built like an infantryman, thin and fit. He is noticeably confident in the way he talks and walks, and impressively alert when conversing with you. He truly listens to your words, looking for how he can help you get what you want.

Scott Sharp. Scott has a casual, confident manner. He is just over six feet tall, built to wear the crossed rifles of the infantry. He has a commonsense approach to missions that makes him fun to be around. Scott emphasizes substance over style, preferring something that works over something that only looks good.

Steve Adams. Steve is a serious man with business in his eyes and intent in his broad shoulders. He is solidly built—a younger Tex Turner. Steve goes full speed ahead no matter what he is doing, working, or playing. People naturally respond to his enthusiasm and focus. Steve is ready to lead but also willing to follow and learn.

Why Barber's Story?

The original manuscript did not include my story. It is uncomfortable for me to have it told now. I struggle with the line between humility and pride and, more importantly, the perception of each by you, the reader. As you read about the characters you must know that the challenges we overcame, the impressions they made on us, and the lessons we learned from them are passed on with the hope that they can help you gain insight into your struggles and show you how to achieve success over them. It is also important for you to know about me as a person. Learning about where I've been and about some of my setbacks and accomplishments will enhance your encounter with the enclosed lessons. You will know that the point of view of the author is not one of an academic, but rather of a foot soldier like you.

My experiences and those of the other subjects of this book are not exceptional in the Ranger community. In fact, they are fairly average. Many people have suffered more and overcome more to achieve greater results. The truth still remains that these experiences *are* exceptional in our society. Through presenting them, we can illustrate leadership principles that are the bedrock of any successful person.

Goals

Before we get to the mud, the swamp, the cold, the sleep deprivation, and the starvation, let's acknowledge that people in and out of military uniform are not that different when it comes to money and financial security. There were only a handful of people that I met in my 15 years in uniform who were not concerned with money and their financial futures. At West Point, mutual funds were a common topic of discussion, and I was introduced to dollar cost averaging in 1986 when I started in my first mutual fund. Officers and soldiers alike were invested in the stock market, dabbling in real estate, or running businesses from their homes. It was a fairly entrepreneurial environment even though the level, due to our workload and mission, was necessarily low. The pervasive nature of concern about income, savings, and getting ahead financially is nearly identical with people in my civilian experiences.

You and I share the common goal of personal financial freedom. Beyond that, there are a million selfish and altruistic desires, but let's assume you still have to have the money to keep a roof over your head and food on the table. And let's assume that it is better to have that money without having to go to work every day, 10 hours a day.

Yeah. Yeah, but what does this have to do with leadership? Leaders achieve goals.

I Had No Idea

I have tried several different approaches to financial independence, and time and again I had to back up and find an alternate route. Remember, I was employed more than full-time in the Army. Though I was happy with what I was doing, it was evident to me that the pay was not going to put me where I wanted to be. As a young officer I thought that having extra money to put away every month into a mutual fund was the way to go. I worked as a security guard in my off time to generate some extra income. On my first detail, I stood at the barricades in front of the stage for an Aerosmith concert, and on another assignment, I shuffled around the aisles of an antique flea market on a Saturday. It wasn't long before I realized there were better things I could do with my time. One of those things, I thought, was building picnic tables and selling them for investment money. I would have made a killing except with my second table I caught the urethane coating on fire and my wife made me stop.

No one has ever accused me of being a genius, but I'm not sure anyone truly recognized my succeed-at-all-costs mentality, even when the cost was seemingly my pride. Wearing a security guard uniform at night after wearing my prestigious Army lieutenant's uniform and Ranger tab during the day didn't bother me. Making picnic tables and displaying them in my front yard with a For Sale sign didn't bother me. Besides torching my profits, they simply weren't good plans for what I needed to accomplish.

I continued to constantly think about the subject of money—how to generate it, and the choices that a lot of it would give me. I spent five years cutting my teeth in sales in multilevel marketing, and, like most people, I spent a lot more money than I made. I traveled to the rallies, I listened to the tapes, I read the books, I bought the dream, and then—I worked. Let me be very clear—the education was well worth it. Truly, the education of a constant awareness and exploration of personal possibilities, along with consistent effort, was priceless.

You may recognize the fact that status and a facade of success didn't interest me. I was concerned about results, and I was going to experiment and work until I had reached my goals. I couldn't imagine making excuses to myself if I ultimately failed. I didn't have a choice. I had to keep going. If you are wrapped up in the image that your car, home, title, office, or boat gives you, but know you are in a hurt box when it comes to your finances and future, you'd better wake up to what's important. You need to set some definite goals and then start working toward them.

I did not achieve my goal of financial independence through all of my initial tries. The money I had socked away in the mutual fund was used to pay off early marriage debt and take a chance on the growing stock market of the late 1980s and early 1990s. You could call my strategy "contrarian." I had a knack for choosing the stocks going the exact opposite direction of the exploding market. Gold! Please, someone shoot me. Then there were the picnic tables. What a bonehead. Then multilevel marketing. What else was a no-business-skill, full-time Army officer going to do?

Though I left each one of these pursuits, I never quit my goal of financial independence or my long-term goal of real choices in life, and having genuine time with my wife and children. Had I failed? Absolutely not. Each of these experiences was treated as research and development. I was reading personal development and leadership books at a rapid pace. I was succeeding exceptionally well as an officer and leader in the Army. I was pressing on like one of my 60-ton tanks going through a rock quarry. Yeah, there were bumps, but nothing that would stop me from getting to the other side.

Out of the Army

Well, crap, I thought. I might as well get out of the Army and get a good job. Armed with my acquired sales skills, I got my first job selling drugs as a pharmaceutical sales rep in Dallas, Texas. It was the place to be for a can-do type of guy who didn't quite know what the future held. After several months in the field, I found myself frustrated at what I saw was the lockstep approach to promotions and a very check-the-box method of leadership. Though my boss was a wonderful leader, I saw the company's progression system becoming suffocatingly rigid.

The truth is that I saw myself on a much shorter path to success.

I was not attracted by the lifestyles of the people with 5 to 10 or even 20 years more than I had in the company. They worked too many hours and spent too little time with their families. I was used to being in charge and responsible for the welfare of soldiers and millions of dollars' worth of equipment, and though I worked a lot of hours, I didn't see the optimum use of my capacity where I was.

I decided to move my family from the psychologically secure home and job in Texas all the way to South Carolina in pursuit of the dream that the Internet held: ownership and financial freedom. I was paid very well, as much as the vice president of operations of the company, and for six months it was great. However, those were the six months leading up to the great Internet collapse of 2001. After losing my job I was surprisingly relaxed. I had faith in a positive outcome to my newly found freedom.

I was 35 and daily getting further from where I wanted to be financially. I had no job, a fairly large mortgage, a wife and year-old son, and no other job prospects. We were 1,500 miles from where we wanted to live. We had very little savings, and in five months burned through that and more. Somehow, I just knew that everything would be okay. My thoughts were dedicated nearly entirely to how I was going to create an independent future for myself.

After the five months of unemployment, we finally sold our home. We packed up all of our belongings into a 24-foot truck, 10-foot trailer, and four-door sedan. We loaded our baby into the car, the dogs in the truck, and drove for four days to Colorado—still with only one job lead, and not terribly excited about the situation that job would create for my family.

After a month of looking and interviewing, I was able to choose between a prestigious consulting position, a standard sales position with a national company, and a part-time assistant position to an individual business owner.

A Route Best Suited to My Goal

That was 23 months ago. I started work as a part-time assistant to an entrepreneur getting ready to take his business national. I was paid $2,000 per month and allowed to sell the business' services to clients I developed, and get commissions from those sales. The owner and I worked together in a crowded 12-by-12-foot office in the back of a coffee shop, and fretted over phone expenses and the cost of gas needed to go on appointments. However, at least for part of the week, I was able to direct my own schedule, work as hard as I wanted to, and create commissions that wouldn't be capped.

As I write this, nearly two years later, I'm sitting in my office looking across the golf course at the Air Force Academy. The front range of the Rocky Mountains juts up behind the white spires of the chapel, and a dark rain cloud is covering the southern half of the sky getting ready to let loose. My business partner (former boss) and I are considering purchasing the 30,000-square-foot building where I sit, and where most of the nine companies we own are housed. My company just bought two H2 Hummers for the owners to drive, and I didn't feel right about my wife and kids in something smaller, so I bought another large SUV for her. When I leave the office today I'll take my Pocket PC, which is so new to the market that the company we bought it from doesn't even have some of the necessary accessories in initial stock.

When I go home, I won't take any work so I can play with my two young boys, 10 months and three and a half years old, and spend time with my wife. My wife and I will talk about our upcoming vacation to Monterey, California, and consider how much we'll miss the kids. We may discuss how much money we will tithe this month and the offerings we'll make with additional money. We will make dinner, watch a sitcom, put our children to bed, and get some rest. Before we rest, we'll reflect and give thanks for where we've been in our lives and the blessings we've received over the past two years. Just as important is our understanding that we have not arrived and never will. We continue to set new goals and push ourselves to greater achievement.

If you haven't guessed, the two years between the drive to Colorado and today is quite a story. The true story, however, is in the developmental times of my life that made me ready for the choices and challenges of the past two years. The most important period of foundation laying for growth and development in my life is my time at West Point and in U.S. Army Ranger School.

Special Note

My purpose is not only to add to the discussion on leadership. I want to promote the pursuit of self-knowledge and personal responsibility. I encourage you to read and read and read some more on the subjects of leadership, management, and self-improvement, among others. There is an abundance of titles available for you to read to fill a lifetime. Some will claim to be the one and only book you will ever need, while others will lay out a philosophy in bullet format so simple you don't even have to think to read it. The importance of these books is how they help you develop your bedrock of leadership principles and add to your learning and experience. A habit of continued reading will reinforce lessons from other books and life's experiences and will keep your mind fertile. This book is part of your reading regimen, but it is not the end or the capstone book for you. It is one in a series of written experiences to allow you to discover another piece of your personal philosophy.

I encourage each of you to write down your leadership philosophy. What is your bedrock? What principles do you base your decisions on? Do you even know? Write them down; record your principles. As a leader with high personal and team goals, you will come up against obstacles and enter into confrontation. You will face conflicting and divergent opinions and forces; your vision must prevail. Without good knowledge of the principles behind your goals, the reasons why you do what you do, you will fold under pressure. Instead, understand yourself logically and be able to develop intelligent arguments to sell, defend, and push your purposes forward. Another saying warns, "You had better stand for something or you'll fall for anything." Knowing yourself and the reasons behind your goals is the beginning of standing for something.

This is so important, and will pay such dividends, that any effort is worth the benefit. If you find it difficult to do this through your own introspection or want validation or coaching, there are experts available to help.

RANGERS

are

PERSISTENT

BRACE BARBER

Persistence does not exist without stress and pressure. You can't persist through a sunny day and an ice cream cone. Your goals will require persistence and patience. How many times do you have to get up after falling? One more time. Persistence isn't dictated by physical beauty or strength. It isn't influenced by a high IQ or perfect eyesight. Persistence is a personal decision made every day or every minute until you have achieved your goal. Persistence is the leveraging of time against the weight of a heavy goal. You'll see that persistence can force actions that are uncomfortable and awkward, and it can compel introspection.

The Decision

Before I attended, no matter how many people I talked to about Ranger School, the same picture remained in my mind. The night is perpetual, and day never arrives to dry the moldy rucksacks on our backs. Slimy vines from the jungle ceiling hang down to slap our dirty faces as we march forward on another patrol. The forest is a maze of trees, always anchored in marshy soil, which clings to our jungle boots with sucking teeth of mud. We march for days at a time, with no specific mission, just weariness and hunger to keep us company. It is a cold, lonely world, meant only for those who have been challenged.

The Ranger School graduates I asked had the same problem explaining the diversity of misery there as I do to the people who ask me now. How do you convey the feelings of frustration and anger at the paradox of being too tired to march anymore, yet aware that freezing is the alternative if you stop, or how the simple pleasure of a cup of coffee was worth more to a Ranger than the company of his girl back home.

Before attending Ranger School, I read the book *Platoon Leader* by James R. McDonough (Presidio Press, 1996). Early in the book he sums up the experience of Ranger School by saying, "It made me realize that I was not as tough as I pretended, but tougher than I thought." If every Ranger student were as tough as he acted, the school would be little more than a nine-week adventure camp. The only learning done by the students would be patrolling techniques, mountaineering, and swamp operations. Teaching these skills is only a small part of the overall objective of Ranger School. The higher intent is to teach each student about himself during situations of intense duress.

The desire to attend Ranger School did not start as a burning desire; it was more of a small fungus that grew into a tree over a four-year period at West Point. I did not even realize that the thought had taken root until it was almost an acceptable idea my senior year. I waffled on Ranger School so many times it became a habit. When I felt strong, "I am going." When I felt weak, "I'm not going." I finally made the fateful move of verbalizing my goal. I told both of my roommates, Pat Mathes and Brent Layman, that I was going to go to Ranger School. I knew that making a commitment to someone else and laying the goal on the table would force me forward. Despite committing myself when I was feeling strong, I still had to stick with my story through my not-so-strong times.

Mentally, I continued to struggle with the idea of putting myself into voluntary hell, no matter the payoff. To feed my hunger for information on the school, I attended a briefing conducted by Colonel

Tex Turner. Colonel Turner was the head of the department of military instruction at West Point, and had at a previous point in his career run the Ranger School.

At the briefing, I stayed in the back of the auditorium as it filled with my classmates. The murmur of the crowd grew and at times got very loud. The cadets mingled and moved around like dark blue ants between the seats looking for a buddy or finding a place to sit. There was a lot of excitement in the room, as they were about to learn some of the truth about their chosen branch. Colonel Turner walked onto stage and the room got quiet.

He spoke at first about leadership and he related a couple of stories from his days in the field. Then he got to the importance of Ranger School. I stood in the back hoping to pick up any little bit of information I could about the course. I was still trying to figure out if it was right for me. Then he said *it*—"There are two kinds of officers, those who are Ranger qualified, and those with excuses why they are not."

For a second I felt it was just Colonel Turner and myself in the room, and he was looking right at me from two feet away. "Well, cadet, what's it gonna be? Ranger—or *EXCUSE*?"

I stuck around for the remainder of the briefing but did not hear much. I left that auditorium a future Ranger. I would not be denied.

Grasp the simplicity and power of No Excuses, and you have guaranteed success.

"Well, what's it gonna be? Wealthy—or excuse?"

"Well, what's it gonna be? Healthy—or excuse?"

"Well, what's it gonna be? A good parent—or excuse?"

"Well, what's it gonna be? A good friend—or excuse?"

"Well, what's it gonna be? A good employee—or excuse?"

"Well, what's it gonna be? A good leader—or excuse?"

If you set goals in line with your personal priorities, and never accept excuses for failure, you will succeed. The accounts in the remainder of this book are acknowledgments that it is difficult to never give excuses when you are shooting for extraordinary success. The characters show that despite the depth of conviction you have for a worthy goal, the pursuit of that goal will be filled with pressures and opportunities to quit. The journey will be full of chances and desires to make excuses and rationalize the abandonment of your goal. If it were easy to be wealthy, healthy, a good parent, friend, employee, or leader, everyone would be. Choose your goal, not the excuse.

This relates directly to leadership because leaders do not make excuses. I figure if you are responsible for others and you make excuses, you haven't led anyone anywhere and aren't a leader.

Be the Frog

I was on the top bunk, snuggled comfortably in my sleeping bag. All was quiet in the barracks except for the shuffling of the fireguard making his way back and forth through the old wooden building. The darkness outside was stiff, threatening the sun to stay away for a few more hours. My mind popped open, my eyes stayed closed, and my body lay still. Cocooned in my sleeping bag the way I was I could not tell what had awakened me. I listened for the commotion associated with first call, but could not hear any. It could have been midnight, or 0200, or God forbid, 0430. I dared not look at my watch, for fear of the last possibility.

I could still feel the weariness of my muscles pulling me into the mattress. The few hours of sleep could not begin to revive the strength I had expended in the previous four days. I drifted, and sleep quickly dragged me back. In what seemed like only a minute or two, I was awakened again by the yelling of the student platoon sergeant (PSG).

He was a large man with light hair and small dark eyes. He had a heavy face, the kind you could compare with his baby pictures and immediately see the resemblance. He yelled only when necessary, and waking up sleeping Rangers was one of those times.

I sat up slowly, letting my feet hang over the edge of the mattress. Invariably Hines, a private first class (PFC) from the Third Ranger Battalion, would sit up at the same time and bang his head into my feet, or get kicked as I swung them over.

Today, 8 November, was a day that found us dressing, although in silence, with a slightly lightened mood. Day five, the last day of City Week, was here, and so was the last physical training (PT) session, the last run, and the last bayonet drill. Something in the back of my mind said, "It's got to get easier after this."

All of my pretraining had been geared toward City Week, toward the 30 minutes of calisthenics and basic training type hazing. I could do push-ups until the cows came home and "run to Columbus just like this." Despite the training, I was tired after the first four days, and I prepared to give my last little bit for this final day of City Week. I swore to myself that I would never do this phase of the school again.

Although the weather in Georgia was comfortable, the mornings could be bitterly cold. We stomped out of the barracks as late as possible for formation. BDUs with gloves, running shoes, and black stocking caps were the uniform. We jogged to the PT pit in formation, stopped and downed our gear, moved into the dark brown sawdust, and prepared to start. To our front was our PT instructor, Sergeant Moreno, a short Hispanic noncommissioned officer (NCO) with a muscular body and a very large mouth. However, what waited behind him is what had our attention.

Behind him was the worm pit, Ranger School's version of an obstacle course. Included were most of the normal stations—pull-ups, crawling under barbed wire, a horizontal ladder, a low-crawl pit, and a rope climb. But all of this was augmented with a foot and a half of muddy, ice-cold water underneath each one.

We did our exercises, then went on a four-mile run, and returned to the PT pit for stretching. Steam was rising from our bare heads, giving us an angelic aura when mixed with the stadium lights around the field. No one had given us a yes or no when questioned about the worm pit. We had slipped by the first four days without doing it, and the hope that the winter might save us was strong among the 40 Rangers who now began to feel the cold penetrate their clothes and hot skin.

Even as the first platoon began moving to the start point to our front, we hoped beyond hope that we would not have to go. We were still stretching when the first set of 10 Rangers finished their pull-ups, and plunged, screaming, stomach first into the water. "Fuck," was the only thought that entered my mind, as I gave in to the reality of what was to follow.

In four days of Ranger School, I had already been kicked, slapped, and thrown in the hand-to-hand pit, and I had jogged down a dusty road with an 80-pound rucksack, but the first smashing, almost unbelievable reality of pain came when I fell into that ice-cold, dirty water at the beginning of the worm pit.

We stood in line, 10 abreast, waiting our turn at the pull-up bars. Each rank drew a different RI to guide them through the course. Much to our chagrin, we drew Staff Sergeant Yovan.

His six-foot, nonmuscular frame was capped with a crooked smile and a skewed mentality to match. I am sure that as a child he twisted the legs off of frogs and pulled his sister's hair until she screamed. He would take sincere pleasure in seeing us suffer through the worm pit under his control.

I let go of the pull-up bar and dropped to the ground. A second later, I was facedown in the freezing water, scraping my belly across the sandy bottom of the lane underneath the barbed wire. A shock had gone to my brain, and my breaths were quick and short as I tried to regain my air. Instantly I began to shiver, and my screams of motivation sounded more like a stubborn car engine on a cold morning.

I kicked with almost panic energy, sucking in more water than air, and scooping sand into my pants with my belt. "Push . . . push . . . push," I thought. "The end is getting closer. Push . . . push . . . push." I must have looked like a frog moving through the water—very little style, but a definite goal. Frustrated, I struggled through the first obstacle, kicking at the sandy bottom that gave way at my feet. My slow progress allowed time to think, to savor the misery into which I had just jumped.

None of us had a choice in the matter, and none had it better than the other. The worm pit was the first major indoctrination exercise into the Ranger mentality. Not a single person there wanted to do it, but we each knew that it was compulsory and expected. We simply had to do it, or leave. Performing a difficult and uncomfortable task was expected of a Ranger when the mission dictated it—no questions asked.

I have read that soldiers in combat do not turn and run in the face of the enemy because of their buddies next to them. People are concerned about their buddies' welfare and also the personal embarrassment running away would cause. It was impossible to think of walking away from the worm pit for those exact reasons. Ranger School had provided our enemy, tapped our basic fears, and expected us to drive on. We did drive on, not even knowing that the worm pit was as close to battle as we might ever come.

I kicked and scratched to the end of the wire obstacle, emerging from the muck resembling a swamp creature. "Arrrrgh! Hooahhh!" we all screamed as we rushed to the horizontal ladder. Through that, we dove once again into a muddy strip of water. There was no wire above our heads, just an RI. We were in the water simply to be in the water. The lane started out wide enough to accommodate all 10 of us, but in its 30-foot length it tapered to a small end like a funnel spout. We all began with the high crawl, hands and knees, moving as far into the funnel as possible. Sergeant Yovan called a stop to that quickly, and had us on our backs doing flutter kicks in the middle of the water. We rolled left, then right, and then we were instructed to continue down the lane doing the snake. He said it was his favorite: hands behind our backs, bellies in the mud, kicking and wiggling to the end of the lane. As the end closed in, bodies began piling up, and those in the lead inadvertently kicked the rest of us who followed.

Winded and tired, we made it through the snake. The end of the obstacle course was looming near, just a quick climbing obstacle, and then the rope climb. We tromped along, dragging our feet and holding our heads up trying to catch our breaths.

Ken stood in a trough of water three feet deep, and stared in distress at the 15-foot rope, which he grasped in his meaty hands. Ken was about six foot three and 230 pounds. He was a large man with a lot of strength, but not for climbing ropes.

"Wrap the rope around your foot, and step up onto that and then move it up as you go," we encouraged him.

He made two attempts at pulling himself straight up, resting his feet on the knot about two feet off of the water. Sergeant Yovan even cheered him on, offering a case of beer if he made it to the top.

It finally became apparent that he was going to have to use the wrap-around-the-foot method, which would have to be taught on the fly. When Ken wrapped the rope around his foot, no one less than Harry Houdini with a buck knife would have been able to free him. His already tired arms tried once to pull up, then again. We were cheering wildly, unexpectedly realizing some of the enjoyment that can come from group endurance.

The final time Ken tried to pull up, his arms gave out, and his hands slipped from the rope. His large, now whale-like body inverted and splashed into the water. His foot was connected to the rope by what seemed to be close to a hangman's noose, suspending him upside down in the water. His arms flailed, slapping the water wildly, as we jumped in to save his life.

He gasped for air as we unwrapped his foot and stood him upright. The RIs commented that they had not seen such a sight since they were at Sea World, and from then on called him Flipper. Ken survived the rope climb with a rope burn on his ankle and a new nickname that he kept throughout the first phase.

The remainder of the worm pit consisted of three-to-five second rushes on packed dirt and gravel. After 10 or so good yells, and knee-banging drops to the prone position, we were done.

Understanding the near-freezing condition we were in, the RIs released us quickly back to the barracks to clean up. Shuffling back to the barracks, I held my arms out from my sides in an effort to keep my cold, wet clothes from touching my body.

Within a minute of reaching the steps, there was not a stitch of clothing on anyone. We used a garden hose to rinse the scummy water off of our uniforms and ourselves. Forty naked butts stood in line, braving the cold morning air and displaying goose pimples and a bright red blush.

I hung my uniform on the clotheslines in front of the barracks and brought my running shoes, which I had forgotten to clean, into the barracks. Bare feet slapped at the floor as guys raced to the showers to clean up before breakfast. Although barely warm, it was an extremely comfortable shower.

Every day we stand at the beginning of our own worm pit, those difficult and distasteful things we have to do to get to where we want to be. None of us want to be there and none of us look forward to the painful parts of the experience. Walking away from the challenge means failure. Discouraging as it might seem, even as ominous and all-consuming as the worm pit was, it was near the beginning of the challenges that lay in our path on our way to Ranger qualification. It may be the same in your circumstances. You may have a series of worm pits that take several months or years to work through before you achieve your goal.

I was a styleless frog bound for a small success, which I did achieve that day. This type of mind-set relates directly to my early efforts at making money. I didn't care what I looked like; I had a goal.

Land Navigation

One of the many tests of City Week was the Ranger land navigation course. Land navigation is just that, navigating cross-country using a map and compass in order to find different points. At each location there would be a code for us to record on our score sheets to let the RI at the end of the course know we had been there. Each point also contained an azimuth and a distance to our next point, so you never knew more than one point at a time. It was built up by the RIs as a difficult course, making us believe that we would be going through thick brush, deep swamps, and hordes of dragons with only a compass and picture of a buck knife. If we were to fail, we would have to repeat the course during the famed eight-hour break while our classmates were out on the town eating real food and buying necessities for the rest of the course. If we were to fail again, recycling or separation faced us. Realizing the stakes of the land nav course, everyone was motivated to make a magnificent effort toward passing the course the first time.

I had had very little experience with dismounted land navigation. During a course set up by West Point prior to the end of our sophomore year, I failed miserably. I wandered in at 1800, one of the last finishers, two hours after the deadline. I retested on that course on the following Saturday. I hoped now that that was not an omen of what was to come.

In the forest, at ground level one hill looks like the next, and one creek is hard to tell from another. The point of land navigation is the development of the ability to tell one from the other, and to locate yourself on a map. When on a course where it might take an hour to get from one point to another, there is generous time for you to start doubting yourself, especially if you are not confident in your map-reading skills to begin with.

We arrived at our start point, and dismounted the back of the truck. We stretched as we hit the ground, standing under a blue sky of what was going to be a pleasant day. The absence of my rucksack made me feel like I could run the whole course. I was not in too much of a hurry. I had eight hours to find a minimum of four out of seven points. I was not interested in getting any praise for finding all seven points. I figured the energy it would take to find the last three points would be better spent elsewhere.

From the high ground where I stood, I could see a large part of the forest into which I would soon venture. I plotted my first point on my map, and then stood up to check whether I could see the general area where it was. Unable to do so, I started the journey. It was November, so most of the leaves of the trees had fallen, making visibility in the forest moderate.

I counted the dips and rises on my map in the direction to my point, and started counting the corresponding features as I passed them on the ground. I figured I would not need to look at my map until I got into the general area of my point. It was rather cocky of me to use this technique considering my past record, but my memory sometimes glossed over my earlier shortcomings.

Soon, I came to a spot near where I thought my point was supposed to be. After a half hour of trying to find the point by checking the area and checking and rechecking my map, I realized I was lost. Fortunately for me, the saviors of all lost Rangers, voices, were heard in the distance. I hurried off in that direction and caught up with several others gathered at a point—my point. "Outstanding," I thought, but it still took me two hours to find.

My strategy for the second point was a little safer. I checked my compass every couple hundred meters as I ran. I still managed to get myself lost, forcing me to move quickly, sometimes without putting my compass back into its small case. It hung freely, swinging from its lanyard and banging into my leg as I ran. I found my second point in about two and a half hours.

I started to feel the pinch of time—only a few hours left, and two more points to find. A quick orientation and off I went running through the woods, compass loose. I ran—I stopped—I looked, and ran again. On a flat piece of ground exactly like the rest of the ground I had seen that day, I stopped to check my progress. I pulled out my map and reached for my compass—"What? Oh fuck! Where's my compass?" I thought. The lanyard hung loose from my load bearing equipment (LBE). I'm sunk, I told myself. I'm stuck in the middle of the forest, I haven't seen anyone for an hour, the sun is going down, I'm not sure exactly where I am, and if I don't complete this course I get to do it again during my eight-hour break. Unthinkable!

I knew I had to pull out all the stops. I oriented my map to the ground and to the setting sun. I had a rough idea where I was. I assumed I was correct and lit off in a straight line toward the sun and my next point. I put on my leather gloves and safety glasses for protection since there was no longer time for skirting around difficult areas.

The beeline I made for the sun took me through some low ground in the training area. These areas were always filled with an overgrowth of wait-a-minute vines and thornbushes, and could be as wide as 30 meters. Each time I came to an obstacle of these multi-armed monsters I moved through them with manic determination like I was in waist-deep water going against the current. At times I looked like the aftermath of an unsuccessful attempt to climb through the barbed wire of an enemy perimeter—caught up in all sorts of fashions, barely able to move. I was fortunate, however, that I was not in a summer class when the leaves and flowers were in full bloom and these obstacles would have been impossible.

I found my next point before the sun set. My heart and mind did not have time to rest. I oriented again on my fourth point and moved out. Heading north, I kept the sun on my left shoulder and went straight ahead. The terrain was clearer on this leg because it was mostly uphill. My time was dwindling as I moved, and my stress mounted. I finally arrived where I had the last point marked. I just knew I was in the right place. "This has to be it," I thought. But where was it? "The RIs gave me a bogus grid," I steamed. It was always easy to blame someone else in these times.

I had already spent too much time looking. I had to enlarge my search area to see if it was just out of my sight. I ran up and down the road like a mother looking for her lost child. Then I walked ever larger circles around the place where I had originally thought the point was located. I was losing hope when I saw movement in the distance at a place that I was certain was not my point. It was, however, the closest thing around, so I moved to there as the sun was disappearing from the horizon and marked my card with the code at the point. I hopped onto the road and ran. My time was almost out, and I still had two kilometers to go to the finish.

Even thought I was tired and unconfident, my heart still jumped when I came over the rise that exposed our base camp in the distance. I walked between the large rucksacks in the formation site and made it to the finish desk manned by an RI. Most of the Rangers were back from the course, sitting and resting or talking among themselves. To my surprise, though, there were many people who had not yet returned. I thought I would be the last one in. The RI took my card, compared it with his legend, marked it "Go," and told me to get some rest before we moved out.

I truly relaxed for the short break before we mounted up in the back of the deuce-and-halves for the trip back to the barracks.

In order to accomplish our goals, we need a lot fewer resources than common wisdom would suggest. What you can't do without is determination. Win our lose, you must give it your all and never give up.

Ken of the Hill

We started anew at the Darby phase. Each of us had already out-lasted many other candidates through the rigorous City Week. The phase was marked by classes and beginner patrols as a squad. My knowledge of patrolling techniques along with my experience in the field was close to zero. Everything seemed new to me, and therefore I took everything the RIs taught in more of an academic light, which I was used to, instead of as general guidance the way it was intended. I wanted to make sure I checked the box on all tasks. I gave the instruction no analytical thought, and simply copied down what they said without seeing the purpose behind each technique or tactic. I really didn't see the big picture at all. I saw only the pieces of the puzzle and tried to shove all of them into my pocket at once, not knowing whether they would make a congruent picture someday. As I pulled the pieces out one by one or a handful at a time, all I made was a mess.

After the planning portion of our first mission, I was terrified to learn that I was leading the patrol during the execution phase. I was only leading a squad, 11 guys, on a simple patrol, but to me I was driving at 80 miles an hour down an icy road on a dark night with fogged-up windows.

"Let's move out," I commanded.

The first part was simple. I understood how to conduct a forward passage of lines. It really was easy; there was an actual checklist to use. I coordinated with the commander of the unit overwatching the obstacle we would pass through, and whose soldiers would be firing into us or over us if the enemy chose to attack while we were walking the path through their defenses.

I read from my handbook: how many people were in the squad, who was going to guide us through the obstacle to our front, who was responsible for covering us and how far out, what we would do if we received fire while in the lane of the obstacle, and so on. Everything was in writing now.

"Bring up the rest of the squad. Let's count them through," I ordered. I took a breath of relief. Everything was moving smoothly. Ken, our 230-pound M60 gunner, was last. He came by, and then I followed.

We mentally prepared to start being Rangers in earnest, walking stealthily through the forest, seeing the enemy before he sees us, and setting up an ambush or a raid to kill and demoralize him before he knows what hit him. All of us were in the lane now, flanked on each side by barbed wire and dummy land mines. Shots rang out from the hill to our front. I froze for a second, pulled one of the pieces of the puzzle from my pocket hoping it was the right one, then shouted, "Six hundred meters north!"

The squad began to run through the lane of the obstacle and as far as we could, maybe 50 meters, until we came to a 10-foot-high sheer wall of dirt and rocks. We were already tired as we began to claw our way up the rise. We looked like children playing king of the hill, going up a little way and then falling back down, trying again, and falling again. We grabbed anything we could hold onto and pulled ourselves, our 80-pound rucksacks, and our weapons up the wall.

The enemy continued to fire, making our effort even more pathetic; real bullets would have wiped us out in a matter of seconds. I knew I had blown it. We finally made it up the side of the wall and continued on our way. It's nice to be in a situation where by all rights you should be dead, but you get a second chance to live and do things properly. We continued to march over the rolling, pine needle–covered hills.

It was a nice afternoon for a walk until the artillery simulator landed to the side of the patrol. I again reached into my pocket and pulled out a piece of the puzzle. "Six hundred meters north!" I yelled again. Damn, it was the same piece as before. My squad members were definitely going to kill me. The first 600-meter run lasted only about 200 meters, but exhausted us all. Depending on your point of view, the next action by the RI either saved me or killed me. He stopped us before we ran and made Ken—Flipper— a casualty.

The RI said, "He's wounded and can't walk. What are you going to do, Ranger?"

"Oh, man," I thought, "I haven't the slightest clue." Shooting him and continuing on with the mission seemed like the easiest thing to do, but I knew that wouldn't fly. A couple of the other squad members, sensing my bewilderment, made some suggestions.

"We need to medevac him. Call for a medevac. We need to get him to an open area where a chopper can come in."

The RI, clearly unimpressed, asked, "Is anyone going to perform buddy aid on your friend?"

Oh crap! Now we need to know first aid?!

While a squad mate chuckled at the possibility of performing mouth-to-mouth on Ken, I looked at the map to see where the closest open area was. It was at least a kilometer away according to the map, but in reality no one knew. I called in the medevac report over the radio, another checklist I could read from my handbook. Then the dilemma was how to move a 230-pound man who can't walk. I was a very lean 140 pounds, and no one in the squad could even consider a fireman's carry. "Okay. Let's get two guys, one under each arm," I commanded.

Ken was lying on his back as two of the squad members started to pull him up by the arms. They each strained as they put their heads under his arms and tried to go from a squat to a stand. It was futile. They looked like they were trying to carry a heavy box that was too large to get their arms around.

We had already been sitting there for 15 minutes. I felt like I had spent hours in a maze and ended up at another dead end. I didn't know what to do. The RI was kind enough to remove me from the head of the patrol. I relaxed a bit as we got under way, a fully healthy squad again, but I also knew that I had failed to meet the test successfully and it ate at my gut.

Leaders are trained. Some people are naturally adept at leadership, but the good news is that anyone willing to work at the subject and take the risks necessary to learn through practical experience can be a great leader. I mentioned at the beginning of this book that I approach the subject of leadership as a foot soldier, not an academic. Thank goodness I was provided with the opportunity to develop as a leader. If the Army had counted on my intrinsic abilities. . . .

No matter what your skills are right now, you have the capability to be a leader. Take steps to learn about the subject through study, through exposure to leaders you have access to, and through willingness to step to the front and lead.

Swamp Skirters

Warmth to a Ranger going through a winter class is precious. Most of the time we did not have it, and when we did, it didn't last very long.

Sunshine was our God, and water our Satan. Therefore, creeks, by design of the Ranger Department, were almost always in the path of our patrol. We would spend as much time trying to plan a path around the creeks as we would on the rest of the mission. When we came upon a creek, we would send out teams to find a bypass before we would just trudge on through it.

On one particular mission at Camp Darby, we wore ourselves out trying to keep dry. We had been moving for hours in the area of Hollis Creek, a long, tangled creek that runs through much of the training area. The solid ground frequently gave way to marshy patches, which we persistently skirted. We hoped, beyond any rational hope, that we would find the *one* path through Hollis Creek that would allow us to stay dry.

As if keeping the patrol's feet dry was as important as accomplishing the mission, the point man or patrol leader guided us around wet areas. I moved as carefully as the rest of the patrol, walking around puddles and if necessary hopping from tree to tree. I knew that one good step into muddy ground or into a puddle would allow water to gush into the sides of my jungle boots through the airholes. Once your feet got wet, especially at night, you were in for a long, painful walk.

Walking on soggy socks for miles with a heavy load is like having a starched collar on a sunburned neck for hours. Your feet are tenderized with each step and your socks bunch up in all the wrong places. The best thing to do is to pull up your socks and tighten your boots down to allow as little movement as possible. Unfortunately, no solution is permanent and we moved constantly, not allowing much time for adjustment. Staying out of the water to begin with was the best answer.

Our movement for about the first 500 meters into the creek was fairly easy. It was messy, but not wet. "I hope to hell we are on the way out of this shit," I prayed. Then our movement slowed. "Why are we bunching up? What is ahead?" I worried.

I could not see what the problem was, but distant splashes warned of our wet future. I guess as a last resort the leadership had decided to move through Hollis Creek. As the line of Rangers moved one by one into the swamp, I still maintained that I would be able to get through this obstacle dry. No one wanted to face the fact that they were going to get wet. Each of us fought the idea with an intensity that surpassed reason.

It was our first time into Hollis Creek, but we were not ignorant of the actual nature of the terrain; rather, we were naive. We ignored the map, which clearly depicted a marsh paralleling the creek for its entire length. Patrol leaders were heard to say, "See here, where the marsh gets real narrow, that's where we will hit it, and hopefully we can stay away from the deep water."

One of the battles a patrol leader was fighting was a political one. Only hours or minutes before, he had been a member of a squad, simply following the column of Rangers; now he was the leader and he needed the remaining members of the squad to help him succeed. He wanted to stay out of the water for more than simple comfort reasons—he wanted to keep the soldiers as happy as possible. He knew that when people get wet and cold they focus on their basic comfort rather than 100 percent on the mission at hand. Couple wetness and cold with exhaustion, and you may have what is known as a no-go patrol. Those are the cases in which the entire Ranger chain of command gets a no-go on the patrol. The Rangers fail to perform, usually due to exhaustion or severely adverse physical conditions.

"If we are making good progress, we will try to skirt the creek to the north. I wonder if the RI will let us take this bridge if we use the proper techniques."

The RIs had seen the Hollis Creek scenario too many times: walk around for hours attempting to bypass the water, then, behind schedule, decide to move through it, only to find that there isn't enough daylight left to see where you are going under the thick canopy. They walk along quietly, every once in a while checking to see if the patrol leader knows where he is. They don't much care if he is right or not, they just want to see what an eventful night it is going to be.

In addition to being naive, we also conveniently forgot the stories of old Rangers who were lost in the swamp for a full night, or spent an hour moving 100 meters in water up to their waists.

We disregarded all evidence that predicted the worst. We were new and did not completely know what to expect from the RIs or the terrain. In brief, what we learned over time was that both could be very unforgiving and unmoved by our suffering.

The denial was part of the survival mentality of Ranger School. In order to keep a positive attitude, sometimes the obviously terrible situation had to be ignored.

We were all new to the patrolling aspect of Ranger School, but from the previous days we knew how the cold could penetrate to the bones even while dry and transform a body into a shivering heap on the ground. A wet uniform was inescapable—a cold that could not be shaken off. To a Ranger student in the dark of the early morning, sitting still in an observation post, it was as permanent as a scar. The only moment you could think of was the current one, and it was a miserable one. You couldn't even imagine the warmth of the noon sun. The cold had a lock on the imagination.

The patrol leader knew that if he took us through the swamp, we would all spend the night as bedmates of the Devil in Dante's Inferno: freezing. It was not only popular but also necessary to the morale of the students that hope remained and that the patrol leader tried to plan around the water.

Patrols, which started with the assurance of the patrol leader that they were going to get wet, automatically concentrated on getting through the water first, and then through the mission.

RIs warned, "Y'all are acting like a bunch of pussies. You're gonna have to ignore the water and consider it a slight unpleasantness if you're gonna accomplish your mission."

We listened and felt less Rangerlike since we weren't that mentally tough yet. They watched with distaste and humor at our vain efforts to plan a dry route. They knew we were going to be soaked by the end of the patrol, and they refused to give advice that was contrary to the true Ranger way of driving on to the Ranger objective despite any obstacle. They knew that at the first sign of water we should march straight through it, and save the energy we were going to use trying to stay dry.

It was now my turn. Three feet to my front was a thin tree, surrounded by water. I could not see a bypass that made any more sense than the path that I faced. I could not see the bottom of the water in the dark, so I assumed the worst. I put my rifle in my right hand, held my left arm out, and leaped to the patch of grass at the base of the tree. "I made it!" I thought, as I grabbed the tree firmly in a headlock. I pulled it tightly to my side. "This isn't so bad. If this is the worst it gets, I'll be able to stay dry!"

It wasn't long before the patrol had lost its bearings completely. To my front I saw five people leaping like fairies out of step, jumping clumsily from one dry patch to another. I was not complaining—I just hoped I could be as successful as they had been, fairy or not.

Soon the darkness concealed the movement all around us. Our column closed in, scared of getting separated as we moved through the creek. The trees then grew out of leaping range, and the water deepened. Eventually, with a leap, a grab, a fall, and a curse, each of us experienced our own mortality and inability to walk on water. The calm of nature was now broken by frequent exclamations of anger as another of our group stumbled in the dark. Movement to my front seemed very distant, and I traveled as quickly as I could through the thigh-level water to keep up.

The water grew in depth at a deliberate pace. At first it was up to our knees, then up to our thighs, yet we still fought it every bit of the way, tiptoeing if possible, and praying it did not get any worse.

The trees once again condensed as we progressed, but the water maintained its high level. Unfortunately, the trees were too large to hold onto with one hand, and the surface-level roots were too slippery to walk on. The water was dirty with the refuse of the forest ceiling, massive undergrowth, and mud from the bottom. Low branches and heavy vines slapped us in the face, catching onto our rucksacks and increasing the frustration of our slow but determined progress. We struggled for each step as the undergrowth and the depth of the water increased.

We found ourselves in belt-deep water, stepping over crotch-level roots. It was an unbalancing prospect, trying to lift our legs straight out of the thick water and over such an obstacle. The bottom became softer, and laid claim to our feet and legs as if we did not have a choice but to leave them there. There was very little solid support around us to aid our balance. Sometimes we were trapped between two converging roots, like a ladder laid on top of the water, the back of our legs touching one rung, and the front touching the other.

The man to my front was PFC Hines. He was very motivated, and very vocal about his anger when he found himself in a tight spot. Because of his short height, I noticed that he was having some problems getting his legs over the roots. At one point, he struggled until he was stuck. If it had not been for the root lodged securely in his groin, we might have lost him forever. He twisted his body vigorously, and grunted with exertion, "Fuck!"

He had already fallen once, soaking himself to his shoulder on his left side. He was upset at looking like a klutz in front of the squad. He had the pride of a young enlisted man who did not want an officer to see him mess up, and in his opinion he definitely did not need an officer's help.

I saw him fighting to free his leg, and decided to give him a hand. I started lifting his rucksack out of the water from the bottom. This was supposed to relieve him of some weight and allow him to work. Unfortunately, my lifting of the rucksack put more weight on his shoulders. With my help, he ended up with his belly in the water, and his head a cat's lick from being dunked. Fighting siblings do not yell as loudly as he did at me. I, of course, refused to help him the rest of the way through the creek, even if he did not need my assistance.

That night we lived through one of those old Ranger stories that will be ignored by the next group of Rangers, and yes, we did get lost.

After three hours of doing the tree-root hurdle, it became too much for our RI. *"Everybody!* I mean *everybody!* Get your fucking flashlights out and let's get this goddamn patrol moving!"* One light appeared in the distance. "Everyone! Come to the white light!" he screamed.

I saw the white light bounce only 20 meters to my front. Until that point, my world had been confined to the dark figures of the man in front of me, the man behind me, and the noises of the patrol moving through the marsh. Suddenly my world expanded, and I could make out the silhouettes of the other members of my squad in a rough line between the light and myself. There were a number of trees between us, but I would soon be there. All of the Rangers at once seemed to assume an admin situation had been granted so they were no longer being evaluated; they started yelling, "Over here! Over here!" or "Hold on! I'll be right there!" It was the reflection of our lifted attitudes as we learned that we would not spend the entire night struggling through that damned creek.

I soon realized that the white light was continuing to move, and very quickly. We all pressed to keep up. The creek ended more abruptly than it had begun, mostly because we did not snake around looking for the dry areas. We marched straight ahead, the water no longer a concern. We emerged from the creek, tired and wet like cats fighting not to drown, and faced the task of concentrating on the long-forgotten mission.

None of us were proud of the way we had made it through the creek, especially of how timidly we had gone into it. We were through it, however, and we hoped we did not have to go through it again to get back.

One of the weaknesses of advice is that it is rarely followed when it is contrary to our personal comfort. Each and every one of us in the swamp that night would have loved to have given the RI an excuse on why the route was too difficult and to have heard in reply, "Hmmm, you're right. Let me call in the trucks and get us around this mess a lot faster." That, of course, was well beyond our reality.

I look around today and see a lot of people only a few meters into the swamp of their journey, hopping from tree to tree, never getting wet. Some have been there a long time, moving only side to side, never forward. What's their excuse? "I'll get wet." Plain and simple, if you're going to accomplish something worthwhile, you are going to get wet. Get over it and step forward. The sooner you do, the sooner you will realize that it won't kill you and the sooner you will reach your goal.

The sideways movement looking for a shortcut that is not there is dangerous because people either give up their hope of moving forward or make a shortcut that no one else is allowed—something illegal, immoral, or unethical.

The business model my partner and I established is unique in the tax industry. In order to establish it, we had to work through many legal, logistical, and support issues that took several years and several hundreds of thousands of dollars to perfect. You could say that we plunged into the water headfirst without a solid plan, besides optimism and faith for coming back up.

In any large business venture you have to expose the details of your business to others, and we did. In at least four cases, we have inadvertently taught our business to less than scrupulous people who have turned around and attempted to compete with us. These are the people who skirt the edge of the swamp and are willing to take what is not theirs. We provided them with what they thought was their shortcut. To them it was not an issue to push us down and walk over us in order to keep dry.

In a couple of these situations, the damage was much more than simply the creation of competition. Our contractors left us without critical services, the loss of which threatened the life of our business. My partner, Darren Oliver, and I have worked extremely hard and on very little sleep over many months to build what we have. In the best circumstances business ownership and creating business growth are difficult. Add to that finding out about these betrayals, setbacks, and the increased amount of work we were going to have to do, and it would have been easy to toss in the towel. We could have made excuses and given solid reasons why we couldn't go on that would have been accepted by everyone around us. We were faced with a question like those posed at the beginning of this chapter, "Well, what's it gonna be? Success—or excuse?"

The preparation that West Point and Ranger School gave me in developing the habit of doing the right thing at the right time and not allowing excuses had prepared me for these situations also. Neither Darren nor I ever contemplated quitting. Imagine the satisfaction that our quitting would have given to the swamp skirters.

If you are at the beginning of a journey and find yourself moving more laterally than forward, who are you allowing to get ahead of you? Who do you see moving forward and gaining the rewards of decisive action? Should you be the one getting ahead, or do you really deserve it based on your actions? It won't be easy, but plunge in.

Prayer

Strength and health and the battle for their maintenance are among the biggest focuses of Ranger students. I had heard that everyone who goes through Ranger School suffers some type of injury. One man I heard about had dysentery and a broken arm, and still made it. As the course went on, I realized that this was a very true statement. In just the first couple of weeks, I saw a broken rib, a busted nose, and a broken leg. In my own body, I felt my right shoulder and arm lose an enormous amount of strength.

I saw this go on around me, and I felt the effects of what it was doing to me. It became a battle to keep healthy enough to stay out of sick call. My largest regret from Ranger School developed out of this situation. I became so concerned with my strength that I would not volunteer to carry the heavy loads of the M60 machine gun or the PRC-77 radio. The plastic blocks of simulated ammunition were distributed evenly among those not carrying extra equipment. I carried as few of those as possible. Marching, or humping as we called it, became second nature, but strength for the rucksack was always a concern.

The course seemed to collapse on top of me and bend my already weakened knees toward submission. The philosophy of living day to day had paid off until now, but now even tomorrow seemed impossible. There was no end to Ranger School, and looking for a light at the end of the tunnel did not enter my mind. There was no way I was going to make it. I almost cried at the realization that I was not making it for the first time in my life. I had never quit or been forced to quit anything before this, and now it was time to face my own weakness. I was devastated by the depth to which I had fallen; yet it was still my choice to stay or leave.

Although I had struggled with the radio during the all-night march down the mountain back to a linkup point the night before, I had made it and was still a Ranger in good standing. Unfortunately, I had used up any reserve of energy that I might possibly have had. My legs were weak and moved slowly, even without the cumbersome rucksack. The feeling in my right shoulder and arm had returned only slightly since the end of the patrol. I did not worry that there might be permanent damage. I just knew that for the time being, I could not lift anything with my right arm.

Mentally my wariness tore at my resolve and made me want the easy way out. "I can't even keep my head up. How can I make it through the rest of this school?" I asked myself. Part of me grasped for the next rung of the ladder, knowing that despite my problems I could not quit. I thought of all of the other people who had gone to Ranger School before me, all of the men I had seen who wore the tab, a couple of whom I thought were weaker than I. "If they could make it, so can I," I thought more than once. It was a motivating thought most of the time. Now it moved me little.

Though I was often alone with my thoughts due to the nature of patrolling, this was different. I had had a duty that kept me from eating with the rest of my squad, so I arrived at the mess hall after the crowds had dispersed. Even the walk to the mess hall through the dark night was peaceful. None of the instructors were around, so I was able to leisurely receive my food and find a place to sit. I deliberately picked a seat at an empty table. I placed my LBE on the chair and my weapon against the table, and sat down. The warmth and quiet were in contrast to the rest of the 22 hours I had been up that day.

My meal sat in front of me, a sight I had dreamed about for many cold nights, but before I began to eat, I bowed my head. I was tired, but I didn't close my eyes and bow my head in order to rest; I did it to reflect. As I sat there in silence, I purposely thought of my family and my friends and the support they had given me. Consciously, I knew that I was praying. Oddly enough, when I lifted my head I was revived. In only a minute, I had an energy and a belief that could not be attributed to anything tangible. It was an amazing feeling that was not only mental, but physical also. I was different when I opened my eyes. I was stronger.

I strongly believe in the power of the mind and that we rarely challenge its limits. What power does passion have when activating our hidden mental reserves? What power comes from faith in action? That night, while teetering on the edge of my willpower and physical capacity, I was fortunate enough to face personal failure and deny it.

Can you gain the habit of successfully dealing with the thought of quitting? Like anything else, you can. What is mental strength besides the ability to overcome intense stress, function capably, and maintain perspective? The habit of not quitting is the Siamese twin of the habit of not making excuses. As you develop one, you get the other.

In My Sleep

Though tired, we all rose to meet the challenges of being a leader. It was a matter of self-preservation, serving the larger team, and attempting to graduate from Ranger School.

"Let me see the following Rangers," the RI said, then read, "Smith, Lopes, Nelson, Mitchell, and Barber."

Despite knowing that I was due another leadership position, my heart still raced a bit. I grabbed my weapon and walked to the RI, who was moving away from the rest of the platoon. He told us to sit down and take notes on the mission. "Okay. Here is the situation," he started, then briefly went through our ambush mission.

We were always concerned about the time of the actual mission. The later the mission, the more likely the Rangers would be droning and only semiaware of their surroundings. Were we taking off in the late afternoon? Did we have to be set up right after dark or somewhere in the early morning? Early morning was always bad. We knew we would still have five to 10 kilometers to walk to get to a patrol base after the completion of the mission, and that was after having been up all night.

The patrol leader was a tall, lanky man with an apathetic attitude even when selected as a leader. He was difficult to get moving when he wasn't being graded and now, surprisingly, seemed no different. There was idle talk of blowing the patrol just to get him a no-go, but that would screw every other leader also. So, like so many plans of justice, it was left in the patrol base when we marched out that afternoon.

I was the weapons squad leader. I had a big part in the ambush because my machine guns would be on either end of the ambush and would most likely signal the start of the firing. Planning, reconnaissance, security, and control are the four principles of patrolling. I was determined to practice the last one, control, beyond normal for this patrol. I was like an umpire watching over a close play at home plate for the entire patrol.

We started movement in the late afternoon in order to be set in the ambush position at 0200. It was going to be a long night. There was no moon so the movement was slow, and our location, as usual, was questionable. On a couple of occasions the patrol stopped for longer than normal and I ran up to the front, where the leader was, to find out what was going on. He was easily identified because he was covered by a poncho liner with his flashlight on.

Being lost or at least unsure of where we were while on patrol was commonplace. Tonight the patrol leader got lucky. As I walked up to find out why we were stopped, I heard the patrol leader telling the RI in an "I'm not so sure I'm sure" tone, "We are here."

The RI, being one of the few who would lend a modest amount of help, asked, "Are you sure *that's* where you are?"

"Well, I think we are. The pace count has us at three kilometers, and we've been going in this direction, so this is where I would *guess* we are," came the hesitant reply.

The RI, continuing to guide, asked, "Do you remember crossing that valley and then going up the high ground?"

"Yeah," the patrol leader squeaked.

I waited outside just to listen and watch until they were done. It was better than going back to my position in line and not knowing when we might move again. I watched the flashlight bounce around under the poncho liner for another couple of minutes. I wasn't bothered at all by the RI's help. It's much better to get to where we were going the first time instead of marching all night trying to figure it out.

"Where do you think that puts you now?" he prompted.

"That might put us in this area, I think," the patrol leader said in a questioning tone.

The RI finished, "I'd agree with you. Now get an azimuth for where you are going, and let's get this patrol moving. You've got two minutes." The RI crawled out from under their makeshift shelter and moved to the side.

I returned to my position in the patrol.

We continued to walk, each in his silent world instinctively dodging branches and following his buddy to the front. The terrain in Florida, when not in the swamp, was made up of slightly rolling hills of very soft, sandy soil. The trees were thin and widely dispersed, not a real challenge to walk between with our large rucksacks. We felt the first drops of a pending rainfall. The rain wasn't heavy, though it was a little cold. As it got harder, we halted so we could put on our wet weather tops. It wasn't a good idea to get wet at the beginning of a night of sitting in a foxhole. We moved for a couple more kilometers before stopping and beginning the reconnaissance and setup part of the patrol.

Once the marching stopped, the cold became a real issue. Our bodies were no longer generating heat, and the sweat or water that had made it to our clothes began to cool. Part of the agenda prior to conducting the non-energy-intensive parts of the patrol was putting on hot gear—long johns and field jacket liners. After a quick transition of outer gear, the majority of the patrol waited in the rally point while a small reconnaissance team left to check out the ambush site.

I found myself sitting in the dark, rain jacket over my head and legs as much as possible. I was still dry, but with the rain beating on my jacket and rucksack. I dared not move for fear of letting one of those streams of water into my dry domain underneath. I was fighting a battle of last defense. If the water made it in, even a little, I was defeated. It rained harder and harder but my shields held up. I was getting colder, but at least I was not wet. Then I felt it, the littlest breach of my jacket, up around my neck. The water began to pour down my back and into my underwear. The water must have puddled in a depression in my hood and then overflowed. I still didn't want to move because I knew it would make things that much worse. I sat there in agony, like being cut and not being able to scream. The reconnaissance party came back, and it was time to start moving into our ambush positions.

I warmed a little as I moved. The rain slowed down to a drizzle while the outside temperature continued to drop. In the preparation of the ambush position I placed my machine guns at opposite ends of the line. The patrol leader located himself in the center-rear of the position, under a poncho, as usual. I went to check with him frequently on my trips of supervision between my machine gun positions. He barely moved from his command post, and I never saw him check the ambush emplacement. I continued to update him until I realized he didn't care. The RI moved around looking at the work being done. My positions were digging in and getting the ammo and shelters ready.

Only a few minutes before we had to be ready, I made my last inspection of the two sites. Exhausted, I came back to the machine gun that was responsible for signaling the beginning of the ambush. They were ready. "Okay, I can sit and wait," I thought. I crawled into the hole behind the ammo bearer and pulled the poncho liner over my head. We looked like two people in a horse costume, except there were three of us and we were on our knees. I put my head on the back of the ammo bearer, partially to rest and partially to enjoy some of his body heat.

Ratta-tatta-tatta-tat. . . . "The machine gun is firing!" flashed through my mind. My head fell off of the ammo bearer's back, and I looked up to see the entire team running out of the foxhole. "Get the fuck back here!" I screamed. "Get back here right now, you sons of bitches!" They were screwing up the whole plan and going to get me a no-go. I was incensed.

The ammo bearer, a classmate of mine from West Point, turned and said, "The ambush has started!"

I came out of the foxhole and followed them across the road to set up security. My head was still foggy.

Once set up on the far side of the ambush site, I asked what had happened.

"You hopped into the hole with us, and not more than 20 minutes later the enemy came down the road," he explained. "We opened fire at the perfect time. Both machine guns fired beautifully. Then the whole ambush opened up. We killed the enemy and then assaulted across the objective, exactly the way it was supposed to go. What's the problem?"

"No problem," I answered with a laugh. "I must have crashed the minute I got into the hole with you guys and didn't wake up until you were starting to assault the objective. I slept through all of the firing of the ambush!"

I was happy I had done the setup work prior to sitting down.

The patrol leader did receive a no-go on that patrol, while all of the squad leaders received gos. There was some justice.

Near the end of Ranger School, even while still dealing with the obstacles of fatigue, hunger, cold, and inexperience, I had developed a level of competence as a leader. Over the course of several weeks, I had gone from seeing our mission as confusing puzzle pieces to seeing the big picture. My new abilities as a leader allowed me to set a framework for accomplishment, and my team succeeded despite my untimely nap. Isn't that the goal of every leader—a successful, self-reliant, and functioning team?

Persistence

The many years since my Ranger qualification have been an adventure, and none more than the past two years. When I chose to work as a part-time employee to a small business owner, Darren Oliver, I had no idea that I was crossing the threshold to business ownership and an entrepreneurial free-for-all. From nearly the first day, I felt like I was water-skiing behind a fighter jet. I began to live a professional life without boundaries.

I immediately accepted Darren's goal of creating a national company as my own. Though I worked only 20 hours a week for him, I made the most of that time and began building working relationships with the people who were instrumental in helping us achieve success. Within a month I was working full-time in the office and squeezing any independent consulting into spare day and nighttime minutes. The amount of work and creative energy necessary for our expansion was astounding. I quickly gained a passion for the vision of the company.

Darren drove his Ford F-350 truck down Academy Boulevard like it was a sports car, though its wheels nearly rode on top of the lane-dividing stripes like a railroad car. He rested his elbow on the open window and leaned to the left a little. "Once we are up to speed, the guys in Seattle should be able to bring in about two million dollars a month, meaning a net of three hundred thousand to us."

The team in Seattle was actually a company we were partnering with that was already expert at creating independent consulting teams. They were taking our idea and creating the nationwide sales team for it. We were busy making sure we had contractors that could perform the detailed tax services that our consultants sold. Our work was minimal considering we already had a great provider and a plan for expansion. Once it was up and running, we would be hands-off while our partners in Seattle did all of the work and gave our company 15 percent of the income. It was a beautiful setup.

After about a month and a half of work, Darren had given me 5 percent ownership of the company, but he always spoke as if I were an equal partner. That was great on one hand, and frustrating on another. "We shouldn't have any other expenses beyond maintaining the materials and ensuring enough contractors to do the work. The rest is ours."

I sat in the right seat doing the math. Let's see, 5 percent of three hundred thousand is . . .

"I'm going to move to an island," he continued. "I'll do my work from a beach somewhere. Somewhere where no one will find me. A quiet place," he said as he drove through a stale yellow light at Union Boulevard.

Okay. Okay, I thought. Where was I? Five percent of $300,000 is $5—$10—$15,000! I was completely involved in thinking about the reality in which I had somehow found myself. The possibility that my dreams could soon be coming true was nearly overwhelming. I silently looked out of the window.

"The income should start by January," he said.

"Do you really think that is possible?" I pushed back a little.

"Oh, yeah. The guys doing the up-front work are experts and are doing more than that in their current business, which is less appealing than what we are offering. There won't be much ramp-up time. Once this hits the street we'll have to actually limit the number of people we accept as consultants."

"You're kidding me," I said in disbelief.

"No. I'm not kidding. You watch," he said. Darren also had a way of being confident in things I had no clue about.

I hoped he was right. It was July and I was still making two thousand dollars a month and living off of credit cards that were becoming bogged down with weight. I had recently applied for and received another card that allowed me to transfer all of my existing balances onto it and pay no interest for six months. I had gained some valuable time, just enough to get me into January and a desperately needed, hefty paycheck. Please let this business work, I prayed.

We pulled into the parking lot and climbed down out of the

truck. We were still operating as a two-man team headquartered out of the office in the back of Darren's wife's coffee shop. If you turned sideways you could squeeze between the door and bookshelf. The entrepreneurial territory I was treading was completely unfamiliar to me, but I trusted my instincts and training. I knew that there were no rules governing the size of a person's office or the magnificence of the entryway that dictated the size of business he or she ran. I was happy with no title and an incredible prospective income, as was Darren. From that office we were not only doing the tax business, but were also partnering in an international trade business and a professional services business.

The people I met were Rangers of the business world. They were already doing millions of dollars of business a year while creating and innovating new techniques and businesses that would dwarf their current production. All of the revenue projections were mammoth, even when cut in half. All of the expansion ideas were national or international, never just local. I was out of my element, but learning that common sense, imagination, and determination rule the day. Quite often in meetings I sat quietly and took notes, while Darren and the others discussed the possibilities, and frequently covered seemingly contentious topics.

Our relationship with the Seattle group had experienced some turbulence as personalities worked to mesh and details of business implementation and money flow were worked out. As in each partnership, the vested interest in making the venture successful kept each of us finally focused on the work at hand.

I sat down at my desk and began reading e-mails. Darren picked up the phone to check voice mail. A minute later I looked over to see him sit back and slide down in his chair a bit. He had a sober look on his face, and he stared at me with wide eyes as if he had just found out some horrible secret about me. I was immediately anxious and curious. He listened to the phone for 20 more seconds before hanging up. His face was red.

"They can't do it," he softly said.

"Who can't do what?" I asked.

"The guys in Seattle have decided that they are going to focus on their current business and not partner with us," he answered. "They have had all kinds of trouble getting our program put together with their writers and they don't want to put any more money toward it."

I was pissed because these guys had deep pockets, a basic knowledge of our business processes, and an existing sales force. They could do this themselves if they wanted, and that's what I assumed they were going to do. "So. Do you think they are going to set this up themselves?"

"Absolutely," he said without hesitation.

In those 10 seconds, we had been set back to where we had started. My easy income and imminent dream had vanished. The light at the end of the tunnel had gone black. We were again just two guys in the back of a coffee shop with only a good idea. All of the potential options flashed through my mind: quit and find a job, consult full-time and forget the national stuff, focus on the other businesses, or set up this business ourselves. I had already decided what I wanted to do.

"Well?" I prompted.

"Well what?" Darren asked.

"Well, are we going to do this ourselves?" I answered.

He just looked at me. I think he was still thinking of ways to get to Seattle in the next hour and rip down their walls. "No question," he said. "We've got to put this together ourselves, and quickly. I want to crush those bastards."

We both knew that we had a daunting task ahead of us. We had to write and produce marketing materials, advertise, and sell. We had to produce a training manual and establish the system to get the services performed, and we had to do this better than the experts. We stood at the edge of the swamp without a map showing us how wide it was and without Ranger Instructors to whip out flashlights and save us if our situation ever became untenable. We were going to put our full lives and incomes into making our business fly and we weren't sure if it ever would.

I was personally back at a common decision point: Do I move forward or do I roll over and pee on myself?

"This way we'll make even more money," he said.

We have faced decisions of that magnitude four times in the past two years. More importantly, there have been hundreds of less critical but immeasurably tiring situations that have demanded a decision to press on toward our goal. There is a straight line between the success habits that I developed in Ranger School and my daily commitment to my current objective. There has never been a question as to our route. We allowed no other avenue besides straight ahead, and we are convinced that no one else understands the determination we share. As scouts in the Army we liked to say, "Move out and draw fire." Darren and I did.

Today, we have over 10,000 square feet of office space and nearly 50 employees.

We were scared and uncertain of the future but confident in our ability to persevere.

Ranger Barber's Walk

From wherever you are now you can start to grow in capacity and competency as a leader. Not surprisingly, that journey takes perseverance and will sometimes find you looking like a frog.

Perseverance is a great place to start because it is the car that brings you to the door of all of the other lessons. If at some point you fail to persevere, all of the educational experiences beyond that point will be lost to you. Perseverance is a prerequisite to any level of success, and its presence is a fundamental, underlying component of all the remaining chapters. It has to be there for you to learn the other lessons of leadership and gain the capability to be responsible for other people. Every successful person has persevered through challenges that their competitors did not survive. They started with rudimentary steps that they are proud of, but would probably be unwilling to share with anyone today. Have you considered Rush Limbaugh's first radio appearance, Nolan Ryan's first pitch, Steven Spielberg's first film, Tiger Woods' first swing, or Norman Schwarzkopf's first order? No doubt you've already taken your first step.

As you move from pulling random puzzle pieces out of your pocket to being able to accomplish a mission in your sleep, you will gain perspective and certainty. The people you lead are expecting you to see beyond today to an end state in the future. They want to have confidence that you have a plan and that today's tasks are moving them toward a future success. People may follow you without this kind of vision, but they will never be inspired.

Much of what I learned about leadership came through recognizing what inspired me. I believe that people respond to worthwhile challenges. Had I not responded to the challenge that Colonel Turner laid before me during the infantry branch briefing nearly 18 years ago, I would not be in my current position. Even though the majority of people respond only superficially to a challenge, it is in human nature to want to overcome and achieve. In today's society, however, where personal choice is paramount and comfort is the pervasive goal, most people will choose not to pursue a worthwhile goal beyond the first hardship. It is part of your leadership terrain to illustrate by example the rewards of perseverance.

You have power to motivate through providing a challenge and a goal, while at the same time you have the task of keeping people focused on that end state throughout the difficulties. It's not just acquiring money that motivates people; there are many more important things you can do, such as listening, appreciating, working hard, and setting the example.

You'll see examples of all of these in Tex Turner's story, as well as hints on how to climb a tree with a motorcycle.

RANGERS

are

HUMBLE

ROBERT "TEX" TURNER

Colonel Tex Turner is a soldier with over 31 years of active Army service, two combat tours in Vietnam, and legend status at West Point and in the Ranger Department. The lesson of his story from West Point through Ranger School and his career is simply to listen. Once he figured out that there was a wealth of ideas in the people he led, he tapped into a way to motivate his soldiers, perform better at missions, and have fun in the process.

Sincerely ask for input from your people and then listen. Listen at meetings, because you may be next in the barrel, and listen to your body so you know when to back off for the good of the soldiers and the mission. Listening takes humility. It takes a humble person to subjugate his opinions and ideas to others through the process of listening and considering. Colonel Turner knew that his role was not to build himself up by dictating and self-glorification through control of the airwaves. He was focused instead on creating successful units that accomplished the mission.

What is your focus? How can you tap into the wealth of ideas from the people around you or who work for you? Or for whom you work?

Thanks for the Sign

I truly believe that all I am and all I ever hope to be as a leader I owe to West Point and Ranger School. I didn't really begin to understand what they had developed in me as a leader until I was tested in Vietnam. In July 1965, I was the adviser to the 35th Vietnamese Ranger Battalion. I became aware of some of life's lessons one day as I sat in a rice paddy, scared to death, tired and hungry, and desperately wanting to see my wife and family back home. Sitting there on the edge of that muddy, stinky rice paddy dike, my feet up on the edge of the water, I was thinking about how much I wanted out of there, how much I wanted away from that place. Feeling sorry for myself, I silently said, "I'm quitting. This is too tough, and I don't like it. I'm hanging up my jockstrap."

All of a sudden I saw a streak of light across the sky. At first I thought it was a tracer, but in the next instant I figured it was coming in at too high an angle. "Can't be a tracer," I thought. When I realized it was a shooting star, I said to myself, "Maybe that's an omen. God is trying to tell me something." My thoughts turned to my past. I survived high school football, beast barracks, plebe year, and three more years as a cadet. I went through all of the welter we had to put up with as a cadet living in that monastery-like environment and then went through Ranger School. I spent eight frigging weeks of pure hell doing all kinds of weird things and then went out and did my duty in the military. I thought, "You know, ever since I got into the military, everything has been pretty easy compared to what I'd done to get there." Then it struck me that I was in pretty good shape.

Perhaps the reason my star streaked across the sky was to remind me that I got to eat every day and I usually got to sleep most of the night, which was much better than at many earlier points in my military life. When you're in combat, it's not like in the movies. You are not in combat full-time. You can get a lot of sleep. Combat has been described as days of boredom interrupted by moments of sheer terror.

It further occurred to me that much of my career had been easy for me because I *had* put up with West Point for four years. West Point is successful in producing quality leaders for many reasons: the academic and physical challenges, as well as the instilling of the values of duty, honor, country, and the ability that helped immeasurably in combat—the ability to get along with people. In combat you have to know how to get along with people so you can survive for months in a foxhole together. I'm convinced that one reason West Point made us change roommates every six months was to teach us that skill. The other reason was to keep us from killing each other if we had to spend another day together. It happened that you would get a roommate you didn't like and as a young man, you had to learn how to deal with those differences just like you have to learn how to deal with guys in foxholes. I thought, "I've already been through all the tough stuff, and I'm in pretty good shape where I am," so I looked up to the sky and said, "Thank you. I appreciate that little sign." From then on I knew where I was going, and I've never faltered since.

What Are Your Actions and Orders

The Ranger Course trains soldiers how to lead in combat at a small unit level. That's what it does! It gives guys confidence in their ability to do the difficult, dangerous things that they have to do. Hell, it defines your physical limits. Every man who's a leader in the Army—and I don't care if he's in the infantry or some other branch—needs to know his physical limits. That knowledge helps him determine just how far he can push his troops in combat. When he starts getting tired, his guys are probably getting tired, too.

The course stresses you out and puts you in command. When you've been wondering around the woods for five days with no sleep and only one meal a day, and then the old patrol leader gets "killed" and the RI says, "Send up Ranger Turner," you start figuring out really quickly how to lead in those conditions.

Ranger Turner stumbles up to the front of the line, and the RI then says, "Ranger Turner, you are now in charge. What are your actions and orders?"

You say, "Duhhh, where is the compass man?"

The compass man shuffles to you and you ask, "God, where am I?"

I repeat, Ranger School stresses you out and puts you in command, and that's what leaders have to know how to cope with. A leader has to get the job done in difficult circumstances, and others have to trust in his abilities and determination to see the mission to the end. The warrior has to live by the "duty, honor, country" code because you've got to trust each other. That code means that I can give you my back and rest assured I'm protected, and you can do the same. If you don't live by that code, I'm not going to trust you on my right or left flank to take care of me. I have to trust that you will get in the covering fire for me *when* I need it or die trying. The course teaches you what it is like to rely on others and know the stress of having others rely on you.

Ranger School puts you in extreme, sometimes dangerous situations and teaches you how to get soldiers to the objective, how to win, and then get them back home. If you are moving through the swamp and the ambient temperature is 30 degrees, the water temperature is 38 degrees, and your people are all getting hypothermia, you are not going to accomplish the mission. You'd better figure out a proper route to get to that objective and, heaven forbid, you may have to build a tactical fire to take care of your troops. Get your soldiers warm, because if you don't get them to the objective to fight, they are not going to beat the enemy. Then you have to get every damn one of them back alive. The level of a soldier's trust in your ability to do that has a direct bearing on the amount of motivation that soldier has to go into harm's way for you.

Revenge

The 29th Infantry out of Fort Benning, Georgia, provided the aggressors (OPFOR) for our class. In Florida they operated as a company led by Captain Burton. They aren't the dedicated OPFOR in operation at the school now. They were a regular Army unit sent to man the objectives and harass Ranger students. One night they were able to haul in a classmate of mine, Frank Herrera, as a prisoner.

The rest of us continued the patrol through to its completion after his capture and then walked back to camp where we got updated news of Frank.

I walked up on a couple of squad mates who were already in

conversation. "Damn if he didn't get his nose broken," said one of the guys. He continued, "I guess he was in the back of the jeep with a barracks bag over his head, struggling to get free when Captain Burton let him have it with his elbow and broke his nose. I saw him when they brought him over to the infirmary with a big old bandage on his face."

The story spread fast, and even though we were tired and hungry, the thought of revenge brought us back to a very aggressive state. It wasn't long before we had a plan put together to capture Captain Burton.

Squatting in the dark, three of my fellow students waited for the captain to walk by. This wasn't a go or no-go situation. It was something they couldn't take back or redo. Burton wasn't large, but he wasn't small, either, so when he walked by, they all attacked with vigor.

They overpowered and gagged him before moving him quickly from there a safe distance into the woods, where they let the real torture begin. They filled his pants up with pinecones and tied his pant legs around his ankles to keep in the cones. Then, acting on a suggestion no one would ever take credit for, they forced him to tie a rope around his dick and pulled the rope backward between his legs and up around his neck. They walked him for several miles in that hazardous condition.

He moved delicately, trying to avoid any permanent damage. Every once in a while they'd give him a prod in the back with a boot to launch him forward and keep it interesting. He must have thought it was best to keep quiet and not fight, figuring, "If they can do this to me, what other sick Ranger tricks must they know or be willing to do?"

Captain Burton returned to the camp area a bit scuffed up and with good reason to think twice about getting physical with any more Ranger students. He never knew who his assailants were. Through the process, however, he gained a lot of respect from us because he never complained or threatened retribution and went along surprisingly well with the game.

Many years later I ran into him at the War College, where I shed some light on what I'm sure was a bit of a strange chapter of his life. His first response was, "So you were one of the little mothers in that class, huh?"

Drop the Rope!

The Yellow River in Florida is probably 50 to 60 feet wide under normal conditions, but on the day we did one-rope bridge training, it was overflowing its banks. In addition to that, we had some early cold weather that year plunging the temperature down into the teens at night. It was cold enough that there was ice in the swamps. There were no rules on how long you could stay in the water based on temperatures like we've set up for Ranger School in the recent past.

We did training on dry land first to learn the techniques of constructing a rope bridge, and then we headed into the water to practice in more realistic conditions. The patrol had a rope bridge team, and each guy in that team was assigned duties to perform upon reaching a creek or a river. We were lined up as a patrol, and at our particular site we were all standing in water about waist deep, freezing our knickers off. Training always seemed to go slower than real missions since the RI had to explain each step in detail and then correct us when we got off track. It was hard to focus on the information when we were focused on our own discomfort, but somehow the time passed, and we were ready to construct a bridge ourselves.

The man in front of me was the poor sap assigned to carry the rope across the river. Once we anchored the rope on a near-side tree it was his turn to link the two sides by swimming the river. I was right behind him, watching in painful sympathy as he soaked himself and then started swimming in the freezing water. He got about halfway across, and the damn river was flowing so swiftly that it carried him downstream. He looked like a drowning dog as he finally gave up stroking and floated with the current. They picked his ass up in a boat down a ways. The big old tough sergeant pointed to me with eyes that said, "You're next."

I said, "What?" I thought, "Oh shit. This is it. This is *the* miserable time everyone talks about." I took off all my clothes to reduce the drag, wrapped the rope around me, and said, "I'm going to get across that damn river!"

On the near shore I pulled myself upstream by the roots in an effort to counteract the fast-moving current. The water at the bank was shallow and was only up to my ankles at places. The icy mud squished between my toes as I had an all-too-personal experience with the shallow water of the river. I approached that black water like I was walking on broken glass and about to jump into a pool of alcohol. I felt pain and burning in my legs as I stepped into the water, and the sensations only worsened as the water level rose with each step toward the center of the river. My whole body was experiencing an ice cream headache as my head went under and I took my first strokes toward the far side. I swam hard upstream and toward the other side and somehow made it.

I don't think I've ever been that cold in my life. I stood on the far side as naked as if I had just crawled out of the bathtub, pale white and covered with goose bumps. I pulled the slack out of the rope, turned around and dragged it to the designated tree. I wrapped it around the tree and began tying it off when the RI yelled across, "Dro-o-o-op the ro-o-o-ope!"

I questioned back, "Whyyyyy?"

"It's the wro-o-o-ong treeeee!" he answered.

I said, "Show me the right tree and I'll hook it up!"

"Dro-o-o-op the ro-o-o-ope, Ranger!" he yelled. I hung onto the rope, staring back in defiance. He read my look even from that distance and then repeated, "I *said*, Dro-o-o-op the ro-o-o-ope!" Reluctantly, I dropped the rope sensing that my condition, which I couldn't imagine any worse, was about to deteriorate. The squad pulled the rope back to their side and the RI then yelled, "Get your ass back over here, Ranger!"

I thought, "Oh my God. I'm going to die," and yet it had a bright side. I thought, "At least I'm out of this one. My Ranger buddy will be the guy who has to take the rope across next," so I swam back across the river looking like a fly caught in syrup. I emerged from the water and went back to my gear, where I began to dry off in preparation for getting dressed.

"Ranger Turner, come up here. Take it across again," commanded the RI.

I thought, "God Almighty." Each demand on me was one more step beyond reason, but it never entered my mind to question my task. Each time, I evaluated my condition and determined I could go on. Minus reasonable excuses, we all went well beyond our perceived limits.

"Which tree do you want?" I asked.

The RI pointed to the far side. "That one." As if I could tell where his finger was aimed.

"Now hold on, I want to get this right. Do you mean the big one closer or farther from the bank?" I asked.

"Farther," he clarified.

"Okay. I got it," I said, and swam the rope across one more time.

This time I guarantee you I got the right tree. I got up as high as I could on that tree and tied the rope off with a round turn, two half hitches, and a slip knot. They finally got it tightened on the other side and came across. I had to wait, like a naked school crossing guard, where I was until everyone was over to undo the damn rope.

Just as the monotonous training had passed, so did this exercise, and I was dressed and back in the patrol moving toward home. We finally got back into camp at about midnight after being out in 40-degree temperatures all day, and though we were wet most of the day, I don't remember anybody getting hypothermia.

Listen to the Voices

By the time we got to Florida, everybody had figured out that my Ranger buddy, Mike Isacco, and I had a knack for direction and keeping patrols on course, so if we weren't running the patrol, we got picked as point or compass man. We were always out in front, and that didn't change when we came to river boat operations.

I sat in the front of our RB-15 wondering how I would do on my first river excursion as compass man. We paddled down the river for almost three hours, me under a poncho with a flashlight with a red filter and map trying to follow where we were. It was quiet on the river, so I listened to the slight sounds of the paddles on the water and the night sounds of the swamp, and took the cues from my buddies to try to track our progress on my map. It was a whole different game being the compass man in a boat: no pace count, no hills or valleys. At night there were just turns.

Every time the river turned the guys would tell me, "The river is turning left," and I'd figure out where the bends matched the map. The first time I took the poncho off of my head was when my calculations had us near the debarking site. The boat continued forward until it was time. "Okay, guys, this is it," I whispered, and we rowed to shore.

From the back of the boat our crafty RI asked, "You boys going to get off here?"

Something in the way he asked the question told me this was not the place. I said, "Wait a minute. Hold it, guys. We've got a little bit further to go . . . I think." I was purely guessing at that point. My confidence was shot, and I accepted the unspoken task of trying to figure out where in the world we were. I threw the poncho back over my head and said, "Keep going, guys."

About 30 minutes later, with me still not knowing where the hell I was, the RI nonchalantly asked, "When are you boys going to get off this boat?"

I threw the poncho off and said, "This is the place, guys!"

We pulled over, got out of the boat, and went on the planned azimuth, which took us right to the objective. We hit the rocket site and went on home. I just knew that the RI didn't want to walk through swamps all night and all the next day just to get a bunch of ugly Rangers to an objective.

Sleep with One Eye Open

The RIs never said much when I went through. They were professionals, like a great platoon sergeant keeping watch over his troops, but not saying a hell of a lot to them. Staff Sergeant Columbo, an RI in the mountain camp, was the toughest, meanest person I could imagine, and though he would really bring smoke on us, we knew he truly loved soldiers. When we were there, he was sporting a large bandage on his finger from almost cutting it off with a machete. Yet during the mountaineering portion, standing at the bottom of the cliff, he demonstrated throwing a grappling hook and rope over the top of the cliff, and then climbed to the top. I wondered, "How in the hell does he climb that damn thing with that big a bandage on his finger? It must hurt like hell."

Staff Sergeant Columbo was our RI on one miserably cold night that seemed to have no sympathy for our condition. The snow was blowing so hard that it was difficult to even keep our eyes open as we marched along. Unconsciously, I prepared for a full night of suffering, but because the cold was so overwhelming I couldn't think more than a minute ahead. That's when Staff Sergeant Columbo said, "Pull it up here. We're going admin. Send out a couple of teams to find a good spot to build a tactical fire."

We couldn't believe it. We had never heard of something like that. "Hell, yeah. Let's do this," we said, but wondered, "What the hell is a tactical fire?"

The RI explained, "Find a place that has a lot of big boulders around it so you can hide the fire from horizontal observation."

That made sense, so we sent out a couple of teams who found an area with big glacial boulders around it. The imminent salvation muted the cold in my mind, and the wind didn't bother me as much as it had a few minutes earlier. I followed the man in front of me up the trail. "I'm going to be warm," was my thought, "and it's going to be soon!" I walked slouched over, head down, to protect my face from the wind. I kept waiting to see these boulders on my left and right, but for endless minutes I only saw the dirty shuffle tracks of the Rangers in single file to my front. Still looking down, I butted my head right into the rucksack of the stopped man in front of me. I looked up expectantly and was happy to finally see our rocky campsite.

We trudged in and claimed a piece of land as home by dropping our rucks. "Where is the fire going to be?" I wondered, and looked around for the most likely place. The best place to sleep was one that was close enough to the fire for easy access, but not close enough that the heat or rotating Rangers would keep me awake when I chose to crash. I picked a place against the rocks just off the open area and then dumped my rucksack there. Blood rushed into my shoulders and back where my rucksack and straps had cut off circulation. It was a cold sensation, but a good one even in the extreme chill of the air because it was a sign that my body was still functioning and one day would heal from this trauma. The next command was for us to gather wood and dig a pit for the fire.

My Ranger buddy and classmate, Mike Isacco, and I took off on a firewood search detail. Dead wood was pretty sparse on the clean forest floor. Our hunt was like searching for coins in a grocery store parking lot. We had gone about a quarter mile away when we finally found a wooden fence around some old farmer's field. Mike and I looked at each other with the same question on our minds: "How much of this fence can we take without anyone finding out?" We hesitated for a second, looked at our handful of twigs, let them drop to the ground, and got to work. Mike and I leveraged our weight against the boards and pried them off the fence. Once we got started on the deconstruction it was like trying to stop eating potato chips, and soon we reduced that area to a sizable gap. It didn't take us long to have more wood than we could carry back in one trip, so we loaded each other up with a maximum load and headed back to the boulders. We were greeted as conquering heroes as the lumber clunked on the ground. The RI was not actively involved in the building of the fire and was off on his own, unaware of what we were using for fuel.

I huffed out big clouds of breath and I tried to get my wind back after the long haul. I pointed in the direction from which we had come and said, "A quarter mile that way. There's all the wood we need." Another group set out immediately with a distinctly posse attitude. They came back a short time later with enough to last several hours and representing damage that would take the farmer several hours to repair the next summer.

We were admin, so the name of the game was to keep warm and get some sleep. The fire continued to grow, and we continued to add fuel. We all scrunched around the fire, and like the rest, I was dozing off. I looked up to see the RI sitting on one of the boulders far away from the fire. He had no field jacket on, like a thinly clad statue immune to the cold. The RIs didn't wear field jackets, so they were more aware of the temperature and therefore more likely to know when the Rangers were cold. In contrast, I had so many clothes and thermal underwear on that if I had fallen down I'd have rolled half a mile. I was so bundled up that I had to use a peter rope to take a leak.

Staff Sergeant Columbo just sat there, looking straight at me, both eyes wide open, concentrating on Ranger Turner. I didn't worry about it and quickly dozed off. I woke up a couple of hours later, and out of habit I thought, "Better check the RI." I looked up to see the oddest sight. Staff Sergeant Columbo had one frigging eye open looking straight at me. My only thought before going back to sleep was, "I hope I get a platoon sergeant like him in my first unit."

Sleep with One Ear Open

I went into the briefing tent ready to relax and watch as the Rangers who needed patrols to graduate got their chance to shine one last time. We were in the final part of our last phase, the mountains, and I had already passed all six of my patrols. Put simply, I was ready to keep as warm as possible for the rest of the time and then graduate. I thought, "These guys would never give me another patrol. I've already had six, goddamn, and I've done well on all of them."

I sat in the tent colder than hell and concentrating on trying to get closer to the potbellied stove. I looked over the shoulder of the Ranger in front of me toward the briefing board, but somewhere in the distance to the board my thoughts dispersed. I focused instead on life after Ranger School, on food, sleep, and warmth. Like flipping through a book at a hundred pages a pop, I could only roughly tell at what part of the briefing we were in or when it might end. It finished way too abruptly.

"Ranger Turner," the RI said, "you're the patrol leader."

I hadn't listened, taken notes, or even remotely prepared, yet there I was, in a tight spot as the patrol leader for the planning phase. I panicked. I didn't take any notes! I was like a lost child. I wanted to be able to look into my notebook and see some legible, applicable scratches that I had subconsciously made, but I had it out just for show, and only blank pages faced me.

"Let me see the squad leaders up here and any volunteers for compass man," I spouted out in a show of confidence, but taking charge was the only step I knew for certain I had to do. Ranger buddies stuck together, and Mike Isacco knew that if I was the patrol leader he was going to play a significant role in getting things done. He didn't know how much he was going to help, but since he was looking for one more patrol, he had taken very good notes. I used all his notes, picked his brain throughout the planning process, and made it to the end of that desperate situation. There is nothing like a Ranger buddy.

I gave the order and started getting everyone loaded up on the trucks when I was "killed" and somebody else took over. Relieved again to be simply a member of a squad, I was thankful for a buddy who had saved me. I knew that there wouldn't always be someone around to pull my ass out of the fire, so ever since then I've always listened up in any meeting because you never know when you are going to get picked to lead the next mission.

RI Fun

I came straight back to the Ranger Department as the deputy chairman of the Patrolling Committee after my first tour in Vietnam in September 1966. Back then the Patrolling Committee was the largest committee in the Ranger Department with probably over 100 guys assigned. We not only conducted the hand-to-hand combat training for the Ranger Course, we also trained patrolling for IOBC and the "shake and bake" Sergeant Leadership Course to prepare them for their trip to Vietnam. Over 25,000 guys a year went through that two-week-long training.

The soldiers and officers I was surrounded by were all dedicated and uncommonly driven. One of my coworkers was Captain Bill Spies. I didn't immediately know why, but his nickname was "Peg Leg." He trained hard right along with the rest of us, making airborne jumps frequently to get in for RI changeover. After landing on one of the jumps I stood up and began to get my bearings when I looked across the way and saw Spies hopping on one leg. "Son of a bitch. This guy's got only one leg," I thought. I stood there dumbfounded as he went over to his rucksack, unstrapped his leg, stuck it onto his stump, wrapped up his parachute, and ran off the drop zone. It didn't take me but a minute to get my gear wrapped up and head to the turn-in point myself, and I'll be damned if he didn't make it there before I did. I now knew why he had the nickname, but I never found out why he had only one leg.

Captains Ski Werbiski and Eric Macintosh, also Vietnam vets, worked for me as the heads of the two different departments. The Army made sergeants very quickly back then to accommodate the war, earning them the name "shake and bake." As professional soldiers we tried desperately to pass on all the little tricks we had learned through our years of service and our time in Vietnam. We wanted to make sure they knew the basics about leadership, staying alert, staying alive, and getting all of their soldiers back in one piece. It was more than training for us. We knew that a poor job on our part could cost someone his life in a very short time.

We worked very hard, and we let out our aggressions with equal enthusiasm. One opportunity for celebration came when a few other guys and I were promoted at the same time. I had finally made major and wanted the day to be noted in a memorable fashion. I went in together with the other guys and threw a promotion party at the Fort Benning officers club. I got so damn drunk at the promotion party that the next day I was so sick I had to turn around on my way to work and come home.

Rangers rarely wanted to have a party on main post because we could end up going to jail. The best thing to do was to rent one of the lodges that Benning maintained out in the woods, set it up, and have the party out there. With that in mind, one night I had a cocktail party at my house in the Custer Terrace housing area at Fort Benning just to get things started before going to the lodge. It was 1967, and since hippies were a big movement at the time, we decided on a hippie theme for the night, and my fellow Rangers spiced things up by dressing the part. They all rallied before heading to my house and came down the street of my neighborhood in a column of motorcycles with their wives or girlfriends on the back. The guys wore long-haired wigs, and their wives were dressed in short skirts, high boots, and long wigs also. It was a scene right out of a Hell's Angels dream. The screamingly loud motorcycle engines stopped conversations on the street and drew frightened stares. So help me, I saw my neighbors coming out of their homes, grabbing their children, and pulling them off the street.

My hippie friends pulled up and parked their motorcycles in front of my building like hitching horses and filed inside. After getting primed we loaded up and took off in a thunder of bikes to the cabin. In my own wig and outfit I saw my neighbors peering out of their doors and windows wondering what in the world was going on. We drove out to Harmony Church and through the Military Police (MP) gate at Sand Hill, where they fortunately didn't stop us.

Once in the woods and out of direct fire range, we raised all kind of Cain, broke the windows out, and had a hell of a good time. The invincibility of alcohol combined with the pride of Rangers coerced us to carry through with the idea of a drag race. We lined up our motorcycles and revved our engines. I could barely focus, but I knew I wasn't going to sit this one out. I had to win, for whatever that was worth. I got the rpm's on my Honda trail bike up high, screaming like a stuck pig in preparation for the signal to go. The handkerchief dropped; I popped the clutch; the bike did a wheelie and threw me onto my ass, and the bike climbed a pine tree. Of course, I lost the race and bent my front fork, but I was alive and had participated. We always had a lot of fun, though it wasn't always safe to be a Ranger—even when recreating.

Planning ahead, we kept a stock of spare window panes at the Ranger Department because every time we had a party we broke most of the windows out. That Sunday we went back out there and put the windows back in. It was kind of like making a bed. We replaced them so we could break them out again.

Along with motorcycles, many of us went out and bought boats, and just like with the motorcycles, we had to be out by ourselves in order to protect the general public. On the lake just north of Columbus we commandeered an island. The one we selected we actually cleaned up, equipped with picnic tables we built, and made into a nice place to visit. We'd go out there whenever we could to water-ski and picnic with our families.

We enjoyed spending time together at work and in leisure. Learning about each other away from work was important because it helped develop even more trust between one another. Learning about a fellow soldier's family and finding out more about the real person behind his everyday work persona drew us closer as a unit, and I'd have proudly gone to war with any one of those guys.

Listen

In Ranger School you always had to be ready to take charge. There was always the possibility of getting the nod. The tough times were when after walking through the woods for three or four days you get called up to the front to take over. The old patrol leader "was shot" or "stepped on a mine," and you were now in charge. The first question from the RI was always, "What are your actions and orders?"

It taught me that you had to take charge totally and absolutely. Whenever you are given a unit, the name of the game is to take charge, take action, and win. When you are given command, you are in command, and you are the one that success depends on. The unit is going to do exactly how you do. It only takes one man, and if you are a good leader, know what you are doing, and know how to execute the operation, it will be a success. However, if you pussyfoot around and don't show confidence, compassion, and control—that is, you haven't taken charge—you will not accomplish the mission. Everything we did in Ranger School was just that: take charge, take action, and win.

I understood that even at West Point because when I became a first classman, I was picked by my tactical officer to be a company commander. I took the position to heart and was flat gung ho about it. That was one of my problems at West Point: I was too damn gung ho, and I never figured out how to be gung ho tactfully. I failed so many times it was frightening, but by the process of elimination I learned the proper way to take charge. The reason I failed was because I wasn't able, as a classmate, to lead my classmates very well.

That was almost impossible to do anyway, but after trying to get them to do something for so damn long, I'd give up, and if necessary I'd slug their ass and they'd walk the area.

Once in the Army I looked back at that experience and tried to figure out ways to motivate guys to get the job done without resorting to punishment. There was always a way to motivate someone, to give them a desire to accomplish the mission, not just because it's an order, but because it will be good for everybody if they do the job properly. One method I used throughout my career was to seek the input of my soldiers.

The five-day patrols in Ranger School were frigging tough, and I had to find some way to motivate the exhausted guys I was counting on. All of a sudden I was thrown in charge, and I had to figure out a way to get everybody squared away. The most effective and easiest way to do that was to get all the subleaders together and find out what they thought. "The mission is to head to here and take out the objective. We are here right now. What do you guys think?" I'd ask.

One of the guys would bring up something like, "You know, we've been crossing these damn fingers for the last three days. I'm tired of going up and down all night. I've got a better route."

"Okay, what's your route?" I'd inquire, and then listen. Sure enough, we'd go that way, and everybody was happier because we didn't climb damn mountains and then plunge into valleys all night long. It taught me to listen to my soldiers and to keep my ear to the ground, because if I didn't, we might not win the battle. I told my troops, "You'd better tell me when I'm headed for a cliff, or I may just take you with me," and half seriously finish, "and if I do, it's going to be your fault, not mine."

I was sincere in being open to receiving input from my soldiers, and they could sense that. Often as a battalion commander I would be stopped by a private as I crossed the area. "Hey, sir, I've got an idea. What do you think about. . . ."

I'd listen and reply, "Damn, Jones, that sounds like a good idea. Let me check that out and I'll get back to you." Sure enough, I would look into it and call Jones or go over to the company and see him. "Where does Jones live? Where's his bunk?" I'd ask. I'd trot to his bunk, grab a seat on his footlocker, and talk. "About that idea you told me of couple days ago, well, I looked into it, and it won't work," or "We're going to try it and see if it does work." Invariably, whether we used it or not, the guy felt important, and then he was motivated. We might not have done what he wanted, but at least I listened, and he felt his ideas were valued.

I think that openness is critical in any unit. You have to motivate the members of the unit to do the daily mission and more. There are a thousand ways to inspire people, and respecting their ideas is one of the best. I learned that at West Point because of my failures, and at Ranger School because of my successes.

First Desert Phase

When I first got to the Ranger Department in 1982, we accepted people from all branches of the Army. About midway through my tour General Foss said, "What we need to do is require all infantrymen to be Rangers." That directive virtually shut out most other branches. There just wasn't enough room. Now it has gotten down to the fact that admission is restricted exclusively to combat arms guys.

The original reason for the Ranger Course when it was set up back in 1951 was to train people from all branches of the Army in small unit patrolling operations. It was a "train the trainer" course where the graduates could go back to their units and teach them how to do those kinds of operations. The thinking has changed over time, with the belief now that guys in non–combat arms branches won't be thrown into a patrolling situation behind enemy lines. I beg to differ. We never thought that a Ranger unit in World War II was going to be put up against a German armor division, either, but that's the kind of thing that happens in war.

In war, even the cooks and clerks have to be prepared to be warriors. You may run out of infantry and armor guys, and you have to take the cooks and clerks out of the bunkers and out of the command post and put them on the line. I saw it happen in Vietnam. The non-combat guys were forced to man the perimeter, rifles pointed downrange, securing our base and their lives. At that point it was too late to train them. They had better damn well know how to use the bayonet, how to shoot, and how to throw hand grenades without the damn things going off in their hands. In Vietnam we even had a trained second lieutenant throw a grenade in front of one of my positions. It hit a tree, bounced back in his hole, and blew his ass off. It didn't kill him, but he had holes all over him. Of course, that can happen in a fit of passion in the middle of combat, so you want people as ready as they can be. Weird things happened, and everybody had to be a warrior.

Primarily, Ranger School was, is, and always will be a leadership school, and I went into my job as the head of the Ranger Department with that in mind. I wanted to train everyone who came through, whether it was an infantry soldier or a supply clerk, to be the best prepared they could be for the next war. I didn't know where that next war might be, but my experiences in the Pentagon gave me an idea. I traveled a lot from the Pentagon, operating in the high and low deserts of the Middle East, Egypt, Sudan, and the Syrian Desert. We had some severe problems due to the lack of expertise in desert operations, and it occurred to me that we needed to train our Army in that environment.

Brigadier General Ken Leure was the assistant commandant at the Infantry School and had helped me get to the Ranger Department. He and I saw eye to eye on training matters, so the first time I met with him I said, "Sir, I want to start a live fire and establish a desert phase in the Ranger Course."

He said, "Do it. Call if you need any help."

One of the ways I was able to get the commanding general to approve my request for the desert phase was to go back into the history books and find some after-action reports that had been written by general officers and colonels from World War II in the North African desert. I highlighted one part (among others) that said, "If one or two guys in each unit, even up to battalion level, had been trained in desert warfare, they might have saved the whole battalion from being captured." Besides the fact that the training made sense to everybody, the resources to do it were to be taken out of hide—from existing resources, money, people, and equipment—so it was no skin off their butt. The commanding general approved it and sent the request to Training and Doctrine Command, who approved it also. Now our mission was to make it happen.

I had some challenges to overcome right away, the lack of time and personnel being the greatest. The school was eight weeks and two days long. I fought furiously for an extra five days because when I put in the desert phase I had to take five days out of the mountains and two days out of the Florida camp.

The live fire was a lot easier to get started, with the first one being conducted in Florida in about two months. It started out as a static ambush because they were pretty easy to set up and control. My initial concern was to avoid getting somebody hurt or killed. Our first actual moving live fire didn't get started until we put in the desert phase at McGregor Range. I figured that by the third phase the Rangers knew each other enough to trust each other on their right and left when working with live ammo.

The desert phase took a little more imagination and flexibility to bring on board. I could only use assets that I already had. I didn't get any extra money, people, or equipment, but I wanted to get the desert phase going fast. The sequence of phases was Benning, mountains, desert, Florida, and then back to Benning to graduate. The plan we put together had the mountains RIs running the desert phase. They would put the students through their home phase in Dahlonega and then take them down to the Benning Airfield, pop everybody on two C-141s, in-flight rig them, and then jump into the desert at McGregor Range on Fort Bliss just north of El Paso, Texas. We put the first class out there in April of 1983.

McGregor Range was a great place to start. However, from the beginning, I wanted to get a better training area. It was too wide open and big for Ranger type operations. There was no place to hide. We needed a place that was a little more compact, where you could get up in the hills and high desert tree line to hide during the day, sneak out at night to make your attack, and then move back into a hide position before dawn. We finally found what we needed at Dugway Proving Grounds, Utah, and moved out there just before I left in 1985. It was your typical high desert, rocky hardpan, sand dunes, salt flats, and close-by hills with ample, low ground cover to hide in.

Dugway was the perfect place for everything to come together. The live fire mission was conducted just about anywhere. All we had to do was pick an area where we could shoot up against a mountain and we wouldn't have a problem. I kept fighting for the extra days and people right up until I left, and although I didn't get them in my time, right after I left, the school received what it needed. Like everything else in the military, you keep pushing for what you want, and if you don't get it, hopefully the fight will continue after you leave. Sure enough, soon they got the additional five days and 90 more men to formally set up the desert phase.

I left the Ranger Department in July of 1985 and went up to West Point to take over the Department of Military Instruction (DMI).

Spirit of the Bayonet

As the head of DMI at West Point, my determination was to pass on my experiences and lessons of leadership to the cadets and encourage them to go in the direction of Ranger School. My purpose has always been to pass on what I've learned to create a better unit and Army. I didn't just talk about the times Turner was a hero. I deliberately told about the times I had messed up. I thought it was important to be able to kid about myself and the dumb blunders I'd made so that, hopefully, the cadets would move out and not make those same mistakes.

I tried to put some emotion into my talks at West Point the same way I did throughout my career. Done right, I believe a little theatrical effect gets people's attention and leaves a lasting impression on them. One of my habits was to stick a bayonet, fixed to a rifle, into the stage wherever I was. At West Point I stuck bayonets into the stages of Eisenhower Hall and South Auditorium, among others. Even shooting the bull with my troops in the field I'd have my M16 with fixed bayonet, and I'd just stomp that thing in the ground right in front of them, put my hat on it and talk. It was a gesture that made a point. In my speeches it said, "This is important," and when I was with my soldiers, it said, "You are important and you have my attention."

I was pretty fired up when I changed out of battalion command, so during my speech I took one last chance to drive home a point. My classmate, Tom Robinson, was taking over command from me and stood on the stage along with the commanding general, General Shy Meyer, while I spoke. At the end of my speech, I reached down, picked up my M16 with bayonet attached, held it over my head, and talked about the spirit of the bayonet to the assembled troops.

I looked out from my elevated position onto the battalion formation. The soldiers stood still and quiet at parade rest, rifles held at a slight angle to the front topped with bayonets. As I spoke, I started hearing the rattle of their bayonets from their shaking rifles. That was like pouring gas onto the fire, and my adrenaline pumped. They liked what they heard, and all 800 guys shook their rifles to my talk. I had that damn rifle over my head, brandishing it around, and I was thinking, "I'll probably go to jail for this one," but everyone loved it. Then I was ready to bring it to the end. I proclaimed, "I now pass this M16 rifle with fixed bayonet on to Lieutenant Colonel Robinson." I turned the point of the bayonet groundward and thrust it into the wooden stand.

The bayonet sunk into the lumber all the way to the hilt and the rifle wobbled slightly. That mother was stuck! I backed off and motioned with my hands to the rifle in a "hoo-ah" gesture to pass it on to Lieutenant Colonel Robinson. I didn't tell him about this before the ceremony, but what he assumed, and correctly so, was that he was supposed to pull it out and hold it above his head. He grabbed the damn thing like trying to pull a small tree up by the roots, but he couldn't budge it. I was thinking, "Oh, shit. We've got real trouble here."

Quickly, after his failed attempt, he put his hand on the butt of the rifle and stood next to it with a look that said, "Okay, I've got it. I've got it." It still stood there bobbing.

He still chews me out about that every time we see each other. "I'm going to kick your ass, Turner. You should have told me about that."

"If I had told you about it, you still couldn't have pulled it out," I answer. "Hell, both of us together couldn't have gotten that thing out. I saw the sergeant major up there after the change-of-command ceremony working the thing back and forth for about 10 minutes trying to get it loose."

I had fun doing that kind of thing even though it didn't always turn out exactly as I planned. I always enjoyed generating that kind of emotion and excitement, so I figured when I got up to West Point and talked to the cadets about combat leadership or whatever, if it was appropriate, I'd do the same thing. It always worked with the troops in the field, and it seemed to work with cadets also. It was important to me that the cadets really hear the lessons I was talking about so they could learn and incorporate them when their time in a unit came.

No Excuse

At West Point I would often say, "There are two types of officers: those who are Ranger qualified and those with excuses why they are not," and I stand by that. It's always that way. If you are standing around a bar or in a command post, invariably two Rangers will start talking about Ranger stories. Even now, guys don't tell combat stories. They tell Ranger School stories. "I swam the frigging Yellow River five times! I was freezing to death. My balls were knocking together. . . ." Then they'll ask another officer standing close by, "Did you go to Ranger School?"

And the answer comes back, "No, I couldn't make it. I was injured. I couldn't get through." There is always somebody who makes an excuse. It is almost automatic. "I couldn't make it because . . . I was in armor and the armor branch wouldn't let me go."

You can't listen to those who tell you that you can't.

Ranger Turner's Walk

Humility has a negative connotation and yet is a characteristic of the strongest leaders. Being humble doesn't mean you are weak. The humility Tex Turner exhibits stems from strength. When you see a leader listening to his subordinates, praising people for their contributions, and deflecting recognition to team members, you are seeing humility. Together these actions are among the most motivating tools you can have as a leader. Of course, unexpectedly sticking a bayonet into expensive wooden things is motivating, too. You need to pack your ego into your rucksack along with your foolproof plans and start from scratch.

There are plenty of people in positions of authority who feel that their position is a validation of everything they think or do. They are severely off target. It's time to utilize the motivating power of listening. When times are tough, people are going to work harder to fulfill plans that were derived, if even in part, from their input. It's called ownership, and it works.

To explore the other side of humility or humiliation, we just have to look at the time Tex was drooling on himself during the briefing for his mission. He certainly wasn't expecting to be the next in charge and was caught off guard. He had to humbly ask for support and had put himself at a disadvantage by fully depending on others to carry him through the mission. He was fighting extreme fatigue in order to stay alert; you will never be that tired and you know ahead of time that you are the leader.

You are paid to be prepared. Your study and work will not only keep your team out of humiliation's crosshairs, but it will provide you with opportunities that can be exploited. The type of preparation you need is not simply the information that comes through standard channels. Like Tex trying to read the map on the river in the dark, your senses have to be alert to unusual signals and nonstandard information. You've got to look for clues wherever you can, do the best that you can, and listen to your team and motivate them so that they are a reliable resource in completing your mission successfully. The type of preparation you need requires constant focus and a militant perspective on success. Our next Ranger, Eric Faulkner, will guide you in those areas.

RANGERS

are

FOCUSED

ERIC FAULKNER

Officers and noncommissioned officers were unable to compete with a young private named Eric Faulkner. Their rank, experience, knowledge, physical prowess, and stamina could not match Eric's perspective. He had the same goal, a gold and black Ranger tab, but he went about achieving it with a completely different frame of reference. The Ranger tab was a side effect of winning the war he imagined and helping his buddies survive.

Eric set those as his goals and achieved the best record in his Ranger platoon. He was focused outside of his personal suffering, which lessened his exposure to self-pity. He set goals bigger than himself that he could reach every day. No matter what your profession or job, the perspective your goals give you will make an enormous difference in how you do your work. What is your focus? Are you creating value for others the way Eric did for his teammates?

Ranger Battalion

It is amazing how people make big decisions in life based on stupid things. While in high school, I saw a really cool Army commercial where a soldier stepped out of an airplane and turned to look at his parents. I noticed his black beret and the Ranger tab on his shoulder, and at that point I knew I wanted to be a Ranger. In high school I did not have a lot of experience to guide my decisions; so like most teenagers, I thought if it looked cool, it was worth going for. My Army recruiter said that mine were the highest scores he had seen in a long time, and that I could do anything I wanted to. I did not hesitate to tell him I wanted to be a Ranger.

After months of initial training that took me from a high school civilian to an Army soldier, I was prepared to enter my unit. Unfortunately, my grand entrance at the Ranger Battalion was performed on crutches. I injured my knee playing basketball in the last days of in-processing into the battalion. I hobbled in saying, "Hi, I'm your new private. Here's my profile," which ranks among the worst things in the world you could do. In their mind I was an oxygen thief, filling the slot of someone who could actually do the job. They loved me for that, I am sure, and things did not improve until after I had knee surgery.

The indoctrination into the battalion was tough. The Ranger Battalions expected a lot out of all ranks and had to have privates who could get up to speed both physically and tactically very fast. The learning curve was steep and with no rest stops. The Rangers were always on the move, going 100 miles an hour, and I had to quickly get used to that pace. However, once I became acclimated to the Ranger Battalion, I loved what I saw. I loved the mentality and the atmosphere. I knew I had made the right choice and wanted to stay. Thirty-six soldiers were sent with me into the battalion, and within two years there were only two of us left. The rest either got injured or quit. It was intense training, like freebasing information; you really had to want to be there.

The only thing that sucked after my indoctrination was that I was still a private and the word "private" was like a cussword. I wanted to go to Ranger School because once I successfully returned from there, I would automatically be promoted to specialist—no longer a private! All I knew was that if I ever wanted to have a life and get out of the crap, I had to get to Ranger School and pass. It normally took six months to a year to get a Ranger slot, but once I made the decision to go, I thrived on the knowledge and studied constantly. I was not the smartest person in high school, so I really had to study hard and put in long hours just to get things right. I did not go partying or to the movies or bars, or do anything that detracted from my goal. I stayed in my room, I worked out at the gym, and I studied.

I memorized everything. I studied Ranger history and the *Ranger Handbook* (*RHB*) in depth. I did not have practical experience in working with an operations order (OPORD), though I had seen my captain give one once for a mission. I thought it was pretty cool how he had his plan put together and organized. Then I got a *Ranger Handbook* and said, "Oh, that's where he got the idea." It was amazing how many things were available to everyone, but only a few took advantage of the sources. I looked for other sources of information on the school. I found specialists who had been through Ranger School and picked their brains. I constantly took notes in my *RHB*, which was already beat up by the time I got to Ranger School. I practically slept with it, and by the time I left, I could literally recite word for word an OPORD. I could tell you exactly what part of the plan goes in where and why.

In addition to the motivation of leaving the private rank behind, I was driven by a desire to make my parents proud. I really respected my mom and dad, and I knew I had screwed around in high school and let them down. I was a punk with long hair, playing in a rock band and going nowhere. My mom always told me, "Eric, you quit everything you ever start. You need to finish something." She was right. I would start something, get good at it, and then quit. I said to myself, "I'm going to start and finish Ranger School."

I earned a slot to Ranger School in four and a half months, pissing off some of the other privates who had been there longer than me. One guy in particular was upset since he had been there for a year. He didn't realize that his focus was not right. His thoughts were, "Hey, I've made it. I have arrived because I'm in a Ranger Battalion." He thought he had status, but he was still a private. Instead of focusing on doing what had to be done and earning a slot to Ranger School, he screwed around and finally got kicked out of the battalion.

Another Injury

Four weeks before I left for the preRanger course, where the Ranger Battalions got their soldiers ready for the school, we did a battalion airborne jump. It was a night jump with very high winds. High winds create a dangerous situation because they make it difficult to calculate where jumpers are going to land. There are calculations used to determine where a person will land based on the speed and altitude of the plane, the type of parachute, and the speed and direction of the wind. All of these can be controlled except the wind, so when trying to hit a small drop zone surrounded with trees, the slower the wind the better. A lot of people got hurt that night, including me.

The inside of the aircraft was dark except for the red lights by the open doors near the tail. It looked like the inside of a haunted house with eerie, dark faces lining the walls. The drone of the engines and sway of plane were soothing, and even the thought of the jump was now a routine concern that did not really raise my blood pressure. Then came the signal to stand up and hook up. I snapped my static line snap hook to the line above my head that ran the length of the plane all the way to the door. The shuffle started toward the door, and we exited the plane like a rapid-fire PEZ dispenser, each one a split second after the other. It was like jumping into dark chocolate pudding. Everything—sight, sound, and time—was muted. My focus was completely on maintaining a closed position with my hands tucked around my reserve chute, packed on my front like a good-sized beer belly. The chance of getting my arm or leg caught in an unraveling riser was not one I was willing to take.

I kept my legs together and felt the yank of my chute opening. My body swung around wildly for two or three seconds before I seemingly exited the other side of the pudding. It was black and silent around me except for the blowing of the wind. Floating to the ground was a peaceful but short experience. As I got closer, I could tell the wind was moving me laterally pretty fast, but I could not control my direction or orientation. Hitting the ground was always a shock, no matter how ready I was, and in the dark it was hard to be really prepared. In a violent counterpart to the unnerving leap from the plane, the landing adds the reality of a vicious collision with the earth. We were trained in the proper parachute landing fall (PLF), but sometimes it turned into a cartwheel of arms, legs, equipment, and dirt.

My weapon, a squad automatic weapon (SAW), hit a mound of dirt before my feet did, slamming it into my side and cracking two ribs up under my armpit before I came to rest on my back.

The timing couldn't have been worse. My newly cracked ribs threatened my approaching departure to the preRanger course. My platoon sergeant kept on saying he was going to give my slot to somebody else, and I kept on telling him, "No. They're already feeling better." I lied, "I don't even think I cracked them. They are only a little sore. I think those X-rays must have seen an old crack or something."

I bluffed my way until the weekend before I was supposed to leave for Fort Benning, Georgia, when my platoon sergeant insisted on testing me one more time. He had me drop to do push-ups, flutter kicks, and the side-straddle hop—jumping jacks to the rest of the world. "Sergeant, it doesn't hurt a bit," I lied again. It hurt plenty, but I wanted to go to Ranger School. I was so focused on my goal that I was not even thinking, "Hey, idiot, Ranger School is not like Airborne School. It's not like basic training. There aren't going to be people there making sure that it isn't too hot for you or that they aren't pushing you too hard. It's going to be abusive." My platoon sergeant bought my story and sent me on to the preRanger course, and from there I went right into Ranger School.

During the first five days, we did hand-to-hand combat, physical training (PT), and many other activities, all physically demanding and painful. Hand-to-hand combat was similar to professional wrestling on TV, but we did it in a sawdust pit, we wore BDUs, and the blood was real. In the first hand-to-hand session my partner, Wade, flipped me and I landed right on my cracked ribs. We were taught how to flip and throw each other to avoid any major damage, but he had thrown me incorrectly, directly overhead, so I was all out of whack trying to land. I was unable to break my fall with my arm, and I reinjured my ribs. I got up and thought, "Oh, my God. Here I am only three days into Ranger School and I'm hurt bad." I told my Ranger buddy, "Look, man, there is no way I can get flipped again. That was way too painful. I've got a couple of cracked ribs. Let me just keep flipping you. I've just got to get through this first phase, then I can put a ruck on my back and hump all day long. It's just this throwing crap that is hurting right now."

"Yeah, no problem," he said. And I flipped him from then on.

On day four we had the last hand-to-hand session, and then the next day, the last day of City Week, we had a five-mile run. After that we would pack our bags to go to Camp Darby where the humping started and I figured I'd be okay. The morning of day four, before the hand-to-hand session, my buddies watched from the barracks doors for the RIs and wrapped my ribs. I held onto one end of a wide Ace bandage while they pulled and wrapped it around my chest. I could hardly breathe. During the hand-to-hand session, an RI caught me not switching out. He lost no time in making the correction: "Hey, Ranger, you need to get thrown now."

My ribs were already hurting from trying to throw my 200-pound buddy. I said to Wade, "Thanks for trying. I appreciate it." Then I turned back to the RI and said, "I need to go to the medic." I went directly to the hospital where they X-rayed me and then sent me back to the Gulag, a wooden World War II barracks where they keep all the soldiers removed from the class before they go back to their units or recycle into a new class.

I was at the Gulag for about a week doing whatever wimpy details the school staff had for me when I got word back from the medical clinic that there were no cracked ribs evident in the X-rays. I thought, "I don't know how they missed them, but *great*! They can recycle me into the next class."

I called back to Sergeant Weldon, my squad leader in the Ranger Battalion. When I told him I was recycled, he went off the deep end. I said, "Look, Sergeant, they thought I had cracked ribs but things look good now and they are recycling me to class three. When my partner threw me wrong, it hurt bad enough that I couldn't go on. But I'm going on to class three."

I continued to work for the staff. Then, with four days until the next class started, I got a phone call from a radiologist, someone who knew what he was doing when it came to X-rays. He said, "Private Faulkner, you have two cracked ribs. You're going to have to come back in for reevaluation."

When I came back from that appointment, I was told, "With cracked ribs you're going to have to go back to your unit for at least six months; then maybe you can come back to Ranger School."

Desire above Sense

I pleaded with the sergeant at the desk, "No, I can't go back. When I walked out of the Ranger Battalion, my squad leader didn't say, 'Good luck, Faulkner.' He said, 'Don't come back without your tab. Don't show back up if you don't have it.' I've got to get this thing." When the doctor told me that I could not go through Ranger School, I was pissed. Now I had to call Sergeant Weldon and tell him I was coming home, which was a worse phone call than the first. I whimpered, "They are really cracked, Sergeant. I have to come home now." He was yelling on the phone, and I wanted to say, "I didn't want to crack my ribs," but you didn't do that as a private.

I was walking around the school area when I saw the next class was starting to show up. The school used to have a noncommissioned officer (NCO) and officer go with the students through the whole course as part of the cadre so the students would have some consistency. It was beneficial because they got to know each person individually and were able to help people out. I recognized the NCO for this new class. He had been my Ranger Indoctrination Program (RIP) instructor when I was preparing to go to the Ranger Battalion. I walked up to him and said, "Hey, Sergeant McClemons, how's life?"

He was happy to see me and wanted to know about the Ranger Battalion and how things were going. It was not long before I turned the chance meeting into an opportunity to get back into the course. "Listen, I've got to tell you my situation."

I told him what happened. "I made it all the way through City Week. I did the whole thing. It was the day before we were supposed to pack for Camp Darby when I got caught. But I can put a ruck on my back and hump until the sun goes down, all day long; it doesn't matter, just as long as I don't have to get thrown. Well, maybe parachute jumping might hurt, too."

He said, "Let me get back to you."

When he found me again, he said, "Look, here's what I did: I put your name on the roster. You're in fourth platoon, fourth squad. At midnight when we load the bus to go to Camp Darby, bring your bags, jump in line, and get on the bus. Your name will be on the roster."

I gave him an emphatic "Thank you!" and even though I had five days to wait as the new class went through City Week, I went back to my bunk to get packed.

The new class finished up City Week, complete with hand-to-hand combat. I was packed and ready to go and just waiting for the appointed time. I had taken the opportunity to get into town and do some shopping. I picked up especially important items like dip (chewing tobacco) and had three logs of Copenhagen tucked safely away in my bags. At midnight the time came and I trucked across the compound like I was sneaking into a perimeter, hopped into the line, and said to the man next to me, "Hi, how's it going? I'm in your squad now."

"Hoo-ahh," was the reply.

I got on the bus and went to Darby, and that was when I started with my second and final Ranger class.

I never called Sergeant Weldon again to tell him that I had gotten back into the class because I wouldn't believe it until I was actually there, and I didn't want to possibly flip-flop again. I just hopped into Ranger School and took off. At the next break I called back and he asked, "What the hell is going on? I've been out of my mind wondering where you are. I called Ranger School and they told my you were in class three. I said, 'Okay,' and left it at that." Sergeant Weldon was smart enough to leave well enough alone. He knew he did not need to know the facts, but he was not happy that I had not kept him informed.

Tobacco and Big Mac

As the new guy in the squad, and being the odd man out, I did not have an assigned Ranger buddy. I was kind of a whore, going from Ranger buddy team to Ranger buddy team. "Hi, can I be with you guys today?"

Class three was in the winter phase, so to avoid cold weather injuries, the school banned any kind of tobacco products, saying the nicotine constricts your capillaries, which carry blood and therefore heat to the skin level. Without good blood flow it was much easier to get a cold weather injury. No one was allowed to have cigarettes, dip, or chaw, and the RIs dumped them all out during the inspection right before I came running over with my bags and three logs of Copenhagen.

We arrived at Camp Darby and went right to work setting up camp. The process was uncommonly unorganized with everyone busy at some stage of setting up their tents. Some people were almost complete, and other Ranger buddy teams were still looking for a place to put theirs up. It was Grand Central Station in the woods.

Everyone was moving in their own direction when I pulled out a can of dip and snapped it against my hand a couple of times to get it packed against the side. The snapping was some sort of Ranger mating call, and the guys swarmed around me like flies on crap. "Where did you get that stuff?"

Thinking fast, I said, "I have only this one can. Weren't we allowed to go buy it at the PX?"

"No, man," they answered.

I exclaimed, "Ohhh, I should have brought some more with me."

I gave some out right there, but did not make the mistake of displaying all of my cans at once to anyone. Initially I thought I could trade it for food, but reconsidered, knowing that we all needed as much nourishment as we could get. It would have been stupid of me to try to take people's food away from them just for dip. After the swarming incident, I let a couple of the closer guys know that I had more.

I rationed it so I had dip the whole way through the school. I buried one log in a waterproof bag away from the billets as soon as we got to each phase. I would run out there at night, dig it up, pull a can out, rebury it, run back, and then empty the can into an old accessory pack bag from a meal ready to eat (MRE). I would put the pack in my pocket and discard the can. I put an entire log into my duffel bag before it was sent off to Florida. By the time I got to the end of the desert phase, right before going to Florida, I ran out and had to spend a couple of days without dip. All I could think of was getting to Florida for more. When I got my bag in Florida, I opened it up and motioned to my buddies, "Come here. Check this out." I unrolled my sleeping bag and there it was. We all looked at it like 10-year-old boys with a nudie magazine, except we knew what the dip was for. We all sighed.

In another case of trying to craftily enjoy forbidden pleasures I was not so lucky. The guy I was Ranger buddies with for a while was the first sergeant of our class. He had a friend who was a specialist who worked at Ranger School. The specialist told him to meet him at the baseball diamond at midnight, and he would provide him with a couple of Big Macs. Since my buddy was in a meeting with the RIs at that time, he told me to go and get the Big Macs.

I was walking through the woods on my way to the baseball diamond when I stopped to take a whiz. All of a sudden I heard something in the bushes. I thought, "Oh crap, it's an RI." I was standing there in a very vulnerable position, unable to move anywhere. I heard it rustling some more, and I hurried to finish up, but that was impossible. All of a sudden a deer with a full rack of antlers came leaping out of the bushes and brushed past me. Startled, I surprised myself when I screamed like a woman. That set off a stampede and a whole herd of deer passed to either side of me. Unrecoverably shaken, I ran back to the tent and left my Big Mac somewhere in the night behind me.

Just a Kid

I was in Ranger School as a 19-year-old E-2 private. I had done basic training, Advanced Individual Training (AIT), Airborne School, Ranger Indoctrination Program, and four and a half months in the Ranger Battalion, and boom I was in Ranger School. I had been a private my whole military life and had never had leadership training. I had always been a follower, getting yelled at and told what to do, never having to think too much. Then I hit Ranger School, where as a lowly private I was an equal with sergeants, captains, and a major. I was intimidated by these guys, thinking they had to know so much more than me. When we talked, one of the first questions was always, "So, what do you do?"

"Well, I'm a platoon sergeant," or "I'm getting ready to be a platoon leader," they would reply.

"Wow," I thought. "Golly gee, I'm a private, a faceless member of the squad responsible for leading only myself."

The first patrol we went on was a wonderful learning experience. I was a super follower. You told me to do something and I did it, no questions. Then I was put into my first leadership position as the squad leader for the patrol. "I've got a map. I'm in charge. God, this is crazy," I thought. My mission was to move the patrol from actions at the objective to the patrol base and then conduct patrol base activities. The previous squad leader had gotten the patrol lost earlier in the day, and we hit the objective at one o'clock in the morning.

I took command of the patrol and took off on what was mapped out to be about a five-kilometer movement. Well into the march I maintained my confidence that we were in the right spot, but some of the other guys disagreed and claimed that we were off target. They started questioning young, "cherry" Faulkner. "Hey, man, do you know where you are?"

Land navigation, as a skill, is a mental game as much as it is a trained talent. In the dark it is impossible to be 100 percent confident you know exactly where you are. As we moved, I translated my upward and downward steps into the contour lines on the map and marked where I calculated we were. Starting with that assumption, I looked at the direction of march on the map and then got a mental picture of what the next leg of the march would look like. The difficult part comes when your expectation of the coming leg differs from what you find. That's the point of question, insecurity, and vulnerability. It takes mental strength to maintain your confidence through the fast and furious second-guessing. You think, "I wasn't really sure that the last hill was this one here, and that valley may have been this one instead of this one," and on and on. However, that night I stuck to my guns.

"Halt," I commanded. "Yeah, I know where I'm at." I could not see anything on the map, so I knelt down, pulled out my red-lens flashlight, and lied, "Yeah, this looks right." It was pitch-black out, so who in the world could tell if we were in the right spot? But we kept moving.

The team leaders made me aware that the guys were exhausted. It was our first patrol, so it was a matter of their bodies not being accustomed to the long movements and physical exertion. People started complaining to me, "Hey, why don't we stop and take a break? We're already late, so let's rest for a minute."

"Yeah, that's fine," I said.

We did that twice before hitting what I thought was the patrol base. The RI gave me an indication that we were in the right spot, putting to rest any questions I still had about my land navigation skills. We were busy setting up the patrol base when the RI said, "Listen, this whole night has been late. Set up a cigar-shaped perimeter and sack out." We had to get up at six o'clock, and it was already four o'clock in the morning. He said, "You've got a long day tomorrow, so get some rest." We all crashed immediately, only to start again two hours later.

The next morning I walked with the RI into the woods, away from the other squad members, and sat down on a log to receive my evaluation. He said, "Faulkner, you got a no-go." He had been around that night listening to the suggestions the squad had given me. "One thing you've got to realize is that you are not here to make friends. They are your buddies and you have to take care of them and help each other through, but you cannot coddle these guys. You can't baby them. A leader is not a position where you are out to make friends and have everybody like you. You need to do what you know is right. If you know you have to meet a deadline, then meet the deadline. If your guys are tired, meet the deadline. They are not going to die of exhaustion. Their bodies will stop them before they die of exhaustion. You took too many breaks."

The other patrols I led I unfailingly did what needed to be done, and from that point on I got seven straight gos. I trusted myself a lot more. I started thinking, "I know how things are supposed to work. I know from the book. I know from people telling me how things have to run, and I know that deadlines have to be met." I thought, "If there are situations that come up, like the guy before me running late, screw it, we are going to make our objective on time." That was what determined my getting a go or a no-go. In wartime I could not say, "Okay. Let's just take a break." No. We would have to get there and take out that radio tower; otherwise our troops could suffer. I did not mess around. If I was given a deadline by my commander, then I had to be there.

Perspective

From the time we started a patrol and crossed the line into enemy territory, in my mind I pictured myself in combat, looking for the enemy. I was in Vietnam. I was in Korea. I was somewhere dangerous on patrol, and I kept that picture to keep myself alert.

One night in the forest I was the last guy in the formation. I was acting as rear security and had to look to the sides and rear. As we moved along, I continually scanned, intensely looking for the enemy in the underbrush and scenery in the distance. My mind-set controlled my actions, wide eyes, alert ears, and soft footsteps. During one of the short stops, the RI came up to me and said, "Here's a major plus. Son, I'm scared. You are making me think I'm in combat and there really *is* enemy out there. I truly believe that you are in combat right now. You are doing a great job."

I was surprised by the RI's recognition of what I was doing. I viewed my actions as the standard, not the exception, but I was encouraged to maintain my diligence.

That same night I was part of the leaders recon and was left behind as security—eyes on the objective. The leaders recon was an opportunity for the leaders to move up close to the objective and get an idea of how they wanted to set up their unit to achieve success. They then returned to the objective rally point (ORP) to finalize the plan and disseminate the information to everyone. They left two men on security, myself included, as a guide point and as a source of information about the changes that had taken place, if any, on the objective while they were gone. It was cold and raining that night, and I made the command decision to tell the other guy to put his rain parka on, and then I put mine on. We did it correctly, as if in combat, even though no one was watching us, one guy at a time. The patrol came pulling up, none of them with their parkas on, completely drenched. "What the hell?! You got your rain parka on?! Major minus," the RI exclaimed, making my spot report balance for the night zero.

Pain

There was a lot riding on my success at Ranger School. If I failed Ranger School, unless it was due to a legit reason like an injury, I was out of the Ranger Battalion also.

We all expected to live with pain and injury during the school, so each of us had to decide how much was too much. We all had to decide what was going to threaten our lives and what was a temporary inconvenience. Anyone looking to get out of the school without signing a lack of motivation (LOM) statement could feign an injury. An LOM was the kiss of death for an Army career and for anyone who wanted to maintain his pride. It was a public announcement of failure and weakness—"It was too darn hard for me." For those who made it through, the opposite was usually true. They denied their injuries in order to keep going.

We moved into the mountain phase where we learned highland patrolling techniques and military mountaineering skills. The rappelling was done very near our billeting area in what looked like a small rock quarry. I had seen pictures of the rappel cliff before I went to Ranger School, and I looked at it as quite an impressive place. I had pictures of different scenes of Ranger School that I had kept and looked at when I was preparing myself for the school. I always kept my goal in front of me. The pictures formed scenes in my head that I was able to match up when I actually got there, creating the feeling, "I've finally arrived."

When we started doing the mountaineering, I began to worry. Rappelling was not so bad, though the buddy rappel, having a guy on my back, was pretty rough on my ribs. The thing I was worried about the most was the controlled fall. I had to tie the rope around my waist, climb up the 34-foot incline, and then fall. I watched others do it, get to the top, yell "Falling," and then drop, allowing the belay to stop their descent. The belay is a safety feature built into mountaineering, a man able to stop an uncontrolled descent by the person rappelling by pulling on and tightening the bottom end of the rope. It was a sudden stop that could hurt pretty bad even without broken ribs. It was at least as bad as parachuting. I was scared to death, hoping that Sergeant McClemons could get me out of it also; he could not.

I got myself focused on doing it, psyched up for the pain. The RIs were making people repeat the drop four and five times, screwing with some and having them do it up to 10 times. My turn had come. I tied the rope around myself and climbed to the top. I thought, "I'm going to have perfect form every time." Prepared at the top, I pushed off, locked my arms, and yelled "Falling." I prepared myself for the yank and the pain and kept focused on my form. The rope snapped tight around my chest like I was in the middle of a violent knot. A scream of pain echoed in my head.

I received a go after each of my first three tries and did not have to do it again. I got to the bottom, belayed the next guy, and was done. I think Sergeant McClemons may have watched out for me again, telling the guy, "Hey, just let him get through it. If he does it right, give him a go. Don't screw with him."

Even though Sergeant McClemons was not able to get me out of the mountaineering fall, he did me a huge favor when he put me down as a "leg," non-airborne-qualified Ranger. I did not have to do any jumps like the one that injured me in the first place.

Since everyone had their patches off, no one could tell the difference between airborne and non-airborne soldiers. However, my uniform should have given away my secret. The majority of it was faded to a light green, except for where the patches used to be. The areas where it was still dark green were called ghost patches. Nobody asked any questions even though I had the ghost scroll of a Ranger

Battalion on my sleeve and the square above my pocket where my airborne wings went. Everyone knew that if you were in a Ranger Battalion you were at least airborne qualified. The story held, and I air-mobiled in by helicopter every single time, not doing one parachute jump.

Beyond the Extra Mile

It was an extremely windy, cold night on Hawk Mountain. We had walked nonstop for a long time, exhausting us on top of our already starving and freezing condition. This was the first time we had reached the point where we knew what real misery was.

I was the patrol leader, once again in charge of the part of the patrol from actions at the objective to patrol base activities. I had proven myself extremely accurate in my land navigation skills, consistently keeping our patrols on the right course and in the right location. It was a rare skill that, if marketable, would have made me wealthy in Ranger School. I would have given it out for free to everyone if I could have so we wouldn't have to suffer through the consistent all-night marches of the lost patrol. I had started getting pretty cocky with my map-reading abilities, and during this patrol, as usual, we were right on target.

We approached the location where the patrol base was supposed to be. Arriving on the leeward side of the mountain, the opposite side of the ridge from where the patrol base was supposed to be, I decided we would pull up short and set up camp there, out of the wind. I stopped the patrol and began to get things moving on the patrol base.

The RI ran up to me and asked in a disturbed voice, "What are you doing?"

I said, "I'm stopping here to go on my leaders recon."

He asked, "Do you know where you are?"

I said, "Yes, I do. We are right here." I pointed to the map. "Sergeant, if we go over to the other side of the ridge we are going to freeze to death in that wind. I decided it would be a better idea to set up over here. I don't see any advantage to that side."

He agreed with my reasons, but insisted, "No. You are setting up on the other side of the mountain."

I did not know why he was so adamant about it, but I had to follow his order. We walked straight up the side of the mountain, and as we came up over the ridge, I saw a sign for the Appalachian Trail. I thought, "Oh, great, there are people just casually walking this trail, and here I am, freezing, no sleep, and hungry." We got to the other side of the mountain and into a biting wind that was blowing like prop blast and just as loud.

The patrol had gone really well, and I was determined to have a strong finish. We established the patrol base, setting everything up perfectly. It was a textbook patrol base, and all I could think was, "Okay, I get to be a rifleman now. I'm going to go be a slug and fall asleep on the line." I was sitting there prepared to switch out, wondering why the RI had not said, "Roster Number 625, you are now patrol leader."

I waited and waited and waited and finally he came over and said, "Ranger Faulkner, you better go wake up your radio operator (RTO) because you've got an incoming encoded message that you're going to have to decode and use to plan for the next operation."

In an astonished voice I said, "What?"

He replied, "You better go wake him up!"

So I went and woke up the RTO, Rice, a pain in the ass who was always sleeping. He took the message, decoded it, and gave it to me. I took the message to the RI like a bright-eyed child with an Easter egg, seeking a prize. "I've got the message. It's decoded," I said. I was certain to be switched out now.

He said, "Wake me up when you're ready to give your operations order."

"Oh, my God," I thought. "Doesn't he know it's time to switch me out?"

I gathered all of my squad leaders and the platoon sergeant together and told them, "Go get some sleep. The RI is racked out in his fart-sack over there, and I have to wake him up when I've got the OPORD ready." Once again, I was being nice to my guys and letting them go to sleep, but I knew that they were tired, too.

I went over to my gear, pulled out the necessary items, and got under my poncho liner. It was then that I did the math and realized I had not eaten for the entire day. I grabbed the frankfurters and bean component from my MRE. The frankfurters had a gel on them that seemed to be ever present, like someone had put apple jelly on miniature hot dogs. The wind was howling around me as I sat there very cold and bone tired. I lay down belly first under the poncho liner, put one foot on each corner, brought the poncho liner over my head, and placed rocks on the other two corners. In front of me I had my red-lens flashlight, waterproof notepaper, pen, bean component and frankfurters, with the gel almost frozen. It was not your normal midnight snack.

I looked at the message and thought, "Okay, paragraph one." I looked at it a little more, ate a frankfurter, started to fall asleep, and thought, "Screw this. Why am I doing this? I ain't writing a whole operations order. I can wing this thing. What are the bare necessities?" I pulled out my map, drew a line from where we were to the objective, and got the azimuth. I determined the distance, got key grid coordinates along the route, and wrote them all down. Finally, I put together the time line. I finished my frankfurters and beans and just sat there contemplating life for a minute. I was alone in the world. I just knew it. The wind was whipping. It was pitch-black outside, and not a soul was awake for hundreds of miles.

I took the little I had written, got up, kicked all of my squad leaders, and got them moved to where I was for the OPORD. I shook the RI, who was in his fart-sack, zipped up all the way with just his nose sticking out. I told him I was ready. "Just tell them to come over here and huddle around me," he said. "I'm staying right here."

We all gathered at his sleep site and actually leaned up against him. It was the only way to get close enough to each other and still be under some sort of cover. "Okay, you guys ready? Paragraph one . . . ," and so started a full five-paragraph operations order. I got to the point where I was about to describe our actions at danger areas, like crossing roads or open areas. "Now, if you look at this diagram right here . . . ," and I described all the activity as if I actually had a chart.

I soon got tired of trying to keep my leaders awake, so all of my squad leaders and the platoon sergeant were sacked out completely, leaning against each other and the RI. I was not worried about the RI discovering that they were asleep because he was still in his sleeping bag, totally covered. When any of my guys started snoring, I punched them and woke them up.

Again I was alone, talking to myself. "Okay, you got that? You got that? Okay, great!" I got further down into paragraph three, actions at the objective, which really required a lot of detail, and I thought, "Whoever's the next patrol leader is going to be screwed because no one is getting this info."

I decided to try to take a shortcut. I started lowering my voice from a normal level, speaking softer and softer, waiting to see if the RI was asleep. If I could tell he was asleep, a snore or a gurgle or something, I was ready to loudly say, "Paragraph five," and jump right to the end. I got my voice lower and lower and lower, and all of a sudden he said, "Ranger Faulkner, speak up. I can't hear you."

Crap. I went through the whole paragraph three, making up the operation as I went along. Fortunately I had studied the OPORD format enough that I knew the five paragraphs inside and out. I got all the way to the end, and I punched all of my squad leaders in the arm. "Okay, you guys got any questions?"

"No." "No." "No," came the answers.

"Great, go disseminate the information," I commanded, knowing that they had not heard a word that I had said. Everyone went on his way, mainly to rack out.

The RI asked, "What is your SP time?" SP is short for start point, the time we were going to cross the SP.

"Zero six hundred," I answered. It was already 0400.

Due to time constraints, we were not going to do weapons checks, but he wanted me to do rehearsals. I had two hours for that and to get some rest. I was at my physical limit. I had to sack out for a few minutes at least. I told my guys, "Just let me lie down, close my eyeballs, just for a second." I looked at my platoon sergeant. "Wake me up in an hour, and if you fall asleep I'll kick your ass." I walked back to my gear, relieved that I was going to get even a few minutes of authorized rest. I sat down and pulled my poncho liner over me and felt my muscles relax. I was still completely dressed, boots laced up and patrol cap over my face. My brain began to shut down as sleep took over. The brain can play tricks as it drifts to sleep, and the popping popcorn I heard in my dream was really rifle fire.

The attacking opposing force (OPFOR) interrupted my rest only minutes after lying down. I realized later that the RI had given our grid coordinates to the OPFOR for this attack and that was why he wanted us in this position. I got up but was completely in a stupor. I had a euphoric feeling of floating. Everything was in a fog around me, and my steps were on legs of cooked linguini. I screamed out cliché commands, "Return fire! Return fire!"

Luckily, the other Rangers in the platoon had enough presence of mind to do what they could. They performed well, even in their weariness, because it would help me get a go. I think the OPFOR penetrated at one point, but we fought them off. We did a search of the ones we had killed and pulled out maps and drawings from their uniforms that we used for the next mission.

The attack ended. We did rehearsals, and the sun crested. I still had not gone to sleep. We got everyone in line, and prepared to move out. "I can't fucking believe this guy is going to make me do this mission," I thought, furious at the extreme to which he was pushing me. The operations order by itself was one complete graded phase of the patrol, so now I had gone through two full graded phases and was getting ready to start the third.

"Move out," the leadership ordered, and the patrol started into the woods.

"Stop," came the command from the RI. "Roster Number 345, you are now the patrol leader."

"Thank you, God," was my mental reply. I grabbed the new platoon leader and pulled him aside. "Do you know what is going on?"

"No. My squad leader didn't know squat when he came back to disseminate information," he answered.

"Okay. Here's the deal," I said, explaining the mission to him. I then ran down the line telling each of the new squad leaders what was going on, ending my briefing each time with, "You are going to have to assess the situation when you get there." As soon as I was done, I was Joe Rifleman again, but the night was over and I still had not slept. I had a full day and evening ahead of me, and I was already beyond exhaustion.

The RI waited until after the mission to critique me. He then graded me and the platoon leader who did the movement from the patrol base to actions at the objective. When he gave me my go for the mission, he also gave me a minor plus. "Faulkner, that was the best five-paragraph operations order I've ever heard in my life. That was phenomenal. I have not heard operations orders that good in bay planning when you have all the chalkboards and support materials. That was so detailed and specific. It was awesome."

I was praying he would not ask for the drawings and charts I had supposedly used. I tried to think of an excuse—I ate them. They fell out of my ruck. They were drawn on toilet paper and I used them. I did not know what I was going to tell him.

What You Gotta Do

In terms of warmth, the song title "If You Can't Be with the One You Love, Love the One You're With" was never truer than in Ranger School. We were in a patrol base and I was on a listening post/observation post (LP/OP) with Staff Sergeant Shipley. He was a big guy, over six feet tall and still with some meat on his bones. Our observation mission required us to be still and listen to the forest for sounds of the enemy. Lying belly down on the pine needles and leaves allowed the earth to soak up our body's warmth, drawing it downward and leaving us shivering. Our lack of movement invited our senses to focus on the one pain we had, the cold. Like magnets attracted to a source of heat, Sergeant Shipley and I slowly started inching closer to each other. By the time we were satisfied, we had laid his poncho on the ground, then his poncho liner on top of that, then him, then me, and finally my poncho liner and poncho, and made ourselves into a warm and comfortable sandwich. I was on top of him in the missionary position, hugging him as he hugged me, with ponchos wrapped around us both. "If you tell anyone," he threatened.

"Don't worry about it," I cut him off. "I'm in the position with you."

"I have not been this close to anyone besides my wife," he said.

Packs of wild dogs were out that night, barking and howling, though I did not know how close. We were thinking they were going to come in and attack us, but we did not care—we were warm. We slept there for an hour and a half before being disturbed.

The T-1 wire-connected telephone clicked. Then it clicked again. "Someone is trying to get ahold of us," I thought. I woke up and grabbed the phone; no answer. I rolled off of Sergeant Shipley just before our squad leader walked up to check the position. "Yeah, we're good," we said.

"Check the connection on the T-1, we were trying to get ahold of you a few minutes ago. You need to send in spot reports every hour," he said.

I replied, "Yeah, I'll check the phone. Maybe one of the connections came loose. Sorry about that."

As the squad leader walked away I felt the earth below me starting to drain my body of warmth once again.

No F-ing Way

When we got to the desert phase I was with the non-airborne guys that were bused to the drop zone (DZ) to wait for the airborne Rangers to jump in. Outside of the bus was nine inches of snow from the night before. The RIs had built fires all around the DZ to allow the pilots to identify it. From the air I am sure it looked like a white blanket with hot coals arranged in a circle. We sat inside the bus with the windows closed, wrapped up like Eskimos, quietly freezing. An RI walked onto the bus. "What the hell are you guys doing still on the bus? Get off the bus!" he yelled.

We stepped off of the bus and into a wailing wind. Getting off the bus served no rational purpose except that outside was the more miserable place for the RIs to put us. "There is no way they are going to jump these guys; no way," I thought. "The wind is way more than 15 knots on the ground." We stood up against the side of the bus for an hour and a half, all of us huddled together, double-timing in place, waiting for the airborne guys to jump. The dry cold of the desert went through our layers of clothes like water through a sieve. My ears stung even with my hands held over them. Our request to go over to one of the fires was met with a definite "No."

We heard the planes in the distance, and we knew our time of inactivity was just about over. The airborne jump did take place, despite the wind. The aircraft rumbled into the distant dusk sky and what looked like a flock of large birds floated to the ground and rolled in the snow with what would easily be the most awkward bird landing imaginable. A consolation for us leg Rangers was, I thought, that at least we didn't have to get into the snow the way they did. The RI released us to link up with our units. I trotted across the drop zone among the freshly grounded soldiers gathering their chutes together and on to the appointed linkup site for my platoon. The stiffness in my legs went away quickly as I started to move, but the snow and the wind on my face made it bitterly cold. We started what was to be an all-night affair of marching.

We moved for 12 straight hours, covering 18 kilometers and getting attacked by the OPFOR all along the way. To survive movements like that I refused to think of the end of the march. I focused on putting one foot in front of the other. Each step taken was one more beyond what I thought I could take but there was no joy in pushing my limits, just a desire to keep going. We finally arrived at our patrol base and set up a perimeter. The landscape was typical desert, open and flat, with nothing to stop the wind. We had no relief from the cold whether we were moving or stationary. The RIs gathered in a tent in the center of the perimeter. They were warm, sitting in there sipping coffee, relaxing, and reading nudie magazines while we were outside soaking wet with the sweat of the movement, freezing to death. We were double-timing in place when they came out and told us to change our socks and T-shirts so we didn't freeze. At that point all of the students silently revolted.

No one said anything. We looked at each other and just kept double-timing in place.

"Do it," they persisted and went back into the tent.

I was not taking my boots off for anyone. I was not going to stop moving. I was scared if I stopped moving I would die. We had been walking all night, and despite my exhausted legs, I was still double-timing in place. No matter what the RIs said, our response among each other was, "Fuck you, we're not taking our boots off. We're not changing our socks."

The patrol leader finally went to the RIs and pleaded, "Something has to be done for them. They're freezing to death out there."

After a couple of guys had to be taken into the tent because they were getting close to hypothermia, the RIs allowed us to build a fire. The flickering of the fire was as mesmerizing to my eyes as the heat was to my body. I could not get close enough, but no matter how hot my front was my back was cold and vice versa. We warmed up our socks before putting them on our feet and savored every bit of warmth we could claim.

We still did a mission that night, without sleep. We were so uncomfortable in the cold that I do not think we slept for three days. We survived on catnaps of a few minutes at a time or nothing at all. The last of those three nights the RIs figured out that they had pushed us as far as they needed to. They must have radioed ahead to the OP-FOR, because by the time we got to the objective rally point they already had tents set up for us.

Suffering had become such a way of life for us that it was unbelievable what was happening. We expected to suffer at every turn. We were dogs that were beaten no matter which tricks we did, and it was okay with us. Part of the reason so many people fall out of the course early on was because they still had an expectation of some level of civility or comfort, and they could not mentally adapt. For us, what was one more night without sleep? Our brief stay in nirvana would not change our expectations, but would give us strength to go on.

We entered the tents and the heated world inside created by running stoves. Inside the tent, the snow had melted off of the ground, so I spread out my poncho liner and poncho, lay down with my head on my rucksack, and covered myself up. I was warm and toasty and convinced I was experiencing a piece of heaven. We spent a lot of time thinking about home, but as I lay there I felt an almost similar level of mental comfort.

She's Breaking Up

Florida was a piece of cake because by the time I got there I had a record of four gos and one no-go on patrols. I was way ahead of the game, and then, to top it off, I got a go on my first patrol. I was tabbed out. I was now five and one and had met all of the course requirements except for time.

In the midst of my success I suffered the worst. I never felt like quitting, though early into Florida I experienced a particularly weak point where several things coincided that made me really want to get it over with. They were not exceptionally severe conditions for Ranger School, but they were bad enough that when the extra ingredient of being tabbed out was thrown into the mix, I was miserable. My mind had pulled out of high gear a little bit, though I was careful not to get a bad attitude. I would not turn into a slug, because the struggling Rangers were counting on me to perform and not screw them over.

We had been walking all day, mostly in the rain, and I was very tired. We pulled into an area to wait out the storm, which had picked up and was pouring down on us. It was not a mid-June, bathwater warm Alabama rain. This was a cold rain where each drop that hit was like the pelting of an ice cube on bare skin. The RI had us sit on our rucksacks, and even though we were already drenched to the bone, pull out our ponchos and put them over the top of us. I do not know how long we were there, but I sat there thinking, "I cannot remember ever being this miserable."

Time to think was often a menace. Being stopped like we were allowed me to pull out my magnifying glass and focus on my senses, which were now being tormented by throbbing exhaustion in my legs, the cold bath of water on my skin, and the knowledge that my condition was not going to change any time soon. Each of my pores screamed, "I'm cold," but there was nothing I could do. I was frustrated. My situation was out of my hands. It was like a movie reel breaking right in the middle of the best part and waiting for the 13-year-old projector boy to figure out the problem.

I had to refocus my thoughts onto other matters. There were a lot of guys who still needed my support. Several students in my platoon were borderline on patrols—four and three, or worse—so the RIs did not want to give them any more patrols for fear that they would get a no-go and then have to do yet another one. Because of that situation, in the last three days I got two more graded patrols and went to seven and one before they stopped grading me. The RIs were giving other guys the easier squad leader positions so they could get a go, while I stayed the platoon leader.

My body seemed to be nearing the end of its productive life around this same time. I started to suffer from tendonitis, and I had an ingrown toenail in my big toe that was infected so badly that it swelled up to the size of a silver dollar and was turning a grape shade of green. For several mornings I took a needle, punctured the area and squeezed out the green stuff to lower the swelling. I then took an iodine swab and wiped it down to avoid further infection. My ribs were holding out fine, but I had had only four and a half months to rehab my knee from surgery before Ranger School so it was starting to ache again really badly.

Up to that point I had gone to sick call twice. One time they made me go in for my foot, to clean it out really well, and the other time my knee hurt so badly that I had to stop. We were allowed only 72 hours of sick call for the entire course, so I was nearing that total and did not want to use my last 24 hours.

I could not believe how cold it was in Florida. The desert was a dry cold, but Florida was a wet cold. There were many nights we just stood, double-timing in place, all night long. On a patrol in the middle of the phase we were going from an objective to a patrol base walking parallel to a creek. The creek curved in front of our path. Though we could see on the map that it was not too far out of our way to go around the bend, the patrol leader went right through it instead of going around it like any reasonable person would have done. I do not know what was going through this guy's mind at the time, but he made everyone want to kill him. Shortly afterward, the creek curved back the other way, forcing us to go through it again before getting to our patrol base on the other side. When you were wet was the worst time to stop moving, but no sooner had we gone through this waist-deep water when the RI told us to get in a perimeter and sack out.

I was going to make the best of a bad situation. I took my boots and socks off, wrapped my feet in my nylon jacket liner and wet weather jacket, and then tied them up so the heat would stay in there. I looked like the bottom end of a sapling whose roots were wrapped and tied, ready to plant. I pulled my poncho liner and poncho over me and sacked out. They actually let us get four hours of sleep that night. The huge irony was that it was so cold and we were so wet that despite how tired we were it would have been better if we got only a couple hours of sleep and then started moving again to warm up.

I was constantly aware of my cold legs, feet, and arms. My body was too lean to create much heat, and it was fighting the determined cold from outside. Sleeping in the cold like that was never really a deep sleep. It was like bobbing on the ocean, sometimes above the waterline, sometimes below.

The next morning I woke up, threw off my covers, and reached over and grabbed my boots. They had turned into green ice sculptures overnight, and my attempt to loosen them by bending and cracking them was almost useless.

Next I took the covers off my feet to find them frozen, too. There are levels of cold, and my feet were well beyond any normal level. Usually, no matter how tired I was, I would wake up if I got too uncomfortable from the cold. I could count on my feet or hands hurting, but now my feet were completely numb, and my other big toe had ballooned up to the same size as the infected one. It was red and shiny from the skin being stretched so far. What a reason to pause—one green toe and one red toe, perfect for Christmas, "Eric, the red-toed Ranger." I thought, "Oh, crap." I had sensation in my heels but none at all in the front of my feet. I massaged the crap out of them trying to get some warmth back into them, but before I could do much I had to put my socks and boots back on and move out with the rest of the platoon.

Our feet were our most precious assets because they were our transportation, so without healthy feet we could not continue in the course. As if to make sure my feet were completely finished off, that day we went out and did a Zodiac boat mission on the river and then were in the swamps that night. The proper position for paddling the boats required us to straddle the sides, which caused our feet on the outside to remain in the water for hours. Even the most robust feet became numb and shriveled from the cold water.

That night the medics went through and did a foot check. Foot checks were routine because the school knew that Rangers were unreliable in reporting how bad off their bodies were, not to mention their feet. It was not uncommon for a Ranger to lie about injuries, even serious ones, to keep from being examined closely and possibly recycled or removed from the course entirely. We sat on the ground in a line, boots and socks to our side and bare feet to our front. The medic came by with a needle and pricked my toes to make sure I could feel them. I watched him closely, and as he stuck me I pulled my foot back, "Ow!" I could not feel anything. I thought I was faking it pretty well, but he caught me.

"Ranger, turn your head," he said. I turned my head, and he said, "Okay, put your boots back on. You're going back to the Troop Medical Clinic (TMC) with me."

He had stabbed my toe several times and I did not feeling a thing. I could not believe I had to go to the clinic and possibly be dropped from the class on the direction of a doctor. I thought, "There's no way. I'm halfway done with Florida." I was already tabbed out but they could still nab me if I did not finish. I was depressed and scared as I sat in the TMC. The whole time the doctor examined me I was telling him it was no problem, that I had to get back and finish the course. He finished my exam and left me alone in the waiting room.

I did get some sleep while I was there but had to settle for my MRE while I watched the medics eat mess hall chow. I kept an eye on their food like a police stakeout, watching from the corner of my eye. I did not want them to know I had designs on their leftovers.

One medic left the mess hall with breakfast—scrambled eggs, sausage, and toast—and came into the TMC to eat. He did not finish it all. Instead he lit a cigarette, sat back smoking, and tapped his ashes into the food before finally putting his cigarette out in the eggs. "Why couldn't he have given me that food," I thought.

Lunch came along, and I got lucky. He left some succotash—corn and lima beans—and red Jell-O uneaten and un-ashed. He went into the bathroom and dumped it into the trash can and came back out. Using my detective techniques again, I went into the bathroom and shut and locked the door. I went to the trash can to investigate. I saw the evidence and immediately started picking out the kernels of corn and lima beans. Luckily, the cup of Jell-O had landed on its base and had not spilled. I ate everything. I even picked the stuff off the bottom of the trash can and downed it, too.

I do not know how or why, but the doctor let me go back to my platoon. There was a level of empathy for the students developed by some of the non-RI staff. Most people felt sorry for us, but there were others, like the medical staff, who knew how badly the students wanted to make it through. When I got the news that I could go back, I did not question the decision—the facts did not count. I believe the doctor took into account my desire and balanced it with any permanent damage that might come from a few more days in the field.

Nothing in Ranger School ever permanently damaged me, though I still cannot feel my right big toe. Just recently I was sticking my fingernail into it. "God, I can't believe the feeling hasn't come back yet," I thought. I maintain my optimism, though.

I made it through the final days in the field, but my physical woes were not over. When we came in from the final three-day patrol in Florida, those of us who were tabbed out were relieved and happy. We were given all of the care packages that had stacked up for us and were allowed to go into the Gator Lounge, where we gorged ourselves. At the Lounge I chanced half a beer and almost passed out. I went back to the barracks, went to sleep, and woke up the next morning unable to open my left eye. It was glued shut by dried, oozing discharge, and I had to peel my eyelid open. It turned out that I had somehow contracted pinkeye. It was fortunate that it happened at the end when we were cleaning gear, because there was not much you can do for pinkeye, and there was a good chance that it would have put me out of the course.

Graduating brought with it a big sense of accomplishment rather than one of relief. I really enjoyed Ranger School. I enjoyed it while I was there. I thrived on that kind of challenge. The whole time I was there I thought, "If I'm here, I might as well make the best of it. I'm not going to dwell on how hard it is because if I do that it is going to be mentally even harder." I kept my focus on the goal, the tab, what it was going to do for me, how it was going to help my career progress, and what an elite group I was going to be a part of when I got done. I saw how the other guys with tabs treated each other, and I kept thinking about being one of them.

When I got done I did not think, "I'm done. I don't have to do this crap anymore," because I was going back to a Ranger Battalion, and people in the Ranger Battalions live the life. When you go to Ranger School you get to experience it. At Ranger School I was just spending time at the Ranger Battalion. It was really intense, but the same type of training.

Focus on Others

I learned that what I thought my limits were were not my limits. Mentally, even today, I put limits on myself. "This is as far as I can go. This is as far outside of my comfort zone as I can go." Those limits are so conservative. I thought I was pushing myself in the Ranger Battalion, but when I got to Ranger School, I broke past those barriers, pushing my limits even farther out. I learned that I can keep going, that I can go through extreme difficulties and endure and that it is all in the mind. If I had kept my original mental limitations on myself I would not have graduated. I would have reached my limit and said, "I've hit that point and they want me to go on but I can't."

You have to be in good physical condition to get through the course, but it is much more a mental challenge. I went through with two cracked ribs and a bad knee. The perception of "physically demanding" is in your mind, too. You hit a certain point where your body is saying, "I can't go on. I can't go on." If you keep telling yourself that, you are right—you can't. You think your body is hitting a limit, but it is your mind telling the body that. When you fight that mental battle inside your head, the physical part gets more energy; you get revived. I think that is why people quit. They hit what they think their limits are, their mental limits, and then in their minds say, "Okay, that's it. That's as far as I can go." Instead, they should have released their minds, not thought about it, and just kept going.

Do not think of the challenge; think of the prize at the end. Focus on the tab; do not count the days. There were guys who put a tick mark on the inside of their hats for each day that passed. That was retarded, I think. Personally I did not care how long it was, how many days I had been there, or how many I had left. I was there until the end. I was not going to quit, get injured, or let myself fail. I was going to succeed. Guys tried to tell me how many days we had left, and I told them to shut up. I did not want to know. I wanted the tab badly. I thought about it all the time. I had a tab pinned to the inside of my hat. I would peel it down and just stare at it, picturing it on my shoulder. I wanted the prize. I did not care about the cost, and that is what you have to do.

It is important to take responsibility for yourself while at Ranger School and afterward as a leader. You must carry your load and be ready to help others. There is not a quality leader out there who relies on his teammates to motivate or guide him. By definition, that person would be a follower and probably not even a good one. You do not have to be the strongest, but you have to have a vision for the future and a desire to get there as a team. My vision for myself included the people around me.

Do what is right at Ranger School. Think, "Take my eyes off myself and put them on other people." Think about everybody else and how they are doing at Ranger School. When they are in a leadership position and you are a follower, think about them needing that go. If you are thinking about yourself and how tired you are, how hungry you are, you are concentrating on the wrong things. I was tired too, but we were all in it together. There were times I literally wanted to beat the shit out of a couple of guys, one in particular. I turned to him and requested, "I need you to make a sand table for me."

He answered, "I'm tired. Can't you get someone else?"

I wanted to butt stroke him. I did not say it, but thought, "Dude, don't you remember the last time, any time, you asked me to do something for you? Did I ever hesitate at all?" I never gave anyone back talk. If someone asked me to do something, I did not care if my leg was broken. "You bet, man, I'll help you out." I had the right attitude because I was thinking of them and all of us getting through Ranger School. It is going to take a team effort to get through Ranger School. If you are in a platoon of slugs and everyone is thinking about themselves, it is going to be hard for anyone to get a go.

Don't worry, you are not going to die of starvation or lack of sleep. They are not going to take you to that extreme. If you are so worried about yourself, you are mentally screwing with yourself and you are going to think, "Oh, I'm too tired to help this guy out." Instead you should think, "I've got to do this. It's all going to come back to me, both good and bad."

I have always thought that you have to be a good follower to be a good leader. If you are a hard worker as a follower and you help other people out, people know you are sincere and that they can count on you. Then, when you need them, they will be there for you.

Ranger School taught me the importance of loyalty to the people I am with. When I go into a civilian job, I still take that with me. "These guys are with me, in the same situation, going the same direction, so these guys are now my Ranger buddies." I don't mentally picture that, but that is the mind-set I have from Ranger School and the Ranger Battalion. I have been given opportunities because people knew I was loyal to them. If people know that I am loyal to them, they know that I am out for the success of whatever organization I am with.

Ranger Faulkner's Walk

If you are still expecting to be able to sit through all of the pictures on your screen saver without interruption and finish your first cup of coffee before you get to actual work, you haven't made the mental adjustment to the level of discomfort necessary for success. Say goodbye to your predictable and comfortable workday. Prepare yourself for conflict and contention, and then go embrace them. Eric Faulkner taught us that in intense environments, extended over long periods of time, the ones who survive and thrive have made a mental transition to an expectation of discomfort.

Don't mistake this for expecting the worst. If you are behaving in the Ranger model, you expect success, but you also expect to have to haul a heavy load on your way, and once there, violently destroy the enemy. Your enemy may be a nay-saying boss, complacent support departments, or competitors; I don't know your situation. But I do know that if you show up to a gunfight with a knife, you lose. You want to show up to a gunfight with a tank and four friends. Expect to work hard to compile that type of power.

This kind of power takes the type of preparedness that we discussed in Tex Turner's chapter, but it also takes the dogged focus and elevated perspective that Eric displayed on his patrols. To keep alert and automatically do the right things, Eric focused his mind to function as though he were on patrol in Vietnam. You have to have an elevated perspective of your situation and consider it even more dangerous than it is. You can't simply be there to collect a paycheck and go home. Your focus must be on your clients, whoever they might be. You must think, "If my team's task is not completed on time and under budget, my client will fail to make payroll. They'll have to lay off 12 people, all of whom have young children and are three months behind on their rent. They'll be evicted, their children will go hungry, and it'll all be my fault." Is that really extreme to suggest? Yeah, but that's the perspective a Ranger takes, and that's why most people don't understand us and why we succeed where others fail. I recommend you become misunderstood as quickly as possible.

As you'll see in the next chapter, misunderstandings and sudden adjustments in expectations are common in Ranger School. You'll also see some of the seemingly odd results of camaraderie developed in this environment along with some powerful leadership lessons.

RANGERS

are

DRIVEN

MARK CHANDLER

It is impossible to challenge yourself beyond the norm if you do not have a drive to be better. Drive is dissatisfaction with the status quo. Drive is when you have a splinter in your finger that is bearable, but annoying, and you won't sleep until you pull it out.

Mark was drawn to test his limits, both physically and mentally. He was driven to look for better ways to get his message across so his patrol could better accomplish its mission. The entire experience of Ranger School tests the drive of the students. The students are dissatisfied with being average. They are dissatisfied with not wearing the badge of their accomplishment: the Ranger tab. They are dissatisfied that they do not have the personal knowledge of their own capabilities. These students use that irritation as motivation to succeed.

Flat out, most people lack drive. They have a splinter of mediocrity and have chosen to live with it. You must develop drive. When you become uncomfortable in your current financial situation, job condition, or relationship, you will move to change it to what you

want. What are you motivated to improve? Do you make the money you want? Do you have the control of your life you desire? Do you have the relationship you need?

Evolution

I first learned about Rangers when I was at Vassar College in 1983 during the U.S. invasion of Grenada. The papers were full of stories about the Rangers and the 82nd Airborne Division, and suddenly everyone was talking about these paratroopers and airborne Rangers.

President Reagan, while giving one of his State of the Union addresses, had a Ranger present, a medic who had jumped into Grenada. He awarded him the Silver Star for heroism under fire. This guy was wearing his Class As and sporting a high and tight haircut. Class As are the Army's way of being businesslike. They are suits like you see on any businessman, but with a nonstylish cut and an army green color. They can get to be colorful, however, when all of the gold insignia, silver rank, and rows of ribbons are added. The high and tight was just that, a skin-close shave on the sides and back of his head, leaving a divot of hair on top.

Vassar College, of course, was the opposite end of the universe from Ranger School. We were all sitting around watching the president on TV, and one guy said, "What in the hell is up with that guy's haircut?" I obviously was not thinking that one day I was going to be like him. I thought, "They must be some sort of psychopaths the Army keeps under rein for special operations like this." There was, however, enough curiosity about the Rangers to hold my interest and eventually lead me to go down their path.

I had mentioned my curiosity about them to a few people, and a short time later someone sent me an article from *Soldier of Fortune* magazine about Ranger School. It talked about what the students went through. It had black-and-white pictures of these guys in jungle fatigues, running around soaking wet with sweat, doing an obstacle course. I shared it with a couple of friends at Vassar, and their response was, "Clearly this must be some sort of exaggeration. It can't possibly be that hard." The article talked about City Week and Camp Darby and how hard the students were driven. I became increasingly curious, and when I enlisted in the Army in 1985, I specifically signed up so I could go to Ranger School. I got what was called then an "unassigned Ranger contract." I ended up going to Officer Candidate School (OCS) and getting branched as an armor officer, so I never enacted my original contract.

Through college and the years after my graduation, my desire to go to Ranger School grew. It represented a great challenge, a rite of passage, the kind I gravitated toward at that time in my life. Ranger School was a personal challenge. It was nothing anyone in my family had ever been through before, so I was stepping out and making my own path. I had been heavily involved in the Boy Scouts in my teens and college years working at places like a scout ranch in Filmont, New Mexico, which offered a lot of challenges that were similar to, though much easier than, Ranger School. The school seemed to be the ultimate challenge the Army had to offer.

There is an argument about that. Some people will tell you that the Special Forces Assessment Selection (SFAS) is more difficult or that the Scuba School is more difficult from a physical standpoint. I would be impressed if any of those courses are much harder. I remember very clearly sitting in the orientation for OCS next to a good buddy of mine and Ranger, John Collier. The speaker got out in front of the class and said, "Officer Candidate School is the hardest school in the Army, bar none."

John shot a glance at me and said, "This fucker has never been to Ranger School." Having now been through both of them, I know Ranger School is easily another order of magnitude more difficult than OCS. That you would even compare the two courses is laughable. OCS was hard because there was a lot of harassment, but we ate three meals a day and could get up to seven hours of sleep a night. It was nothing like Ranger School.

After OCS, at the Armor Officer Basic Course (AOBC) at Fort Knox, Kentucky, I got a chance to compete to go into Ranger School. AOBC was a real gentlemen's course, so the physical training (PT) that the average AOBC lieutenant did was pretty lightweight. For anyone who wanted to go to Ranger School, there was a special PT program. The special PT was conducted every morning, five days a week. The first morning we showed up it was overseen by a captain from the Armor Officer Advanced Course (AOAC). This guy smoked us; 30 minutes of nonstop calisthenics, then a sprint of a run. It was a good introduction to the program, but the captain never showed up again. I think he realized that he was in no kind of shape to maintain that sort of intensity. He ended up leaving us to our own devices, and we ran the Airborne and Ranger PT on our own.

We had a couple of guys who were really into it, including Kurt Roddy. They enjoyed pushing themselves and the rest of us. We worked our asses off with a really good self-designed program. The motivation was always there. The more we worked now, the less it would suck at Ranger School.

A Ranger Course was starting within two weeks of our graduating from AOBC. However, the commandant of the basic course kept us from that class because he thought we needed another month to get in shape. Whether that was true or not did not matter—the delay was fine with us.

During that month, we did nothing but work out in the weight room and run six to seven miles every day. We did not have classes to worry about anymore, just a monthlong slide into an inevitable conclusion: Ranger School. Kurt and I lived together during AOBC next to a park in Louisville, Kentucky. The park had a huge hill in it that we would run up. The first time we tried it, we both barely got to the top without breaking into a walk. Near the top on that first run, my lungs burned and my legs were weak and wobbly. I prayed to see the crest of the hill, hoping the tiny steps I was taking would get me there quickly. A month later when we were ready to go to Ranger School, we were both running up it seven or eight times in circuits.

We also did the necessary runs up Agony and Misery, the torturous sister hills at Fort Knox. The hills were just far enough apart that between them there was time to reflect on how tired I really was, and they were out far enough in the woods that if I succumbed to my weakness, my body would not be found for weeks. Knowing that there were a couple of obstacle courses at Ranger School, we also took our turns at the Fort Knox obstacle course, the same one as in the movie *Stripes*. We worked out on that course for a while, getting good at climbing ropes and jumping walls.

Finally, we were close enough to going that the preRanger fitness test was scheduled. We met at the PT field, prepared for the worst but also knowing we were in great shape. There were a bunch of new AOBC lieutenants with us who wanted to go to Ranger School at the end of their basic course five months down the road, and they were apparently ready to get a taste of Ranger PT.

The commandant was Ranger qualified and helped conduct the test along with some psychopath who was not Ranger qualified but wore a black beret anyway. I don't know what the hell his deal was besides being a sadist who just wanted to smoke some poor lieutenants. They worked us over for about 40 minutes, one guy after another, leading us through exercises in a sawdust pit under the warm morning sun. We finished up the exercises, did pull-ups, then went on the five-mile run with "rubber ducks," the slang name for molded rubber M16s.

We had to finish the run within six feet of the guy leading the run in order to pass. The leader ran us at a pretty brisk pace, probably a little over six-minute miles, but all three of us who wanted to go to Ranger School—Bill Tackasc, Kurt Roddy, and myself—made it. Our poor companions, the new lieutenants, were left in the dust; not a single one of them finished the run within the standard. That was their equivalent of the Ranger PT introduction that we received from the short-lived captain. We three each easily passed the final hurdle of scoring over 290 on the regular PT test by scoring the max of 300 points. In the Army's eyes, we were now qualified to go to Ranger School.

Arrival

In the small break between the test and the beginning of the course, I drove home. During that trip, a strange coincidence occurred when I ran into a guy from my basic course at a rest stop on the highway. We had left from two different places going to two different destinations but stopped there at the same time for a break. We sat down at a picnic table and talked about several things, including the subject that occupied my mind, Ranger School. As a Marine, he did not have the chance to go, but he knew the military and had some encouraging thoughts to share. He explained, "When you get there, they've got to in-process you, and they can't do anything to you while they in-process you, so that's got to take a day. Right? Then you've got to get your physical and turn in your medical records. Then you have to draw your equipment, and that takes time. Right? Just look at how long it took at OBC, the first three days. Then at the end of the school, you've got to do all that stuff in reverse, so that's got to take another three days. Right? So it's 61 days long, but you take three out at the beginning and three out at the end, then you do all this traveling between the four places, that's got to take a day or so each. Right?"

It seemed logical to me as I sat there at the picnic table listening to the hum of the highway. "Sure. It's all got to take time. The actual hell of Ranger School might last only . . . let's see . . . maybe 51 days!"

I made the last turn on my journey into the Ranger camp to report for day one on July 1, 1988. Driving up, I saw the old World War II era buildings straight ahead, a field to my right, and a fenced-in area to the left. I followed a couple of other cars obviously going to the same hell I was. They moved into the fenced area, which was the secure parking area where we would leave our cars for the duration of the course. I pulled my truck nose-up to the fence, shut off the engine, opened my door, and came out. It was only seconds before I was leaning over into the truck bed getting my bags from the back. In that short minute since I pulled into the lot an RI had appeared and was standing at the parking lot entrance.

He had a guy doing push-ups right outside of his car on the 110 degree blacktop. He yelled, "Recover! Get down to that building!" The new Ranger took off at a full sprint dragging and carrying his heavy duffel bags. Then the RI pointed to his next victim and yelled, "*You!* Get down and give me 20!" This was only seconds into Ranger School. The thought that they were not going to lay into us because we had to in-process was ludicrous; they were not wasting a second.

Within hours we got in-processed, all of our equipment was issued, and we even sewed cat eyes on our patrol caps and alice packs (rucksacks). That first day lasted until 0445 in the morning, when we were allowed to go to bed and rest until the first call at 0515 for PT. We literally got 30 minutes of sleep the first day we were there, and they did not let up on us until the very last day. The intensity of the school went right up to the very last second.

It felt like we were being controlled by lunatics, like we had stumbled into the enemy's camp and now they had complete power over us. It was a terrifying feeling that the people in charge of us had no regard for our safety or our comfort. All they wanted to do was make it as hard and as miserable as possible for us. It must be like being a prisoner in some ways. The cadre obviously was not going to shoot anybody or physically harm us, though I felt as if the RIs around me wanted nothing more than to see me fail. As time went on, however, there were a couple of really gratifying moments when the RIs did come across as a little more human. It was possible to win their respect and get the feeling that you were being treated like an equal, but it was rare.

One of the first RIs I had was a staff sergeant who took part in the grueling Best Ranger competition that the Ranger Regiment holds every year. He was a hell of a guy, and I was thankful that I had somehow managed not to make that many mistakes in his eyes. I saw him as a leader whose respect I wanted to earn, and he naturally pulled out a higher level of work from me. He actually gave me one of my minor pluses.

RIs were able to reward extraordinary effort or failings with an administrative merit or demerit called pluses and minuses. There were two grades for each, majors and minors. The pluses and minuses canceled each other out at the equal grade; that is, a minor plus and a minor minus equaled zero. We were threatened with major minuses because if you received a net of three of them you could be kicked out or recycled. In reality, it was odd to hear of a major plus or a minor minus; the common ones were minor pluses and major minuses.

The first week of Ranger School was as challenging as anything I had ever done. During City Week, we woke up early, and they smoked us in PT. It was an unbelievable 45 minutes of rotating RIs who had us do push-ups, flutter kicks, mule kicks, and many more. Then they took us on blazing-fast runs.

The formal PT sessions stopped at the end of that week, and though the other phases did not have any PT, we still did push-ups when we screwed up. Fortunately, when a couple hundred guys were doing push-ups all at once, there was no way the RI could see you specifically. No one did perfect push-ups, especially as emaciated as we were, and I don't think I could do 20 by the end of the last phase. Every muscle was gone except those in my thighs, which were strong from humping a rucksack. I had to go into the school in phenomenal shape if I was going to make it through. Even though PT was not an emphasis for the remaining 55 days, that first week was enough of a physical challenge to demand my best.

After that, it was the mental part that took over. The physical challenges were still there. We had to carry a heavy rucksack and a weapon all the time. We had to climb up the steep Tennessee Valley

Divide, hump in the soft Florida and desert sand, and be able to fire and maneuver. Since we were already weak, it took emotional strength to carry us through. Mental toughness ultimately became more important than physical strength, and the amount that was needed in order to get through the next 55 days was staggering.

Overambition

I personally do not think any place was more hostile than Camp Darby. Each phase was bad for its own reasons, but Darby seemed to be one of the most inhospitable places. It had an awful thicket, which in the summertime was unbearable. We were on our first patrol—a recon, like all of the early patrols were—and everything went wrong. I was fortunately not part of the leadership, but I was with the squad leader, Second Lieutenant Creighton, during actions at the objective, and he wanted to get a really good view of the reconnaissance site. He was in charge of one of three reconnaissance teams. The other two were trying to get views of the site from other angles using the same low-crawl techniques.

The site, a usual one for the OPFOR, had a tent and a couple of guys hanging out by a huge fire. It was the middle of the night and Creighton crawled to within about a foot of the perimeter. Another guy—Sergeant Lynch—and I were right behind him. He must have been having flashbacks to some Vietnam War book he had read, wanting to sneak up unheard, slit their throats, and leave undetected by the others. We all crawled up, bellies on the ground and faces in the pine needles, not believing he wanted to get that close.

The light from the bonfire was just about shining on him, and he was still trying to crawl up farther. We stopped as one of the soldiers walked nearby. He did not suspect anything. We just happened to be so close he was on top of us without realizing it. Creighton, perfectly still, face at ground level, stretching to see out of the top of his eyes, was unable to avoid contact. The OPFOR soldier in his normal stride stepped right on his elbow.

Creighton jumped up and took off running back the way we came, apparently not ready to fulfill his Vietnam dream. He tromped right between us on his retreat, showering us with leaves and dirt. The sudden commotion took the OPFOR and all of us by surprise.

The two of us who were remaining got up and started to move in the same direction, but the OPFOR soldier grabbed Lynch by his weapon's dummy cord and stopped him. We all had these ridiculous dummy cords that tied our weapon and equipment to our load bearing equipment (LBE), and though they served their purpose when we were tired and prone to lose things, when we were in the middle of an operation they were a pain in the ass. I stopped to try to fight him, to free Lynch, not with fists or a butt stroke or anything dangerous, more like really bad wrestling. There was nothing I could do besides biting his hand to break his grip on the cord, which I was not going to do, but an effort had to be made. Creighton left us there and did not return.

On our first patrol, two of us were captured by a nonaggressive and resting enemy, humiliating us and proving that the impossible could happen at Ranger School. After an administrative halt to allow the two of us to link up with the rest of the patrol, we prepared to go on from there. When we arrived back, we were greeted by our RI, who read us the riot act for getting captured. Understandably, the squad leader never said a word. At times like that you just let the RI vent. No excuses or explanations were required.

Head Count

Prior to starting our patrol again, we did a head count. The thicket there was so dense and dark you could not see your hand in front of your face. We did the head count the way we were supposed to: The first guy whispered into the second guy's ear, "One." He turned to the third guy, "Two," who turned to the fourth guy, "Three," and so on until the last man was counted. Then he stated his number to the previous man, "Ten," and that number was passed back to the front as the total in the same whispering manner. If you were standing two feet away, this whole process would be completely silent. We were sitting in the underbrush within a foot of each other. If it had been daylight, we would have looked like small children sitting around listening to the teacher read a story. There should have been 11 of us. But even after three times, we kept coming up one short. How could we be missing somebody? The RI began getting pissed off. First we got captured and now we could not get a head count right.

With more than a normal level of speaking voice, he said, "Let's get a head count. This time do it out loud." We went through the routine, but the out loud head count did not produce our missing person, either, though we were able to figure out that it was Ranger Fly who was missing. "Fly! Where the fuck is Fly?" the RI yelled. Finally, he was absolutely furious, and we were scared. "Everybody close your eyes," he said. He took out an artillery simulator, pulled the pin, tossed it a short distance, and let it explode. We had to close our eyes because of the flash of the simulator. In the middle of pitch blackness it would have blinded us, and we would have had a horrible time trying to even walk with an indelible flash in front of our eyes for an hour. The blast shattered the night. The RI yelled, "Fly!"

About eight inches from me I heard a weak "Yes, Sergeant?"

"Where the fuck have you been?" the RI raged.

This was the very first night, way too early to be droning, but, of course, he had been sound asleep, even with all the moving and talking. These were the kinds of incidents that began painting a picture of each individual that we stored away and called on during our peer evaluations.

We again got ready to move out. The RI asked the squad leader, "Where are we, and which direction are we going?" But the squad leader had no idea. "Team leader," the RI demanded.

"Here, Sergeant," he answered.

"Show me on this map where we are and where we are going," the RI repeated. The team leader did not know, either. The RI was pushed to his limit. "All right. I need somebody to take fucking charge of this thing," which, of course, everyone thought would be like walking into a bullet. The RI was furious, and whoever took that mission was definitely going to get a no-go. No one responded. "If one of you fucking pansies cannot take over this patrol, you all are going to fail."

Finally I said, "I'll do it," and took charge of the patrol. We got out of there without any more incidents, and I received a minor plus for stepping up.

We had all been excited about making it through City Week and moving on to the patrol phase, but that first night made the course seem like it would never end. If every patrol went like that, we would die in the woods. It was like starting a 12-hour drive and going an hour in the wrong direction to begin the day. We had to make up some ground just to get to zero.

Like everyone else, I ended up getting a couple of major minuses for silly things, but I got a minor plus for that and one for getting all of my points on the orientation course. You had to get five points, but if you found six you received a minor plus. When they reviewed our records for the first time in Florida, though, the RI said I was 4–0 on patrols and had two major minuses. I said, "And two minor pluses."

"You have two major minuses. What don't you understand about this, Ranger?" he replied.

"But I got—" I started.

"It's not on your record," he reiterated.

Not much I could do.

I Wasn't Sleeping

My weakest point was day seven in Florida. Darby was bad, but Florida was awful, too. This day was the worst. We were on a very long patrol, and I was confident that there was no way I was going to get called to be the patrol leader again because I had already received a go in Florida. I was simply droning, moving along with the patrol, not even trying to keep track of where we were. We hit our objective and moved back to the objective rally point (ORP), the traditional place to switch patrol leaders for the movement from the objective to the patrol base. In some ways it was the worst leg to be a patrol leader because everyone was exhausted. Whatever adrenaline people had left had been used during the mission and was now gone. It was also two o'clock in the morning, dark, and not the best time to move to a patrol base and try to establish it. People were falling asleep on their feet, and you had to somehow pull everyone together.

We were going through the swamp when our movement stopped. Word came back through the column that the RI wanted to see Steve Larr, one of my good buddies on the team. He was a Special Forces qualified lieutenant who went through OCS with me. He was very competent, but right then he shit a brick. He had been just like me, droning, not expecting a patrol. I almost felt bad for him, but even though he was my good buddy, at the same time I thought, "Thank God it's not me."

He turned to me and said, "I'm going to need you on point."

God was punishing me for that thought. Now it was me on the spot, and I had to deal with my own lack of attention. I didn't know where the fuck we were. I did not hesitate to tell him yes, but I was scared.

I was completely taken by surprise. I was mentally ready to just get to the patrol base, dig into a position, and try to get some sleep, and now I was helping lead this patrol. I quickly pulled out my map and tried to figure out where we were and where we had been. I knew Steve was just as lost as I was, so I got the best info I could from the outgoing patrol leader. Trying to lead from that point was seemingly impossible. I was exhausted to my soul. I set on an azimuth, now the lead man on the patrol. All of the trees I passed and hills I climbed and valleys I went through looked the same. I could match almost nothing with the map. I relied on the pace count and azimuth and just walked.

It's impossible to say what automatic system in my brain kicked in and provided me the skills to operate competently when I was so exhausted, but somehow we got to the patrol base and set up.

Normally, I was pretty good at staying awake, at keeping my shit together even when I was completely tired, but that night I just could not. I had hit the wall.

I was lying on the ground behind my weapon, staring off into the darkness, too tired to be happy that I wasn't point anymore. I let my muscles relax and felt their weariness. I became aware of all the minor pains and aches that go unnoticed during the greater stress of movement. I was thinking of home or some other distant dream when suddenly, and seemingly out of the blue, I realized there was a boot right next to my head. I was thinking, "God, when did that get there?" There was the RI standing over me, and the first thing that came out of my mouth was, "I wasn't asleep." I did not realize right away that he had slipped a flower into the barrel of my rifle and on my head to demonstrate that I *had* been asleep. The only two major minuses I received in the course came that night because of my inability to stay awake.

That situation is played out hundreds of times during each class. It is midnight or two o'clock in the morning. Either way, it's dark. A Ranger and his buddy are sent out to act as flank security.

They walk a hundred meters past the last man in the main body and find a good spot. Only seconds after setting in position and lying down behind his weapon, despite his best intentions he is asleep. It is as subtle as a feather landing on morning dew and more compelling than free tickets to the Super Bowl. The RI, fulfilling his role in this mini-drama, walks out to check the security, not even making an effort to be quiet. He finds two Rangers lying still, their heads cocked at an awkward angle, sleeping. The RI wonders how he should play his hand before kicking each in the boots. In the flash of a second, even before their eyes are all the way open, they say, almost in unison, "I wasn't asleep." The RI asks, "Would you like your weapons back?"

It was not an exceptional night for Ranger School, but for me it was the point where I had gone as far as I could go awake. Like a curious child playing with a sharp knife, despite my first major minus I was pulled as if by gravity toward that knife again, and yes, I got cut—again.

Mail Call

The school ran a traditional mail call like those seen in old war movies. We stood in formation and waited for the mail distributor to call our names. We prayed he would call our names. This was our link to the real world, letters from family and friends. This was real, while all of our thoughts in the field about the outside world were diluted dreams.

"Williams," the RI called.

"Here, Sergeant," came the answer and a raised hand. He jogged out to the front of the formation and darted to the side to try to catch the letter the RI had just thrown at him like a Frisbee.

"Thomas," came the next name before Williams' letter even hit the ground. The hope of having your name called was equal to the anticipation of hearing your name called after the final tryouts for the high school football team.

This particular mail call was special because we were going to get our packages. Normally, any boxes or envelopes with food in them were discarded or set aside for the RIs to eat later. We were not allowed "pogie," food of any type. The RIs, of course, gave us the letters but never the food. At the end of the Florida phase, however, we were allowed to receive uncensored packages that people had sent to us while we were there. The desire to hear my name was intense, causing butterflies in my stomach. "Chandler," he called. It happened. My heart jumped, and I ran out to pick up my box from home. I could not open it in formation, so the rest of the mail call had me itching in anticipation. What did I get?! What did I get?!

Immediately after getting the boxes, we hopped onto a bus for the trip back to Fort Benning. We got on the bus and ripped our packages apart. It was mayhem, each person focused on the box in front of him like a 10-year-old opening up a Christmas gift. Those who had not received a box, and there were plenty of them, must have felt abandoned, but they looked on in anticipation anyway because the next best thing to family was food, and they knew their buddies would share.

During the five-hour bus ride, everyone ate the summer sausages and all the other crap that we had received in the boxes. We pulled into Fort Benning, a busload of satisfied students. We had all eaten our fill and gotten a few hours of sleep. Our muscles ached, not used to the relative comfort of the bus seat, and we were a bit more weary than usual. I think our stomachs were still digesting the food.

An RI hopped up the stairs at the front of the bus and faced us with a stern expression. "All of the boxes and food remain on the bus. Don't bring that shit off, or I'll have your ass." We filed off the bus while the RIs watched for unusual bulges. They pulled a couple of guys aside and discovered that these brave souls were smuggling summer sausages, a horrible contraband. Both people got thrown out of the course for that indiscretion. I personally did not have the balls to test that rule. As the course went along, I realized I was closer and closer to maybe getting the tab, and I did not want to fuck it up.

Our next phase was the desert, so we prepared to fly to Dugway Proving Grounds, Utah.

Motivation

I was one of the minority, non–airborne qualified, "leg" Rangers at the school, which meant that while the airborne guys were doing their prejump checks and getting some rest, we were doing another patrol. For safety reasons, regulations required soldiers to get at least a few hours of sleep before a jump. It was often miserable for us to do a patrol, then link with the guys after their jump, and do yet another one. Many of the less informed Rangers thought that the leg Rangers had it easier because they did not have to do the jump. They were mistaken.

When I made it to the desert, the last phase, I was 5–0 on patrols. We needed a go in every phase, better than 50 percent on all of our patrols, and a go in a patrol leader position in order to graduate. I believe there was a lot of luck involved in my success to that point, and I was really lucky when we flew into Utah. Instead of the legs flying in early to do a patrol, we waited until after the airborne jump and then we landed and did a patrol right out the back of the C-130. We hit the ground, went out the back of the plane in a wedge, and did a reconnaissance patrol. I was one of the patrol leaders and I ended up getting a go on my very first patrol, six hours into the desert phase. I was set—two more weeks to graduate from Ranger School, and I had all the patrols I needed. I was tabbed out. I was in a great position, but many people were in danger of not graduating if they did not get at least one go while in the Desert. I assumed again that I was not going to get chosen for another patrol.

My assumption was supported through the first week, but fell in the last week of the phase while getting ready to do the live fire. Steve Larr and I were sleeping in our shelter half, freezing our asses off, trying to take advantage of the little bit of time we had to rest. I was tabbed out, qualified except for the passing of time until graduation. The last thing in the world I expected was someone waking me up saying I was going to be the next platoon leader; but sure as shit, in the middle of the night the call came. I heard somebody walking around outside. "Chandler. Chandler," he called in a high whisper.

"Yeah, what is it?" I asked.

"The RI wants you," he replied—which was the worst thing in the world I could hear.

"What do you mean?" I checked again.

"You're the platoon leader. He wants to see you," his voice was raised a little.

I was thinking, "There is no fucking way. I've already got

my gos." That was a horrible attitude to have, and I knew it. "Are you sure?"

"Yeah, I'm sure," he said.

I stumbled out of my shelter half and went to the RI, who, sure enough, informed me I was the next platoon leader. Fortunately, I had been the radio operator that day, following the platoon leader around, and I had a pretty good idea of what was going on. It turned out that I was the victim for good reasons. The RIs wanted to pair up the guys who had their gos and really good records with the guys who did not have very good records so they would have a better chance of getting a go. It speaks to the fact that by the end, the school was trying to get people to graduate. They looked at the people they believed could make it and wanted to see them finish. For me, however, that situation created a crushing feeling.

It was one of those times I knew I had not been paying the proper attention, even though I knew I needed to. Taking over in my uninspired condition, I had absolute confidence that I was not going to do well on the patrol, and the RI we had was a genuine jerk. It seemed that the conducive conditions the school was trying to set up for the guys in trouble were threatened from two sides: my lack of enthusiasm and the RI's lack of compassion.

All the RIs were tough, but in the end, there were ones you respected, and there were others you realized were just sadists—nothing redeeming about them. Some did not give a shit about anybody, and this guy was one of them. He would do things just to be mean and to make people suffer. Other RIs made things difficult. They would yell and scream when things went wrong, but I felt like they were trying to teach us something.

The patrol went as expected—for me, a no-go. I found myself unable to recapture the motivation to excel as a patrol leader, though the guys in trouble were given a chance to shine and get their gos.

There is nothing physical about motivation. It is completely in the mental arena. The only thing that had changed for me was the incentive. I still wanted to look out for my buddies, and I did, but I didn't have the greater incentive of doing something for myself. I was already taken care of. If the goal is large enough and the reward great enough, the motivation will follow.

During one of the following patrols, a Ranger student came upon this RI's rucksack sitting by itself and unceremoniously emptied it onto the ground, spreading his stuff all over place. When the RI found it, he was understandably pissed. "My rucksack is missing some things and we are going to search for them, and if anyone finds food, you'd better return it." Like the other students, I wandered around the trees, head down, simply wasting time, not really looking for anything. Shuffling my feet, I kicked a gray packet. I looked close to see a jelly packet. The mental picture I had of giving him his grape jelly packet back was silly, so I put my foot over it, protecting it from everyone's sight. I squatted down, keeping my eyes on the people around me like I was picking up a dollar bill that fell out of the pocket of the guy in front of me, and later I split it with my Ranger buddy.

Spitoon

There was a kinship developed between all of the people who had struggled together to that degree for so long. It was a semidemented brotherhood. Right at the end of Ranger School, hours away from graduation at Fort Benning, Georgia, we were all sitting in the barracks cleaning weapons. Each of us had our weapons disassembled on the floor around us as we worked on one component at a time with a rag or punching rod. The air was thick with talk, bullshit, and loads of manly banter. Several of us were dipping (chewing tobacco), using one canteen cup among us as a spittoon. As natural as tying his shoes, one of the guys took it, went into the bathroom, emptied and rinsed it out, filled it with coffee, and brought it back for us to share. No one thought twice about it. Of course you have to drink your coffee.

While still in the barracks cleaning our weapons, I saw Kurt Roddy, my roommate from Fort Knox. The last time I had seen Kurt was when he came up to me at the hangar in Florida after he found out that he was being recycled. There was nothing I could say to him at the time to comfort him. To say something like "I know you'll make it through" just seemed so hollow and empty. The school had parked him for two weeks to wait until the next class began the Florida phase. He came through the barracks while I was in the latrine, and when I came out he was sitting and laughing with a couple of the guys. When he saw me the smile left his face and he said in all seriousness, "You look like you just got out of a POW camp. You look emaciated." I was never alerted to my condition since the change was gradual enough that for me I looked the same. The only difference I noticed was that my belt had a lot more spare length at the end. The pictures I look at now show that I resembled a toothpick with a set of birth control glasses.

Friends, Family, and Food

There were a couple of different theories on how to best get through all of the mental anguish of Ranger School, but they boiled down to two: family and food. Ranger Fly believed the best thing to do was talk about food, which to the rest of us was the most infuriating thing for him to do. We were all starving, and this guy always said, "You know what I'm going to do? I'm going to have lasagna as soon as I get home." We told him to shut up, that it drove us nuts. We were trying to make it through and *not* think about food, and this guy thought and talked about it constantly.

Personally, during the difficult times, I thought about my family. When I was down was when I really sorted out what was important in my life, and I found that I thought about my family all the time. I realized how important they were to sustaining me.

My parents, brother, and sister were very supportive. Knowing what I was going through, they wrote to me all the time. I cherished receiving and reading each of those letters. Knowing that somebody in the world was thinking about things other than patrols and major minuses helped a lot. My parents mailed me the classic swashbuckling novel *The Prisoner of Zenda* page by page so it would not be found by the RIs. I could read a few pages of that and have a chance to go somewhere else in my imagination for a short while.

Another perhaps more obvious source of support came from my buddies, and I am confident I have never been as close to anyone in my life except my wife.

After arriving at the patrol base during a patrol in the mountains, I began pulling my gear out when I realized that I might be missing an MRE. I did not want to admit anything until I had done a thorough search, but I knew that one of them was not where I had packed it. As I completely emptied my ruck, I had this frightening feeling that I was actually missing one. I tore through my ruck, looking everywhere for it before believing my MRE was gone for good. I am not sure to this day what happened. I may have left it out, or it may have fallen out of my pack at night. To accept that kind of loss was like saying, "I'm missing my pancreas." It was the scariest feeling in the world. "How could I have done this?" I wondered. We were on one and a half provisions a day, a starvation ration for the amount of energy we burned, and now two-thirds of my day's food was gone.

Nothing was more important than food. Tobacco, sleep, and everything else took a backseat, at least for me. There were two different currencies at Ranger School. There was tobacco, and there was food. Nobody ever traded food for tobacco. You traded food for food. Food was as good as romance was in the real world, and I was missing a good portion of mine with no one to blame but myself.

The hunger pangs in my stomach were now acute. The hunger was bearable when I thought I would soon satiate it with food, but now I had no hope. I really took pride in pacing myself with food so I would have enough to last the entire four-day patrol. I would eat only two rations a day for the first two days, and that allowed me to have three rations a day for the last two days. Beyond throwing my ration cycle out of whack, my loss jeopardized my stamina and ability to keep up with the pace.

Steve Larr was there as I experienced this catastrophe, which was one of the most miserable moments of my life. I was beating myself up. "How could I have done this? I'm such an idiot. Now I'm going to starve." Steve, once discovering the tragedy, threw me a package of apple sauce, which was like giving me a kidney. We covered for each other, and though it might seem silly now, that sort of gesture was absolutely one of the most trusting gestures I could have ever imagined.

Another example of charity was when Mike Ryan got sick. He had pulled a partially eaten egg sandwich out of the Dumpster behind the Dixie Diner in the desert, eaten it, and become nauseous. He had to go into the infirmary for what everyone assumed was heat exhaustion, but a couple of us were laughing because we knew the real cause. He came back out to the field a day later, having rested, but without receiving any additional rations. Sick call was not like real sick call where they actually take care of you. It was more of a kill or no-kill situation. If the injury was bad enough to kick you out of the course, it was a kill; if it was not, they said, "Here's your Motrin. Deal with it." A no-kill.

Shortly after that, we were in a fighting position on our bellies looking into the open desert beyond the perimeter when I asked him how his stay at sick call went. Seconds later a Snickers bar landed in front of me. It might as well have been a Krugerrand. While on sick call he had sneaked into the Dixie Diner, this time getting food from the proper end of the diner, and bought three Snickers bars, demonstrating that he had more balls than I would have had.

Despite having guts, being a great guy, and being solid Ranger, Mike was terrible at keeping his stuff together. In the mountains while on patrol he lost a flare. Loss of equipment accountability was a serious issue, and the RI threatened, "We are not going back to get dinner in the chow hall tonight unless that flare is found." The value of that meal was enormous since it was one of the few hot meals we were going to get for the whole 61 days. Everyone, of course, was going to crucify Mike, kill him right there. Mike felt bad, like he had gotten us all killed or captured. Even I was pretty angry about it, but he was my buddy, and it was bad luck that it had happened to him as opposed to me, so I tried to comfort him. We put in an extra effort on our search for purely selfish food reasons, though those of us who were close to Mike may have rationalized it was for him. The search was successful.

Loser

There were some dark lessons learned going through that struggle. I learned some of the worst things about humanity. When the chips are down, you really learn what people are made of, and people who you thought would be reliable when the stress was on them ended up being unreliable. On the other hand, some of the people you thought would be worthless ended up really measuring up. Lieutenant Knight, who seemed like the nicest guy in the world when we started Ranger School, turned into a real dick when he was starving and deprived of sleep.

On one particular night in Florida I was the weapons squad leader overseeing the M60 machine guns and assistant gunners (AGs). It was the second night in a row that I had worked with the machine guns. The night before I was part of the weapons squad, carrying the tripod as an assistant gunner. The AG position always seemed to be the most thankless. I carried the tripod, which was very heavy, and in addition to that I carried the extra M60 ammo, yet the position did not receive the recognition of the M60 gunner. Carrying the M60 sucked, but being the assistant gunner was even worse.

We knew from the beginning of the school that one of the things you were not supposed to do was sit on your ass when you stopped—the rucksack flop, we called it. The rucksack flop looked like someone sitting up against a stump with his knees bent, only in this case the stump was strapped to your body as a rucksack. When we got to a stop we were supposed to go to our knees, then onto our bellies, and face out.

That next night Lieutenant Knight was the AG, carrying the tripod and extra M60 ammo. We were all exhausted. It was another one of those horrible nights in Florida where we moved seemingly forever. When we finally arrived at the patrol base, Knight did the rucksack flop right in the middle. This was like a fire alarm in church—that evident—and the RI was bound to take notice and screw the leaders. Knight was obviously thumbing his nose at his buddies, in essence saying, "I don't care about you."

I went over to him and said just about as nicely as I could in that setting, "Hey, I know we are all exhausted, but you need to get on the perimeter."

I really believe I was compassionate in the way I spoke, and he looked at me and very deliberately said, "Fuck you."

"Man, you are only going to fuck yourself, and you are going to screw your buddies," I said.

"No, fuck you. I've been carrying this tripod all night, and I'm not going to get on the perimeter. I am fucking exhausted," he said.

I was angry, but there was nothing I could do about it without drawing more attention.

The next morning he came up to me and apologized. "I'm really sorry. I was really tired."

I said, "You fucked up. You had your chance." A bunch of the guys had not liked him before, but I had reserved judgment on him. At that point I threw my hat in with the rest of the crowd. I thought this guy was a worthless piece of shit.

Later, he further confirmed my belief. He was the squad

leader in charge of distributing the day's chow. I watched him divide up the MREs for the platoon. He took the box of MREs aside, opened it and dumped it out on the ground. After searching, like looking for a favorite pair of socks in a drawer, he pulled out the ones he wanted. That was another explicit no-no. One of the most elementary rules of leadership in the field is that soldiers eat first and officers do not get special treatment in any way. Not only was he a lieutenant in real life, but he was acting as one of our unit's leaders for this exercise. He knew better. He should have pulled out his MREs just like everyone else, not looking at them until he got them. That was as good as the law in Ranger School. Justice is not always swift, but he ended up getting weeded out of our class in short order.

It was a very dark lesson. People can really change when they are under stress. There do not seem to be any indicators while times are good as to how someone will react under pressure. I guess everyone has their own instinct that they follow that says, "I think I can count on this guy in a crisis," but until you are really there you do not know. In the workplace it is rare to see that sort of stress, but you do get glimpses of it, even in the more sensible work environments. In medical intern programs it is very realistic. I believe that for a short time interns are under an amount of stress similar to what we were under in Ranger School.

Intent

I learned the value of planning, even if the plan is not followed. There is no place in the Army where planning for an operation is emphasized more than at Ranger School. The operations order (OPORD) and the operations order concept are central to Ranger School. Even if you are forced to abandon the details of the plan, having a plan puts everybody on the same sheet of paper at the start.

The two most important parts of the OPORD are the mission and the commander's intent. They transfer over to almost any situation where you have to coordinate people. You must know what the mission is and what the commander wants to accomplish. That is much more important than that the commander wants every soldier to carry three magazines and one signal flare or that the enemy wears yellow jumper suits. If everyone knows what the objective is and knows what the commander wants the end state to look like, you can carry on. I have used that idea in civilian circles with great success.

When you are in a leadership position, one of the questions that is asked of you again and again is, "What's important here? You are giving us all of these ideas and details, but what is the important stuff that I really need to know?" Ultimately it comes down to the mission and intent. It does not matter if you follow the letter of my instructions. What matters is that you know what we are trying to accomplish and you understand how I am trying to accomplish it. If you have to use your own initiative for whatever reason, you are free to do so. This was very important in outdoor education, which I worked at before going into medicine. As a doctor I will not have the foremost expert within arm's reach to turn to and ask, "Well now, this situation has come up. You did not brief us on this, so now what do I do?"

"Well, remember what the mission is and remember what my intent is, and use your judgment." It has tremendous application value.

Goal

For me, Ranger School was kind of a Holy Grail, a goal that was out there for me for five years before I had the chance to do it. I always held it as the ultimate test. Would I be capable? Would I be able to measure up to it? Knowing that I was capable of it was a tremendous feeling. I was not let down by unmet expectations. There were times during Ranger School that I thought, "If this were much harder, I don't know that I would make it through." I was never close to quitting or throwing in the towel, but I was frequently thinking that if they made something a little bit harder, I wouldn't be able to do it.

I learned that I could hold my shit together when things went down. I was fortunate enough to get very good peer evaluations all the way through Ranger School, and that surprised me because I did not feel that I was on top of my game a lot of the time.

Frame of Reference

It is a cliché, but when faced with a challenge I now have the luxury of saying, "As shitty as this is, at least I'm not back at Ranger School."

The challenges that are now appearing in my life are different from those in Ranger School. They are mainly intellectual challenges, but there are some similarities: the duration, the stress, and having to make a decision when the chips are down. I have had some experience in that, and it gives me confidence in my ability to make a decision, maybe not the perfect one, but at least I know I can make a decision, and that is more important than most people realize. The importance comes not necessarily from making the right decision every time, but at least not failing because I was incapable of making a decision. This is going to come into huge importance as a doctor. I could sit there while somebody is dying in my hands and be absolutely frozen because I do not know whether to use this drug or that one. I have to decide quickly whether to enervate or not to enervate and though I have tons more to learn on that very subject, I do know that ultimately I am going to be able to make a decision, and that is gratifying.

There are many people—some I am in school with and some I answer to—without that level of decision-making maturity. Going through Ranger School would have been the smartest thing for some of them. It is important for people to go through some rite of passage in their lives that can act as a frame of reference, something difficult, some sort of challenge that will build their confidence and self-esteem. I felt, at that time in my life, in my early to mid-20s, that I needed something that was extraordinarily challenging, something that was going to test me. You find in history and literature dating back to the earliest records where men, and women as well, needed to prove themselves. I think that combat served that function for a lot of people.

The Army and Ranger School represent the most acute example of that in my life. I did not realize how important that experience was until I began to see the people in my current professional setting, as a physician in training. Some of the surgeons and doctors I observe see what they are doing as the most difficult and the most challenging thing that they have ever had to do, and it very much is, but they end up treating it like a Ranger School. They, like myself, felt they had to challenge themselves in their youth, and they found that challenge in medical school, internship, and residency. Now that they are in charge as the surgeons and doctors, they look back on the people who are following in their path and think that they should have an experience just as difficult and challenging. They believe that the people going through the system now should suffer what they had to suffer through. To me, their focus seems misplaced. In this setting you learn how to be a good doctor and surgeon. There is no real place for harassment and abuse. My belief goes back to the point: "What is the mission and what is the intent?"

It is interesting how much significance Ranger School has taken on now, not only for myself, but for the people I associate with. I find that Ranger School is what people know about me. To most of the doctors and medical students that I work with, Ranger training is such a bizarre and different world that they label me as "that person who went to Ranger School." By my simply mentioning it to a couple of people at medical school, that fact circulated throughout the student body to people I was not associated with and did not even know. Without knowing my name, to them I was still "the Ranger guy." People try to associate me with Ranger School the way so many people are categorized—just because it is easy. If you meet a lawyer and you do not get to know the individual well, then he or she will end up being, in your mind, all the things that a lawyer is generalized to be.

Something that I am frequently asked to do by my close friends, especially when things are arduous, is to compare medical school to Ranger School. It is too difficult to compare the two. They are apples and oranges. The bottom line is: There is not a day in medical school that I would have traded to be back in Ranger School, not for all the money in the world. Medical school is really hard from an intellectual standpoint. In that sense it is many times more difficult than Ranger School ever was. But to be out there in that fucking swamp again, I would not swap three days in medical school for a second of Ranger School.

One thing that comes up is the sleep issue among medical interns. As an intern you do not get much sleep. Recently, some interns were trading war stories about how little sleep they got: "I worked two days without getting any sleep," and so forth. I said, "Gee, I did some training in the Army where we got very little sleep for a long time." They asked what training it was, and I replied,

"Well, you know, there is this Army Ranger School I went through back in 1988."

I did not think it was that dramatic, but a hush came over the room, and a couple of the guys questioned me—"Ranger School?"—to confirm what I said.

The public has recently seen more of the Rangers. A couple of movies have come out that Rangers figure in prominently, so there are some mental pictures generated in even the most civilian of civilian minds when the word "Ranger" is mentioned. People are becoming increasingly curious about them.

Finally, I was at the point where I was explaining how little sleep we actually got. It seems most nights we got maybe an hour or two, and there were stretches where we worked on about an hour of sleep a night for maybe two weeks. It would vary, but I do not remember any time in Ranger School getting more than four hours, and that was during the bus or plane rides between the phases.

The interns were mostly unbelieving. One woman giving voice to the group said, "You cannot go 61 days with that little sleep; you'll collapse."

I simply said, "Well, you know, you weren't there." It was a different reality for them, one they could not conceive of because it was so uncommon, and they had never been through it. Believing that they are tapped out at their limit now makes it seem impossible that something could be that much harder. The fact is, medical school and internship are phenomenally difficult in ways that are very different from Ranger School, but it is nothing like the sort of physical and mental endurance that Ranger School demanded.

Ranger Chandler's Walk

To harp on the importance of expectation again: When it's time to start working, it's time to start working. Expect to be doing push-ups on 110-degree blacktop in the first 10 seconds. We naturally want to rationalize a level of civility and normalcy, even in the world of high achievement. That's a fool's fantasy. It's brutal and unforgiving, and it lasts from the time you step into that arena until the time you step out. The good news is that by being in that arena you have given yourself the only chance you have at real success.

As a leader, you certainly must have the expectation of success, but you also have to manage the expectations of your team. Mark Chandler's experience shows good examples of how that can be done. People do respond to challenges and over time can really internalize a goal. You wouldn't expect that Ranger School would be one of the challenges that a Vassar graduate would seek; yet the seed was planted well before the test began. Lay some groundwork before the time for real work begins. Allow people to prepare.

The other expectation management tool that Mark pointed out was the use of the Commander's Intent, or what we'll call the Leader's Intent. When you spell out what the important characteristics of success are before setting out on a mission, you have provided a great deal of priority information to your team. There are always a lot of details to a plan, but when you answer the question, "What is *really* important here?" you've set expectations. You've set a guide rope in place and clearly established the environment. Creating this framework first is essential for any team to show innovation and flexibility later.

A practical example: Your mission is to read *No Excuse Leadership* and complete it no later than three days from now. My intent is that you understand, internalize, and integrate the leadership lessons contained herein. Notice, there is no mention of where you read it, how many pages a day you read, or what you should eat for breakfast between now and finishing the book. Your expectation of work is set, your understanding of the goal is set, and you are free to use your own imagination and ingenuity to fill in the details. Try this with your team and send them on their way. You'll find a bright new world of accomplishment and you may even get to share a warm cup of MRE coffee from a former spittoon with them one day!

Leader's Intent will be taken to the next level execution in our next chapter about David Stockwell. You'll get to see how rehearsals can add significant clarity and make you an extremely efficient leader.

RANGERS

are

INSTINCTUAL

DAVID STOCKWELL

The instant that Somali bullet shattered against the door frame, peppering his temple with fragments, Major David Stockwell was guided by his survival instinct. His instinct was not a simple fight-or-flight response. It had been trained through the stressful situations of his Army career starting with Ranger School more than 10 years earlier. With bullet fragments in his head and blood flowing from his wounds, he functioned coherently and moved swiftly.

Where training and education leave off, instinct begins. Even as a lieutenant, David combined his deep desire to succeed at Ranger School with a trust in his gut feeling. The situation was not life-or-death at the time, but it was critical that he pass his patrol. He rehearsed the plan with his platoon because he couldn't think of a better way to get his message across, not because it was a checklist item. It worked! Lieutenant Stockwell was focused on function not fluff, substance not style, and went beyond the current doctrine to accomplish his goal. Do you have a deep desire to succeed that will activate your instinct and innovation? Where in your job are you ignoring your instincts?

Return to Arms

I was prior service, having enlisted in the United States Army courtesy of the last draft of the Vietnam era. When I reentered the service I headed to Officer Candidate School (OCS) and the officer ranks. When I went through basic training the second time, my drill sergeant was Sergeant First Class Donnie Black. He was Ranger qualified and had served in a Ranger Battalion and with the Marines in Vietnam. He was someone I naturally wanted to emulate. He was a great example of someone who earned the Ranger tab and maintained a dedication to excellence that made me look up to him. He was the first example of someone who encouraged me to go to Ranger School, not by his words, but through his actions.

Because I was older, prior service, and going to OCS after basic training, he made me his platoon guide. On his suggestion, our platoon did things differently. Instead of marching to the rifle range, we patrolled through the woods. He acted as patrol leader and taught me assistant patrol leader (APL) duties. I had been out of the military for six years, so this was a real immersion into the culture and some of the skills. As we went through this process, I became physically stronger and militarily smarter.

Originally, upon my return into the service, Ranger School was something I considered well beyond my grasp. My brother-in-law was Ranger qualified and I had read about Rangers, so when I came back into the service it was something I was interested in doing but considered a monumental task and probably beyond my abilities. I believed that when you distinguish yourself that way, you are elite. I was more concerned with finishing basic training first, then I would look farther down the road. It took a period of over a year to finally get strong enough and gain the confidence where I saw Ranger School as being within my grasp.

OCS graduates were the last in line of the officer commissioning sources to pick their branches and assignments, so I ended up as a signal officer. The Signal Corps had a very poor record of graduation from Ranger School, so it had a demanding preRanger program of physical and academic preparation, and I was one of just a handful of guys from my basic course who passed and earned a slot to Ranger School. Later on down the road when I went to Fort Knox and they needed a Ranger program, I used my experience from OBC to fashion the program that I put young armor officers through.

When I reported in, I was 28 years old, 10 years older than the majority of my classmates, a bunch of 18-year-old guys from the Ranger Battalions. I had slowed down a little bit in those 10 years since I was their age, and I had never been really strong in my upper body, so I still had some doubts. I knew being older I was a little more mature than my classmates—not smarter, but I had been through high-pressure situations before and could stop and figure things out a little more easily than they probably could. They, of course, had the bull strength that I did not have. At the time I did not know which attribute would be the most important. Either way, I knew I was in for it.

Ominous

Ranger School created a concentration camp–like atmosphere at the physical training (PT) pit. Large stadium lights stood around the perimeter of the area, and their glow cut through the blackness of the early morning. It gave us the eerie feeling that tall fences and armed men in watchtowers were just beyond our vision in the darkness. We could see bugs flying around near the lights, and it looked like the lights were focused directly on us. The pit was a flat, sawdust-filled area circled by railroad ties, bordered by the worm pit exercise course on two sides, and us, the POWs, in the middle.

We stood in rough box formations doing the various exercises commanded of us. After warming up, and especially after running, our heated bodies gave off steam like hot cups of coffee on a cold morning. In a way we were trapped, though voluntarily. We had signed our lives over to people we didn't know with the expectation that they would subject us to pain. Ranger students aren't necessarily guided by their left brains.

Thanks

One of my best friends in life is my Ranger buddy, Vance Nannini, a field artillery officer, who jumped into Panama with the 1st Ranger

Battalion when he was their fire support officer. We went through jump school and Ranger School together, and it was a rather special relationship that we had and still have.

We were in the field during Thanksgiving. Vance was the unfortunate patrol leader. The stark contrast between our current condition and our usual existence before Ranger School was brought to the forefront of our minds as each of us thought about the Thanksgiving holiday and then about our one C ration for the day. Mine was tuna noodle, not even turkey. I opened the can with my P-38 can opener, a tiny little metal handle not more than an inch and a half long and a curved blade that hinged off of the handle. I crushed up the cracker, stirred it in, and made a little stew. Looking at my meal gave me little solace at missing the normally joyful holiday with my family. Meanwhile, in the reality of our day, Vance needed some things done for the patrol and was having no cooperation as everyone moped around at half speed and thought of home.

A couple of days later, at the end of our five-day patrol, we returned to Camp Darby. Expecting business as usual, we were surprised to receive what was called a super supper. The school held a belated Thanksgiving dinner for us. All of the officers from the Ranger School cadre wore their formal blue uniforms into the old World War II style barracks that served as the mess hall and acted as the servers for the meal. An RI put a serving on my plate, then looked at me and piled more food on top of it. They were a bit worried about me because I had lost a lot of weight and must have looked pretty gaunt. The turkey, stuffing, and all the fixings on my plate certainly made that tuna casserole look like shit. Sitting and eating in the mess hall was not like being at home, but the din of the conversation and the rise in spirits that the surprise food brought were certainly worth being thankful for.

Back to Hell

On a dreadful December night in the mountains, Vance was the patrol leader again, extending his streak of unlucky circumstances in which to be in the spotlight. We were walking through the woods when we were ambushed by the opposing force (OPFOR). The RIs set the OPFOR into position, gave them guidance on when to attack, and then walked us into their kill sack. Their machine guns fired rapidly, and only a split second separated the first pops of their rifles and the eruption of the whole forest with noise.

The flashes of their muzzles were within feet of us off to the right side. Instantly, we abandoned our rucksacks, dropped to the ground, and fired wildly in their general direction. At the moment in time when an ambush started, all other concerns of life were forgotten. Hunger, weariness, and dry uniforms were all disregarded as we fell to the muddy trail belly first and crawled for cover. We were conditioned to hit the ground where we stood and return fire.

The yelling of the patrol leaders trying to gain control filled the night along with the weapons fire. We quickly regrouped and attacked through the enemy and defeated their ambush. It was always good to finish an operation like that because it was rare that it would happen twice in a night, and we could relax and move to our objective.

Just after recovering from the ambush, we got ambushed again. "Damn. What is this?" I thought. "Not again." It was an odd ambush. The shots were sporadic but much louder. We realized in a panic that the shots were coming from rifles with *real* bullets. Screaming, we hit the ground again and scrambled for cover. The firing stopped. Some hunters had mistaken us for deer and opened fire. Fortunately, no one was hurt, probably due to the alert our screaming gave to the hunters.

We were on the side of the Tennessee Valley Divide, a very steep portion of the Appalachian Mountains. One of the Rangers had jettisoned his ruck on his way to diving to the ground, and it rolled all the way down the side of the mountain. Our rucks were so packed that there were no flat parts that might stop a roll, and his 80-pound sphere kept going. We had to wait as he went down, found it, and humped back up. After the excitement was over, we focused on the most proximate enemy, the weather, and it continued to get worse as the night went on.

While in the field and on patrol, the rule was that if it was overcast in the afternoon, the night would probably be pretty warm, since clouds hold in the heat. As can be expected, general rules are sometimes wrong. In this case the clouds that should hold in the heat were holding much more than that. On this particular night the clouds let loose a big ice storm, freezing everything. We built completely inadequate poncho hooches to protect us from the elements. The freezing rain caked on them heavily, soon collapsing our flimsy structures. The RIs would not let us build fires, so all we could do was pair with a buddy and huddle up. We put our poncho liners together and hugged each other. No matter how embarrassing the picture might seem now, we knew it was the only thing we could do to keep from freezing.

Vance and I sat there listening to the drops hitting the poncho liner over us and tried to get even closer to each other in an attempt to share as much heat as possible—two grown men reduced to cuddling. To pass the time and somehow fill our minds with something besides our current situation, Vance and I made lists of food that we were going to buy on our eight-hour break. Topping the list were chocolate bars and a jar of peanut butter. We then made a list of all the places we were going to go. "First, we'll drop off our laundry, then to Arby's to get roast beef and gravy, and then to Ranger Joe's and Arco's because they've got free pizza." We giggled like little girls at a sleepover.

In the midst of our talking and planning our weariness was able to gain a weak foothold, and each of us slipped in and out of consciousness throughout the night. The irony of that situation is that we were in the clutches of misery and yet were so tired much of it was lost through lack of awareness. Even our tragedy was mitigated by our exhaustion. Being totally awake for that experience could have sent us both into hysteria and insanity. We could hear hunters shooting in the distant valley and the snaps of rain on our ponchos. We were blind in the darkness, so only the sounds and the intense bone-deep cold kept us company. It was an otherworldly type of night with thoughts of dying right there where we sat.

The next morning found us alive, and as daylight came the rising sun revealed the snow-covered ground. It would have been beautiful if I were looking at it through a living room window. We moved surprisingly fast in recovering our collapsed ponchos and repacking our gear to start the march. It was the only way to warm up.

As the compass man, I led the patrol off the mountain. When we reached the valley, we were able to build fires to warm up and dry out. At least that part of the horror was finished. It was true that some patrols were easier than others, and you hoped to get an easy one. Unfortunately, Vance seemed to have the bad luck of being stuck as patrol leader during the "memorable" times.

As darkness gives way to light—and no dark is so deep that a tiny candle cannot penetrate it—Ranger School breaks for Christmas. It is not a normal Ranger School break of a few hours or like Thanksgiving where they gave us a normal amount of nourishment and acted like it was a gift. We were actually able to spend the holiday at home!

Our bodies were in a poor, weakened condition, each of us having lost a lot of weight, and we more than welcomed the chance to recover a little. I had frostnip in my hands and feet and had lost most of my toenails due to the cold. My hands were thick and cracked, and I couldn't even lace up my boots.

Vance and I drove from Fort Benning, Georgia, to Fort Gordon, Georgia, where my family was for the Christmas break. Upon arriving home, Cheryl, my wife, laid spaghetti on the table in front of us. Eating was the first order of business—the only order of business. We were hogs at a trough, and before she could get us another plateful, we were diving into the brownies. We could not really use our hands for more than scoops, so we just shoveled the sweet blocks into our mouths. Style was not our strong point on that day, nor for the rest of the holiday. It was nice to live like a normal person again, but there was not enough time to get over the long deprivation of food. It was an obsession with us, the way a person raised in poverty might hoard money as an adult. You never knew if there was going to be more. Our break ended way too soon.

We returned to the final phase in Florida. It was not easy reporting for Ranger School the first time, and this was only a small fraction easier. The feeling in my hands and feet had just returned. I was on a normal sleep cycle and had put on some of the weight I had lost, and now I was putting myself back into the situation that had weakened me so badly. Having to go back knowing I had three weeks to go, 12 days of which were on patrol, was a pretty low point for me. The visions of the pleasant life outside of Ranger School were at the front of my mind, but the knowledge that this was the final phase was consoling. My continued focus on achieving the Ranger tab encouraged me to proceed.

From Weakness, Strength

I was the platoon leader for the planning and movement phases of an assault patrol on day five of the 12-day patrol in Florida. It turned out to be a comfortable outside environment. It was a picnic kind of day. The sun wafted in and out from behind the clouds to shine down through the tall, scattered trees onto my platoon. There was no rain, and that makes for a good day in Florida. We were in teams of two sitting in foxholes in a triangular patrol base of about 30 meters per side. I was in the center doing the planning. Everyone was recovering from our last mission and preparing for the next, the normal cycle that never ended. The priorities of work, the orderly way in which we got everything done in a limited time, went smoothly. Things like food and sleep were supposed to be part of the priorities of work, though they were often ignored as secondary to preparing our equipment and planning for the mission. Today there was more time, and guys got some chow and rest while I did the planning for the mission. We got a lot done in the relatively pleasant circumstances.

Due to an insecurity about myself and my planning for the mission, I took an extra step in making sure the concept was passed down to all of my leaders by doing a reduced force rehearsal. My personal doubts came from where I saw I fit into the group around me. I was a signal officer, not even combat arms, in the middle of all these guys from the Ranger Battalions who had gone through the Ranger Indoctrination Program (RIP) and other pertinent training. I thought that due to their background, they had a better concept of these missions than I did. I did not feel that a verbal operations order (OPORD) would be enough to have them understand the mission, so I chose to do a walk-through. I didn't have any problem with their ability. I had a problem with mine, and I wanted to make damn sure that they understood what I had in mind. I was also looking for ideas for improvement to cover areas I had missed. I figured as we walked through the mission they might come up with something better, and that was okay. It was a collective approach that would make the mission better and hide what I saw as some of my weaknesses.

I grabbed up the key leaders. Within the rather large patrol base we did the rehearsal. I carved out little landmarks with the heel of my boot and piled up sand for the high ground to depict the geography along our route. I lined the key leaders up in the order we were going to move and then walked through the mission from the beginning. We walked from one key point to the next phase line or checkpoint, and then I had them explain to me what they were doing at each location. It turned out to be a good rehearsal, with each person getting a better understanding of the mission and how he fit into its overall concept.

Afterward, I finished the planning and then led the platoon on the movement to the objective rally point (ORP) before I was switched out as the patrol leader. During the switch of leadership, I was able to quickly pass on the concept of the mission to the new patrol leader, and because everyone else was familiar with what we were doing, the assault went very well. I was happy to be a simple member of squad for the remainder of the mission. The walk from the assault to our new patrol base was long, and I drifted away in thought as usual.

We arrived at our new patrol base early in the morning and started the cycle of work all over again. When we switched out RIs, the outgoing RI debriefed all of the patrol leaders from the previous day. The technique in Florida was that they did not tell anyone whether they had passed the patrol to avoid students getting a "tabbed-out" mentality. For some reason he ignored that rule and told me I had tabbed out. He said, "I have never seen a reduced force rehearsal in the patrol base. Even though we teach it and talk about it, most people never go beyond a map rehearsal. You did a great job and you got a go."

I simply wanted to make sure they understood the mission, and in doing so I gained a valuable technique for leading people. Throughout my career, whenever I have been able to use it, the reduced force rehearsal has been the key to success. One big difference in that event was that I did it for real, not just to check the box for my patrol. It must have shown through that it was not just some sort of "meeting a requirement," and that is why I think the captain told me I got a go. When he told me the good news, I thought, "Hey, hey, I'm home free." What I forgot in my brief moment of glee was that Ranger School was not going to treat me any differently or celebrate with me. I was reminded on night 11 of that patrol how harsh a reality it can be.

The reduced force rehearsal is still the standard I take to the field. When I was a platoon leader, when I was a troop commander, and when I was the acting squadron commander at the Joint Readiness Training Center (JRTC), we did reduced force rehearsals. "Rehearsal is the key to success" is a quote that I became very fond of teaching my subordinates.

A Different World

During the long walks of nothingness, moving for hours, it seemed as though we were going through places no one had ever been before. It was the most beautiful terrain I had ever seen, nothing like the scenery viewed while passing in a car. Part of the attraction was that we were way out on our own. There were no motorcycles, dune buggies, cars, or four-wheelers around. I particularly liked the mountains and the pretty forested hills in Dahlonega. As I walked I would think, "Wow, what if I built a house there? That's where I want to build a house." We walked on a bit farther. I would think, "No, I want to build a house over there." The thought of living out in a place where few people ventured was alluring. I did not picture a rustic log cabin type home but rather my own home sitting there. For some reason, wanting to live out in the wilderness like that, with the solitude yet with all the modern conveniences, appealed to me. Every time we were at a place that was very scenic or picturesque I wanted to build a house *there*.

It Never Ends

The last few days of Florida were unlike any series of days I had ever lived through before. It started on day 10 of the 12-day patrol. The arrival of a tropical storm forced us to cease movement and seek some kind of shelter and warmth. The whipping wind and heavy rain made it impossible to see, so I found a tree and squatted with my back on the downwind side. Our RI took a trip flare, piled a bunch of wood on it, and then set it off. Even though the wood was wet, the flare dried it out enough to start a fire.

We had only two days to go in the course, which aided in our perseverance, but even that late into the game one guy was pushed past his limit. Anderson was a kid from one of the Ranger Battalions who had joined my squad as a recycle in the mountains. He quit that day. It was impossible to tell why he tripped that close to the finish line. The obvious causes do not tell the whole story. We had all suffered through the physical discomfort for so long that if we were going to quit because of that, we would have done so well before that day.

It was miserable and cold, but what snapped in Anderson that day was not a physical threshold. It was a mental one. He must have been pushed so far that he accepted the vision of a different, non-Ranger future for himself. The decision to go to Ranger School was never entered into lightly, and it meant accepting and wanting a future of personal pride and professional respect. Everyone still at the school with only two days left had been pushed to give up that dream on many occasions but successfully kept it. Quitting Ranger School did not simply mean he went on to his unit without a tab. He was headed back to a Ranger Battalion. At the Ranger Battalions when you went back without your tab, they threw all your stuff out the window and ripped your scroll, the Ranger Battalion patch, off of your uniform. He was beyond caring about the consequences and the long-term changes his decision would have on his life. The misery of the moment—the wind, rain, and cold—can only be understood when taken in that context. That misery pushed a tested soldier to give up the future he had dreamed about and risk the condemnation of people he respected. I wanted to quit every day, but I kept making a new decision to stick with it just one more day.

At the beginning I questioned the balance between youth and its physical strength and age and its maturity. I believe now that mental strength was definitely more important than the physical strength. If you can stay healthy, you can get through. It was the big chiseled guys, the football player type guys that I always looked at and figured were shoo-ins for this type of stuff. Surprisingly, those were usually the guys who did not make it. It was the little geeky guys like me that made it. A big reason for their failure was their habitual reliance on their physical strength and not their mental strength. There is always a danger in generalizing, but I saw it happen over and over again. Our mental strength was tested almost from the beginning. The school quickly tired us out, all of us losing our physical strength, and then it was all a matter of "Who's too stupid to know when to quit?"

I had done really well in my patrols, passing one in Darby, two in the mountains, and my first patrol in Florida. I got a fifth patrol on night 11 of the 12-day patrol, now one day of field time from the end. I was the platoon sergeant, which meant that I spent the all-night move running up and down the column straightening people out and avoiding breaks in contact. The patrol leader was having trouble and might not graduate, so I put out an extra effort. It turned into another Bataan Death March—a night from hell.

One of the Rangers, a Pakistani in my squad, created an amusing image. He looked like a rat as his hunched-over silhouette walked through the woods led by his big nose. It was the typical night when guys put quarters in trees to get a soda or fell asleep leaning against trees they thought were Ranger buddies. One guy physically fell over. He went to sleep standing up and only woke up when he hit the ground. I ended up passing that patrol, but it cost me an entire night of sleep. By the time the sun came up the next morning, I was relieved of my platoon sergeant duties. I was happy to be Joe Snuffy again.

Day 12, the final day of field time in Florida and Ranger School, was upon us, and all of us were thinking that we still had the big mission of attacking Santa Rosa Island. We were ready to move to the water, load up RB-15s with our gear, row out to the long barrier island just off the coast, and attack an objective there. It was a famous mission in Ranger School, and we knew we would not leave without doing it, so we held our excitement until that necessary threshold had been passed. What we did not know was that there was a big storm out on the island, and we were not going to do the mission.

I was extremely tired, so the next hours passed as normal. I was in a half-dazed state, awaiting the order to move. The next to last mission was planned, and we moved out toward the objective. Without a leadership position I was able to simply follow the man in front of me during the march and try to forget about my weariness and pain.

My feet were torn up from being constantly wet and damp the many days in the swamp. They were like a wet newspaper that was used to scrub a driveway. A day earlier I had gone to the medic, who put a total of 54 pieces of moleskin, adhesive tape, and Band-Aids on my feet. Bandaged the way they were, I could not get my feet into my boots, so I peeled the wrappings off, put my two pieces of hamburger into my boots, and drove on. A fortunate self-defense mechanism our bodies have is to become numb to repeated signals to the brain. Every step I took shot the signal, "Ow! Quit it!" to my brain. In time my feet became numb. My entire body became anesthetized to the pain. The incredible lack of awareness that I required to allow me to perform adequately was provided through some natural means—that is, until we began to assault the objective. As soon as someone expressed a need for me to do something besides walk, I woke up to how tired I was. You can sleep in a car with ice on the windshield, but do not try to drive it. I discovered that I was absolutely lost. I had no idea who I was or where I was. I was like a bum, begging coins from passersby on a busy New York street and babbling to myself.

I stumbled around lost while the battle raged around me. I assaulted the objective, taking tiny, painful baby steps. It was the opposite of a runner's high. Instead of endorphins being released into my bloodstream and making me feel great, it seemed everything had been taken out of my blood, and I felt like crap. Literally crying from confusion, I asked Vance, "Where are we and what are we doing?"

He said, "I don't know. Just follow me. It'll be okay." Like the unconscious patient who wakes up in the hospital, we came through the mission and were awakened by the news that that was our last mission. There was not going to be a Santa Rosa mission. We were done. There was unadulterated joy at the reality that we had finished.

Expectation of More

I had the misperception that once you did something like graduate from Ranger School you didn't have anything to prove anymore. I thought it was like winning the Super Bowl. You've won it. You show off your ring, and nobody expects you to win it again. What I learned, though, was that if you are Ranger qualified you don't simply *wear* the tab; you *bear* the tab. And if you are worth your salt, you must earn it every day. The lowest form of creature is a tab wearer instead of a tab bearer.

The Rangers I watched and emulated and continue to watch and emulate have all set great examples. Whether they were younger or older than I was, whether they were specialists, sergeants, or generals, I have seen great role models from the Ranger fraternity. When I see the tab, I look for that intangible, indefinable extra in the person that made him go so much farther. And conversely, when I see someone without the tab, it is almost as if I can identify that intangible, indefinable character trait that is missing. It does not mean that he is bad. It does not mean that he is not a great leader and a great soldier. It just means he is not a Ranger.

I have absolutely seen a difference between those officers and soldiers who are Ranger qualified and those who are not. They carry themselves differently. The first thing that we Army guys do when we meet each other is sniff each other like puppy dogs to see what badges and tabs we are wearing. When you are Ranger qualified, the younger troops look up to you and expect you to be better. The person who has the tab senses that he is an example above and beyond the norm, and he stands a little straighter, marches a little truer.

When I'm Tired

I learned my limits through the Ranger School experience. In some ways I was not as good as I thought, and in other ways I learned I could exceed my perceived limits and a whole lot more. Lack of food did not bother me, whereas the lack of sleep really smoked me. To this day, I know I am getting really tired when my mood changes. I found it unflattering about myself that I can be pretty judgmental, usually as a subordinate looking at the leaders. When I was tired was when I was the hardest on others, the same way I am sure they were on me. We were all living up to the same high standards, and I did not want weakness on my team, either as a peer or as a leader.

I gave my lowest peer rating to a lieutenant who got recycled at Camp Darby. We were preparing for the three-day patrol, and he could not handle the fact that he had only three meals for three days, so he ate all his chow in one day. His weakness and hunger during the next two days made him a burden on the rest of the squad. His lack of self-discipline caused him to rely on the rest of the squad to share their limited food with him, bringing down the entire readiness of the squad. His conduct was as selfish as I had ever seen, and I did not want someone like him with me in combat.

It is much easier to make sound decisions when you are rested.

What Ranger School did was teach me how my mind works when I am exhausted, how to recognize that, and how to still make effective decisions. I also learned to recognize and control the unattractive aspects of my personality in those situations. I have effectively applied those lessons in stressful environments as a leader around the world since I graduated.

These lessons from Ranger School have not consciously changed how I do business. The changes were subconscious. Going through that experience changed the way I viewed and did things without me noticing. I expect more out of men and women, out of younger people, and out of my kids because I know that they can far exceed where they think their limits are even though they don't know it yet.

Good with Bad

I cannot imagine not being Ranger qualified in the Army. As a second lieutenant I became the commo (communications) officer for the 2nd Squadron, 1st Cavalry Regiment, in the 2nd Armored Division. The commo officer position is not associated with gung ho type actions, yet I was Ranger qualified while most of the tank and scout platoon leaders were not. The squadron commander was not Ranger qualified due to an injury he sustained while going through the course as a young man. He piled the responsibilities on me, saying, "You're a Ranger. You can handle it." I don't know his purpose in giving me so much work. It was probably 50 percent legit and 50 percent spite.

On the positive side, my commander used me for some good. Our unit ran one of three air assault schools in the Army. My first summer there a large group of West Pointers came through and filled one entire class. A West Point TAC officer accompanied them through as the "big toe," or mentor/coach, like Sergeant Hulka in the movie *Stripes*. He was the glue that held this class together. It was a very successful class with everybody graduating and getting their wings. The following class was a class of ROTC students, kids from colleges from across the United States, not just one location like West Point. As a result, they did not have a dedicated active duty officer to go through the class with them.

Lieutenant Colonel Hoover sent me through this air assault class as the only active duty guy. I was not the class leader—they had student leadership—but my role was to talk with them, counsel them, and make sure they did not quit. I took care of all sorts of big brother type duties.

The course was physically rigorous, and as a 29-year-old on four-mile runs in boots I thought, "You know, I've done this before, and it's bullshit. I'm really getting too old for this crap. I can't keep up with these young kids." It smoked the hell out of me, but I didn't show it. My class did well, which meant my mission was a success, and I got my wings out of it also. My commander and I were heroes.

I received the extra duties because of my Ranger tab, and because I succeeded at them, when I requested a branch transfer to armor the leadership endorsed it. The tab gave me opportunities, and because I was willing to continue to put out an extra effort, I succeeded and differentiated myself.

Instinct

I had been in Somalia for a month, having arrived there at the end of March 1993. The United Nations was not going to take over until the first week of May, so the Marines were still in control of Mogadishu. I was a public affairs officer (PAO) with the UN forces gearing up to take over. I had just left the Pakistani Brigade commander's headquarters on my way back to the UN military headquarters a few miles away. I had been getting ready to put him in front of the media, so I was teaching him how to greet the press, about a press brief, and how to take questions, among other things. I was driving back along a major artery, 21 October Road.

The city was fairly quiet. The Marines had called Mogadishu secure, so we wore flak vests for our torsos but berets instead of Kevlar helmets on our heads. I had a Norwegian shooter, Kel Nickolson, who rode in the passenger seat with a rifle. He was a big bear of a guy I called Iron Mike. I drove our white Jeep while Kel remained ready to respond to a threat with his weapon. As we drove back, we noticed that the road up ahead was clear. In fact, it was not only clear, it was void of movement—no pedestrians or traffic at all.

We were always taught to look for obstacles that stopped or slowed movement as a sign of an ambush. If there was an obstacle in the road, assume it was covered by fire, and that was an ambush. Well, the converse is also true. If the road is absolutely clear with no pedestrians around, it is probably not a good place to be. Iron Mike and I had a deal. Whenever we were in the city, as we often were, we kept our windows rolled down. We did not use the air-conditioning even though it was hotter than blazes. That way we could better hear, feel, and taste the environment around us. It was like employing a sixth sense. I had never heard a shot fired in anger up until that point, and it is true that you do not hear the shot that gets you.

I was going a good clip, about 50 miles per hour, through this stretch of road. There was a *snap* on the door frame to my left front, and instantly the right rear window of the vehicle blew out. We did not know we were being shot at or that I had been hit by a bullet from an AK-47. We had no idea what was going on. When the round hit the doorjamb it exploded and peppered the side of my head with bullet fragments. When the right rear window blew out, we thought we were getting hit from the right. Then all of a sudden all sorts of firing erupted, and I punched the gas to speed through the kill zone.

I looked in the left rearview mirror to see why my ear was ringing and saw blood spurting out of my temple, not just running, but spurting out as though an artery had been hit. A thought flashed through my mind as I remembered seeing autopsies done on Marines who had been shot in the head from close range. Looking at myself, I thought, "Boy, I've seen better-looking corpses than this." I wondered, "Am I dead? Is this an out-of-body experience?" It was very ethereal. I felt like I had been there before in some of my training. Still under fire and moving quickly, I took out a bandage from my LBE and held it on my head.

I watched the blood run down my head, still holding the bandage and not really sure of what had happened. "Mike, I'm hit, but I don't know if it was a bullet or a rock," I said.

Iron Mike asked, "Do you want me to drive?"

I said, "No. If I pass out from blood loss, here's what we'll do . . . ," and I went through a five-point contingency plan. We worked out how we were going to get back to the headquarters. Mike got on the radio and called ahead to the American Hospital. I was very disoriented. It was much like the confusion in Ranger School where you are tired and hungry but you still have to get to the objective. Somehow you find the fortitude to get there.

I was driving, in control of our fate, and though I was not certain I could maintain consciousness, I kept going. I felt in control enough that I told myself, "Steady. Steady. Control your breathing. Let's get the bleeding under control. Calm the fuck down. Everything is going to be all right." I scanned left. Iron Mike scanned right. We were waiting to be hit again, our tires to be shot out, or some other violence. We did not know what lay ahead of us, and as it turned out, I drove all the way to the hospital without further incident.

I think the shooters were a bit disappointed that they didn't bag the kill, but some days you count the bear; some days the bear counts you. That first shot was aimed at my head, but it was slightly off the mark.

That was the first time I had ever been shot at. I forced myself to go back out onto the street and face the potential of another such incident. From that day on we wore our Kevlar helmets, and I carried my .9 mm handgun locked and loaded with the safety off in my right hand. We still kept the windows rolled down. If the driver's side window was up when the bullet came through, it would have shattered and I would have been blinded. As it was, one of the bullet fragments that hit me came very close to putting my eye out. Of course, had the guy been a better shot, I probably would have been dead. On the other hand, had he missed the other way, he would have missed altogether. I ended up being in many engagements in my year in-country.

I became a little more thoughtful of my time on earth. I was scared, but I did not want to cower behind the wall. I did not want to get bucked from the horse and have the horse win. I got right back in the saddle and went out into the streets again. A few days later we were out in a very crowded section of town and came to a place where I had to slow down for traffic. Somali kids were known for their thievery, and one of them came up and took the sunglasses right off of my head. Fortunately, I had the presence of mind not to shoot him, and I could have. A Marine had done that a few months before—shot a kid who had taken the sunglasses off of his face as he drove—and he was court-marshaled. I had the perfect excuse. I still had bullet fragments in my head. I was justifiably jumpy, and I could have shot and killed somebody and gotten away with it.

I trace my ability to act effectively under stress directly back to the experiences I had at Ranger School. It is not a superhuman trait. I am not better than anyone else, but I had, in a sense, been there before. It gave me the presence of mind to deal with situations under extreme stress. Had I not gone through Ranger School I probably would not have gone back out on the street. I would have made the mistake of staying behind the wall. To do my job as PAO properly, I needed to go back out and see things as they were. I had to take the right precautions, helmet and .9 mm in hand, but I did not let it stop me from doing the things I knew I needed to do.

I did not get wounded nearly as badly as a lot of other guys have in that or previous conflicts, and sometimes I feel guilty for wearing a Purple Heart. I still have a chunk of Kalishnikov round up against my skull, but I am not missing a hand or anything major like that. I am very lucky. There are many guys who were hurt worse who deserve the Heart more. If there is ever a pecking order devised, I will gladly relinquish my right to wear my Purple Heart in deference to them.

The situation relates again to learning where your limits are. In combat I actually got more sleep and more food to eat. I think that Ranger School is a lot harder except that in combat a guy can get killed, and Ranger students do not experience the fear of combat. The ambushes in Ranger School were canned, and unless they were hunters using real bullets, you knew they were blanks. Having faced adversity and having faced my weaknesses before being shot helped me get through Somalia. Ranger School gave me a place I could go mentally to draw strength and a knowledge that I had been pushed before, and I could gain confidence that I could do it again. By the time I was in Somalia, I had spent years internalizing the lessons of leadership and the high standards of Ranger School and the Army. What it meant was that all of the training worked. I don't know how or why it worked; it just did. Even for a public affairs officer, which is the capacity I was acting in at the time, it worked.

The Pentagon tells me that I am the first and only PAO wounded in action while serving as a PAO. PAOs are not known for their bravery. They stay behind things. I bring that up because in the office of the chief of public affairs for the Army in the Pentagon there is the picture of a captain in Vietnam who was a PAO and won the Medal of Honor posthumously. However, he was not serving as a PAO when it happened. He was an infantry company commander. Every year Public Affairs hands out awards in the name of a major general who was killed in Vietnam, but he was a division commander at the time, not a PAO. Being the only one is quite a distinction. Maybe I should have stayed behind a wall, but I wouldn't have as good a story.

Perks of Proof

In early 1997 while at Fort Bragg as the chief of war plans for the 18th Airborne Corps, I was trying to get down to a unit to get branch qualified as a major. Unfortunately, the Armor Battalion had gone away, so Armor Branch wanted to send me to Fort Stewart, Georgia. In an attempt to get a job on post at Fort Bragg, I walked down to the cavalry squadron where the executive officer (XO), S-3, and commander slots were all aviation officers. Fortunately, the commander was Ranger qualified, and he hired me. Though the 82nd Airborne Division still had the ability to veto that decision if they wanted to, they didn't. Being Ranger qualified was the biggest reason I got the job and was allowed by the 82nd to serve there. Had I not been Ranger qualified, the squadron or the 82nd would have forced me to look elsewhere.

There were a couple of infantry majors who were not Ranger qualified who were serving in Infantry Battalions as XO or S-3, but they were very rare. They got and kept those jobs because they were somehow politically connected. I was told by the division chief of staff that the singular credential he had for hiring me as the chief of war plans was that I was Ranger qualified. I had no connections. I had never been to the 82nd and was not part of its "mafia." As it was, I served a year in the division and had the distinct honor of being the senior armor officer in the division. Fifteen years after graduating, my Ranger tab was still at work for me. It still provided the differentiation I needed and put me in positions where I could prove myself through my actions. It was powerful in the world of competition where I lived.

In the cavalry squadron I was the grand old man in the unit, and after our commander broke his leg I led the squadron runs. You have not lived until you are a squadron commander on payday activities in the All-American Division. I had the color guard, the bright flags of our unit, and the squadron in formation behind me. The Infantry Battalions were in formation flanking and facing us. Being in an armor unit in the mecca of the infantry attracted attention on a normal day, but on a day like that, with the PT pageantry, I felt like the spotlight was really on me.

Payday activities are an Army tradition that occurs on the first of each month. Soldiers get off work at noon to allow them the rest of the day to pay bills and run errands with the new wad of money they have in their accounts. The morning is highlighted by an "esprit building" unit run.

As a cavalry unit, our red and white guidon stuck out in the sea of light blue infantry flags. The infantry soldiers were in great shape, a bunch of self-styled butt kickers. They had "Death from Above" tattooed on their hearts and "Mess with the best, die like the rest" coming out of their mouths. This attitude was not just in the younger ranks. It went all the way to the top. We were in the middle of the famous 82nd Airborne Division holding our own as the representatives of the Armor Branch.

We ran down Ardennes Street, which is the main street of the 82nd Airborne Division. It was an incredible feeling of pride leading the unit. The one disappointment came from the young soldiers who fell out of formation. I did not run very fast anymore. The years had slowed me down. I thought, "Good Lord, what is their problem? If I can do this, they can do it." My expectations of the soldiers were not unreasonable. Maybe that was a dangerous way to look at things, but I set a standard, and I expected them to meet it, especially when they were a whole lot younger than I was. I believe that their failure was a result of them having never pushed themselves and having never been pushed by someone else. They had yet to find out where their limits were. Fortunately, when I was younger, I had learned mine.

Ranger Stockwell's Walk

Instincts are great, but you can't buy them off the shelf. They are developed over time almost indiscernibly in the background of whatever your primary task is. It is important to recognize that it does take time, so you will never have good ones without first having persistence. Once trained, instincts make you a better leader and decision maker, yet how they play that role is harder to define. Instincts are like mixing different colors of paint. The resulting color is a unique mix and hard to define, no matter how well you can name the individual ingredients. While you can't define instincts, you can define the mission elements through a reduced force rehearsal. When David Stockwell sensed his weakness he trusted his instinct about the value of rehearsals and went about doing what he knew in his gut was right.

The benefits of a rehearsal are multifold. On the surface you and your team gain a clearer understanding of the mission and the leader's intent through the process of methodically walking through each phase of the plan. Through the clarification of issues identified early, you automatically narrow the potential divergence from the true intended goal—Leader's Intent. If you recall the guide rope in Mark Chandler's story, you realize that the rehearsal shines a light on the entire length of the rope.

I've found rehearsals to be more of a labyrinth in the corporate world, yet the basics are still the same. Instead of scratching out a map in the dirt with the heel of my boot, I put an outline of key events on a whiteboard. Instead of having my leaders walk along from phase line to phase line and explain their actions and ask questions, we step down the outline and do the same thing. Realize that detailed planning has already gone into the entire process, and the rehearsal is for clarification, adjustment, and accountability.

The other unmistakable lesson of David Stockwell's experience is his self-accountability—setting the example. You must be a tab bearer like SFC Donnie Black from his OCS class and you must get back out into the street after being shot in the head. You may not be leading a thousand troops on a run or a dozen cadets through a difficult training school, situations where setting the example might feel much plainer than at work. However, your accountability in your attitude, work ethic, integrity, and work product definitely affect your team.

Your example is followed—period.

As we look at setting the example and the importance of personal integrity, Lance Bagley shows how they can save the day, motivate people, and make the sale!

RANGERS

are

HONEST

LANCE BAGLEY

If you are living a lie, you will be found out. You will not find long-term success. You will fail in at least one of two important areas: your job or your emotional health.

Lance Bagley came to the decision point one early morning in the woods when failure stared him in the face. He had to decide whether he was going to play his role as a conformist Ranger student and suffer certain defeat or he was going to do what he knew in his heart he had to do. Later in his civilian sales career he faced the same demon, and fortunately he had battled it before.

The first step in living in sync with yourself is figuring out what principles or philosophies govern your actions. What are your morals? You then have to decide how to react to situations based on your convictions. Acting in line with your beliefs will allow you to reduce stress, sleep at night, and become predictable to your leaders and subordinates. You become a steady force that people can count on to do the right thing because you are honest with yourself.

Do you know what principles guide you? Are you swayed by the popular trend or have you studied and contemplated the beliefs that make up your bedrock? Write them down. What areas are creating conflict for you now? How can you confront them honestly and change them?

Environment

Camp Buckner was our second summer at West Point, an eight-week sampling of all of the different branches of the Army taught by real soldiers brought in from different units, usually the 101st or 82nd Airborne Divisions. For most of us who entered West Point straight out of high school it was only our second experience of spending time in the field, the first being Camp Fredrick, which was the culmination week of our first summer at West Point. Camp Fredrick was tame as field time goes, but we lived our lives out of a tent and wore Army BDUs instead of cadet semiformal uniforms. After that first taste of living out in field conditions, the next summer I went into Camp Buckner swearing I was not going to the infantry branch. During infantry week at Camp Buckner, our infantry training intensified, including assault drills and an all-night mission after a day of digging foxholes.

My Camp Buckner experience reinforced my view that being in the infantry meant doing three- to five-second rushes, tearing the skin from my knees and elbows, and standing in water-filled foxholes all night. I thought, "Who cares if there is a properly dug grenade sump at the end of my hole? A foot of water will dampen the explosion." Then, of course, there were the bayonet drills and pugle stick competitions. I'm convinced they were designed to wear us out and entertain the cadre as we inexperienced cadets beat the crap out of each other with giant Q-tips. After experiencing all of this, who in their right minds would want to go infantry? But somehow something unknown got under my skin during infantry week at Camp Buckner as we froze in the night and prayed for sleep. A combination of discovering that I really enjoyed being outdoors living under a hooch and the camaraderie that was developed during our small struggle encouraged me to go infantry.

The goal of Ranger School became valuable to me as my natural competitive instinct responded to the indoctrination of West Point and my ability to conquer the multiple obstacles grew to be a matter of personal pride. I wanted to be among the best. The people I respected in the military and those who had encouraged me to go to West Point in the first place were Ranger qualified. The officers I saw at school, the ones I was impressed with, were all Rangers, and each spoke highly of the experience. I wanted to be a Ranger. I wanted to have that tab on my shoulder. After sophomore year, I was irretrievably going down that path.

My change of heart did not come about all at once. It was preceded by West Point's systematic encouragement and pressure. Though I did not originally see myself as an infantry officer, there was a constant barrage of Ranger motivation and mystique that managed to sink into my subconscious. Even before I decided to go infantry and shoot for Ranger School my view was positive. If the United States was going to send boys to war, it was the infantry who was going to take the ground and win, and the Army needed the best leaders there. The director of the department of military instruction, Colonel Tex Turner, a muscular man with a crew cut and cigar, kept telling us, "If you want to be a soldier, you want to be a Ranger," brainwashing us. West Point threw out a personal challenge: "If you are going to be in the Army, and if you want to be all you can be, then you will be in the infantry and you will take the ultimate challenge of Ranger School."

At a class briefing with my entire class seated in Eisenhower Hall, Colonel Turner came onto stage chomping on a cigar. Screaming something Ranger-related, he fixed a bayonet on his M16, then turned the rifle upside down and speared the bayonet right into the stage. The M16 twanged there, butt up, with the blade firmly set into the finely polished wood. He was theatrical and over the top, but he got his point across. After constantly hearing the Ranger message, I wanted to be a part of it, part of the excitement, and I wanted to take up the challenge to be a member.

I don't think I could have made it through Ranger School without having had that year of mental prep. It grew to be something that I wanted more than anything else, and even on the worst days of Ranger School that desire to belong kept me going. It was the golden ring. The tab was the ultimate symbol of achievement. It did not matter who a person was or what job he had. You realized that if a guy had his tab, he had accomplished something. The tab was a call for instantaneous respect for the professors and others we saw walking around West Point with it. For me, I wanted to have that tab on my shoulder more than anything. I relate it to the struggle at West Point. If you did not want it more than anything else, you would quit. It could not be your parents' or friends' dream. Unless you in your heart wanted it more than anything, you were not going to stay. Unless that was everything, then on your worst days—and you would have the worst days of your life there—you were going to leave.

The two to three years of building up what "Ranger" meant made it personal to me. The emotional experience that Ranger School was to me continues to carry over in my daily thoughts, 10 years later. Defeating the giant that Ranger School had become to me and the self-confidence and satisfaction that I received from the experience are still very important to me today.

For the three years prior to graduating I questioned whether I had the intestinal or testicular fortitude to make it happen. There was a lot of testosterone floating around West Point. Routinely, there were challenges to overcome, and Ranger School was presented as the next hurdle. Yes, I was scared, but at the same time my time was coming whether I liked it or not. I was drawn to the fire. It was something I had to do. The commitment was made. I had burned my bridges, and the only thing I had to do next was report.

Veal Man

"There are two types of infantry officers: those who are Ranger qualified and those with excuses for why they aren't" is a Tex Turner truism. I was not going to make excuses, and it irked me to see those who did.

During my senior year at West Point, our company tactical (TAC) officer was an infantry officer without a tab. He was soft, pasty white, and without the good muscle tone you look for in an infantry officer. His common name among the cadets was Veal Man. Even as cadets we knew that infantry and Ranger were interconnected, the way you expect to see a mouth under a nose. It attracted attention when you didn't.

The lack of a tab was the first thing we noticed and one of the first things he justified.

"When I was getting out of the basic course, the Army was just starting the Bradley fighting vehicle course, and I had to choose one or the other. Because the Bradley course was so new and that was the focus of the Army, I went to the Bradley course."

Everyone who heard the story looked at each other and thought, "What the hell is he trying to pull on us? It just doesn't fly."

I saw him three years later and learned that he had the enviable position of being a TAC at Sandhurst, the British equivalent of the U.S. Military Academy. Standing at an airport in Germany I had the same type of thoughts I had when I knew him at school. How is this guy at Sandhurst when he is not even a Ranger? There were some good qualities there, but it is hard to overcome first impressions. Fair or not, this was the mentality at the time. If you didn't have the tab, people asked why.

If you are not a Ranger in the infantry, there is always that stigma of why aren't you? What happened? What is your excuse? I wouldn't have people silently asking themselves that about me.

Human Skull

I drove to the Ranger Training Brigade sign-in site with a friend, discussing the only subject on our minds. We were talking about helping each other through when I asked, "Who do you *not* want to be your Ranger buddy?"

Ranger buddies were the real things. They were your other half through Ranger School. They were more important than all of the other buddy teams we'd had up to that point. Ranger buddies were built up to the point where we thought we should buy rings and hire a priest. The question of who do you *not* want was much more than "Who do you not want to sit next to in math class?" This was your life. Your Ranger buddy could make or break you.

Both of us, without prompting, answered, "Eric Werner." Eric was a unique individual, six foot five, 250 pounds, and neither of us wanted him because he generally had a skeptical attitude. I met him on the first day of West Point and got to know him well over the next four years. I liked him, but he was a rebel, almost antiestablishment, which is a risky attitude to have in the West Point system.

Though different, he was intriguing to be around. He got into trouble at West Point for making a pentagram poster when we played football against Holy Cross, a poster the commandant ordered taken down. He had obtained a card certifying him as an ordained minister in some newspaper church and another card certifying him as a member of the Communist party. He strove to avoid the cookie-cutter personality encouraged by the system.

Once, we visited New York City, where he bought a real human skull for his desk in protest of being allowed only one knickknack on his desk at school. Another time with him he wanted to find *Mein Kampf.* He searched the city for it and finally found it at the Port Authority bus station, of all places. Unfortunately, intriguing was not what we wanted for the next nine weeks, and we both agreed this was the kid we didn't want as our Ranger buddy.

I do believe God has a bigger plan for all of us. Immediately after signing in and separating into our platoons and squads I was standing next to who else but Eric Werner. This was the lotto I didn't want to win, but we lined up by height, and I was the second biggest person in the squad. At six foot, 190 pounds, I was right behind Eric's six foot five, so in the first half hour of Ranger School he and I were paired up as Ranger buddies. Strike one. This was not a good sign.

I avoided looking at Eric, believing that I was already in a weakened position right from the beginning. My attitude was in the dumps. It was a dark painting, splashes of disappointment at missing the opportunity for a special Ranger buddy relationship thrown onto a black background of dread. It wouldn't take long, however, for me to realize that the man doing the painting knew what he was doing.

If I had chosen my own Ranger buddy, I would have missed out on a great relationship, and as it turned out, I have never laughed or cried as much or respected somebody as much as I do Eric. He helped me get through as much as I helped him, and I cannot imagine going through it without him.

Ranger buddies provided support and looked out for each other. When one was down, the other would lend a hand and vice versa. The Ranger Department knew that the reason men stayed and fought in battle despite overwhelming fear was because of their friends in the trenches with them. They didn't want to see their friends get hurt, nor did they want to look like a coward to them. It worked the same way in Ranger School. There was unspoken camaraderie, friendship, and competition that bound us together like no other experience could.

Tedious

After a joyous graduation from West Point and Infantry Officers Basic Course (OBC), I reported to Ranger School on 3 December, 1988, the day of the Army-Navy game that year. In stark contrast to the mass attention Americans were paying the cadets on the gridiron, we stood in formation for hours on a dirt road in front of a wooden World War II building, forgotten by everyone except some family and friends.

I stood in formation with 200 other bald Ranger wannabes awaiting our first instructions. I was impatient and wanted to get started with something, anything. I was already tired of doing nothing. An RI came out of the building, standing straight in a starched BDU and wearing the small tab on his shoulder. He looked every bit of what I wanted to be. My heart pumped, anticipating his order to move.

"Army is losing to Navy," he said. Then he went back behind the closed door.

Finally, after over an hour of standing in formation, we were told to get our gear laid out for the first RI inspection. We dumped out our carefully home-packed bags and arranged the items on a poncho. When everything was ready, an RI emerged from the building, inspected our gear, told us to repack our bags, and withdrew into the building again. I packed, though much less exactly than I had done at home. We returned to attention and waited. It had turned into some type of game. Soon we went through the routine again, dumping, inspecting, repacking, and standing. For hours this went on, us at parade rest or attention for no reason, warping the mental picture I had of a professional, challenging school. I understood that they were trying to get the people who would quit right away to quit, but I didn't think this tedious crap had to be a part of the process.

Among so many Ranger students and with quiet time on my hands I got a chance to revisit my trepidation and apprehension of what I was on the verge of. Can I make it through this? Look at all of the guys who really look like they belong here. Will I measure up? Two-thirds of the people here won't make it, I thought. None of us were tested yet—our knowledge, our stamina, or our strength—but we all looked the part, ready for battle. I eagerly anticipated the test and the opportunity to persevere beyond anything I had done before. Without a word I felt the challenge to answer the question that was on everyone's mind about every other person there: Can this guy tough it out and make it through Ranger School? Only time would tell, and I was eager to get started.

Tigers' Tails

By day four we were already at muscle failure before doing any exercises, a condition that initiated a strange dance of cat and mouse. During the calisthenics portion, conserving energy for the run was the paramount concern, so we worked at looking like we were doing the exercises with vigor while really operating at minimum energy output. We had to keep an eye out for the RIs who wove through the formation like thunderclouds waiting to strike. Our slacking was with an eye toward survival, and we developed a sixth sense of knowing where the RI was and which way he was looking. Early on this day I knew I was in trouble.

I had an RI right next to me like a good workout partner. "Ranger, you aren't going down far enough. Touch those toes," he commanded.

I'm doing the exercise right, you bastard, I thought, and you know it. Muscle failure or not, I wasn't prepared to slack in front of this guy. Any sign of weakness and he'd swoop like a vulture on a carcass. For some reason he had it in for me, and there was no place to hide. I was vulnerable to his abuse, so I kept turning the other cheek. Strike two, I thought.

"What kind of fucking school do you think we are running here?" he asked. "We don't let slackers through, and I think you're slacking. You *best* go all the way down." On and on he continued. Then at the end he came up to me and said, "Ranger, I want to see you after the run. What's your name?"

"Ranger Bagley, Sergeant," I spouted. I thought, "Oh shit. I don't need this."

The whole time on the run I worried about what this guy was going to do. We arrived back from the run and were about to break for breakfast when my RI ran out to the front of the class formation. A couple of hundred of us were standing in rows.

"All right. I want to see a Ranger . . . Brailey. Where are you, Brailey?" he yelled and started walking through the ranks.

Brailey? I knew he meant me. I was the only one he messed with during PT.

We all looked the same: steaming bald heads protruding from damp and dirty BDU tops like turtles standing upright. I chose to take a chance and stay in my spot. Though he wasn't close to me, I knew he might miss me even if he walked right in front of me.

"I know you're there, Brailey. You'd better step out," he commanded again.

I don't know if Eric or the other squad members knew that I was this Ranger Brailey or whoever the hell he was looking for, but I stood fast. I thought, "This guy is going to find me, pull me out, and kill me. He is going to put me in the worm pit and break me."

After several minutes of unsuccessful searching he finally yelled, "Brailey, you got away today, but I'll find you." He returned to the office. We broke for breakfast and continued on with our day.

That was a tense moment for me. I swear I benefited from divine intervention. I thought, "God really wants me to be a Ranger." I am not proud to say that I didn't step out. It was a tough decision I felt I had to make to survive. It was a calculated risk, one of many I faced in Ranger School.

I went out to PT the next day physically more tired than the day before, praying not to run into that RI again. I knew I had at least some chance to avoid him but no chance to avoid an even greater nemesis: the five-mile run. We had to complete the run to move on from City Week to Camp Darby. I had never been a strong runner and didn't enjoy it, so to me this was my biggest early challenge. I knew, however, if I could pass the run, I would have a good shot at graduating. We were already pretty worn out with lack of sleep, lack of food, and a week's worth of heavy physical activity.

"Halt!" the RI screamed to end the flutter kick exercise. An hour of wide arm push-ups, buddy-assisted sit-ups, and rolling around in the sawdust had taken its toll. Lying on my back, clenched fists to the sides of my hips, legs extended, I held my heels as close to six inches off the ground as possible. My stomach burned as if someone had poured boiling water on it.

"I didn't tell you to rest, Ranger!" I heard the RI yelling at a student behind me.

My eyes closed and my jaws clenched, but I had to drop my legs for a second. My stomach just couldn't hold out any longer. The break for my muscles was instantaneous but just as quickly I put the load back on them to avoid the worse situation of an RI's attention. My knees bent uncontrollably and my head turned slightly in the two-inch-deep sawdust; 15 seconds had passed since we halted the exercise.

"Platoooon, ateeeen-shon!" The command finally came, and like rakes stepped on, we popped out of the dark mess and came to a standing, nearly erect, position.

Then came the words we were waiting for: "Even numbers recover. Assemble to the right." We moved into a tight formation and stood there preparing mentally for the run.

The common paradox of Ranger School was that the end of one hell marked the beginning of another, and somehow that was okay. The person who said that variety is the spice of life really hit on an axiom. Even in misery variety is good. I stood now with weak thighs and abdomen wondering how I'd make it through the next mile, let alone five.

We turned and marched to the road, tallest to the rear, which placed my Ranger buddy right behind me. There was a brief rest in the short walk, but like the turning of the cylinder in a six-shooter, our turn in the barrel was coming fast.

"Double time.... *march!*" our cadence caller yelled, and we stepped forward in a jog.

My legs were tired, very tired, and my thighs struggled to push each additional step out of my feet. I settled into the rhythm of the run in the first tenth of a mile. That was all the time I needed to determine what aspect of the run I would struggle with more, my wind or my muscles. Today it was my muscles; like rubber bands stretched too far for too long, they seemed to hang there.

I plodded along in front of Eric with heavy steps. At the three-mile mark I was at the point where I did not think I was going to make it. My legs were rubbery, and I had no breath left. That's when I heard Eric running behind me. He had steady rhythm, breathing, and footsteps, and I thought, "If he is making it, I'm going to make it. I'm not going to let him beat me. I'm going to use him to push me." I kept thinking, "As long as he is here, I'm going to be here."

Switching my focus allowed me to continue and finish the run. Nothing physical had changed. I plodded on the same legs and tried to suck oxygen into the same lungs, but my focus was no longer the same. It was on Eric and the competition. Afterward, dead tired, I said to him, "I appreciate you pushing me like that."

He said, "What? I saw you running in front of me, and it looked like you were running so strong, and if you were going to make it, I was going to make it."

I said, "You've got to be kidding. I heard you in back of me, and that was the motivation I needed to push me forward."

It was that point right there that solidified for me what a Ranger buddy was all about. That started our team and the alternating roles of leading and following that made us work. It was him pulling me along when I was tired, and when he was having his bad days, I pulled him along. We were two tigers chasing each other's tail and running to keep the other from grabbing it.

Pull Out the Stops

Every once in a while we found ourselves in the midst of a two-patrol day. The timing of the day's first patrol was such that it could be completed by 2330 or so, which allowed time to quickly plan and hit another objective. What we did not want, what we feared, was to be called as the patrol leader for the second patrol of the night. We knew ahead of time that everyone was so dog tired that the probability was that it was going to be a no-go patrol.

It was a bitterly cold night two days before the end of the mountain phase, and we all waited to see who would have the second patrol of the day. Collapsed backward on my ruck in the middle of the dark forest, I mentally weighed the odds that I would get pegged as the patrol leader. It had been a few days since I had been a patrol leader, but I had done well, and there were plenty of guys who needed a patrol before me. RIs were great for destroying the optimism of rationalization. "Ranger Bagley, you're the next patrol leader. Get your ass up here!" one yelled.

My heart sank. I mean, I could feel it bumping through my stomach and leaving a horrible sensation in my lower intestines. Now I had more than my own exhaustion to deal with. Everyone—from the guys on flank security, who we expected to fall asleep, to the squad leaders helping with the planning to the assistant patrol leader—was falling asleep, and that was like the groom falling asleep in the middle of his vows. I knew I was in deep trouble because it only became worse as we finished planning and began to move.

Short halts were dangerous because in the short minute or two that we weren't walking, people were checking out. At one short halt called by the RI, I watched a guy keep on walking. He was dragging his rifle, automatically putting one foot in front of the other. He wasn't quitting. He was incoherent. We were all so tired that all reason had left our minds. Guys would have snuggled up to a fire ant hill if it meant they could get a half hour of uninterrupted sleep, and I would have joined them.

When a person was that tired, he virtually had an on-and-off switch. Exhaustion would flip that switch off without consulting conscious thought, making it the burden of the mind to find a strong enough reason to flip it back on. This was an arm-wrestling competition no one wanted to win. As the selected leader, my motivation was just enough to keep me awake, but many of the platoon members that night were unable to lift that switch back up and, therefore, dozed off regardless of whether they were lying down, kneeling, or standing.

I was fearful, knowing that I was going to fail if things stayed the way they were. I had to make one of the biggest decisions of the course for me. I had to do something drastic, and the only course of action I could think of was the tried-and-true butt chewing. I stopped the patrol. Guys moved to the left and right of where they stood and took a knee. I stood up in the middle of the dark woods and screamed at the top of my lungs, "We're going admin on my call!"

I yelled at my team, "Whether I get a go or a no-go doesn't matter. We are in Ranger School, and we are going to be Rangers. We're going to go to this objective. We're going to take this objective, and we are going to succeed because we are Rangers."

If you had listened closely you could have heard the national anthem softly playing in the background and seen the giant U.S. flag from the movie *Patton* hanging behind me. I didn't ask the RI if it was okay or really contemplate the negative side of this. I was going to push-start this rig or push it off a cliff. Either way it was going to move.

Eric just shook his head, and the RI behind me did not say a word. He sat there and watched, certainly thinking, "What the hell is this kid doing?"

After my tirade we went back tactical, did the raid, and moved to the patrol base. We arrived at about sunup and the RI switch-over—there would be no sleep that night.

Many of the guys came up and said, "Way to go, Ranger. Way to take the lead," and sure enough I got a go on the patrol. Even though I screamed, "We're going admin!" the RI appreciated my purpose and the results. I am certain that if I had not done that, there was no way I was going to get a go.

That night has helped guide me in decisions I've made in my civilian career. On my first job after the military, I had a difficult time learning the technical language of the medical industry. Being a medical equipment salesman was much different than the military profession. My sales manager was a guy who was very smooth, very salesmanlike, and that wasn't me, not my style. I was really having a tough time when I finally said to myself, "Listen. If I'm going to succeed, it's going to be based on my own personality, my own style of leadership. I've got nothing to lose. If I'm going to fail, it's going to be because of me, not because I'm trying to be somebody else." From that day on in sales I took that approach and have had great success. To turn the corner in that first position, I simply faced the truth. "I've got nothing to lose. I've got to put it on the line. I've got no other options." If I had played the game my boss's way, I would have failed. I chose another path, one that was sustainable for me, and succeeded.

Spooning

We woke up a few hours later, spooning, Eric with his big gorilla arm draped over me and my back tight into his chest wrapped in a poncho liner. I wasn't warm, but I wasn't freezing, either. Sleeping in such a marital manner was a necessity in the cold forest, especially with each of us undernourished and unable to create enough body heat to keep us comfortable on our own. One sleepless night of shivering on the ground was memorable enough for a lifetime and the best argument in the world for spooning with your Ranger buddy.

Lions

We picked up the patrol base in preparation for movement. The Florida sun was behind the trees to the west, filling the air with dusk. It seemed we had done this drill a hundred times before, and right on cue my mind started to fill in for the sensations my eyes no longer provided. I heard the song, "The Lion Sleeps Tonight," also known as "The Weema Way" song. Every night that song echoed in my mind for hours. Just before heading into our patrol, I told Eric, "I have a song that plays in my head every night as we walk on patrol."

He shot back at me without letting me ask him if he had the same mental radio station. "My God, you don't even have to tell me the name of the song. I know exactly which one you're talking about."

I don't know what psychic closet deep down inside of us was opened every night, but he and I both had the same song playing in our heads. Soon we stepped off onto patrol and into the quiet jungle with "The Weema Way" song echoing in our minds.

I Had Quit

We had done longer patrols and I had been hungrier, but to me the cold had just gone beyond what I could take, and I couldn't get into that water again. The water crossings were so cold they were painful, and another was planned for tonight's patrol. I had been shivering for days, and the thought of getting into the cold stream and pulling myself across the rope scraped through my mind. Many times we did not stop to change out of our wet clothes on the far side. We just got up and started walking again. I could not continue to freeze through another night.

I had gone through all of the years of mental and physical prep, but at that point I was willing to give it all up. I thought about all of the things that had brought me to this brink and I still insisted to myself, "I'm not going to do it. If we do this, I'm going to quit—I can't take it."

For the entire movement through the cold January forest I convinced myself of my conviction to quit. Now, though I never spoke a word to anyone else, I silently decided I had had enough. I do not know if anyone else felt the same way. We did not talk about quitting to other people.

We came to the river, which stopped the progress of the patrol. This was the decisive point. I stepped to my right and took a knee. My M16 rested on my raised knee and pointed into the woods the way it had a thousand times before. It was comfortable there, and I hated to give that up. The routine of being a warrior in pursuit of the enemy, or in the noble hunt for the tab, was nice to have developed, but I had gone as far as I was going to go. There was no Ranger motivation or external stimulus that could win my internal battle or erase the cold on my skin and hunger in my stomach.

Staring into the dark, I could see the pictures of my thoughts and see the events of the next few days unfold. I could feel the full night of sleep and my family's homecoming that awaited me. I had already started to think of explanations. This was my last night in the field, I thought. The man in front of me stepped to me and whispered, "Six."

"What the hell are we doing a head count for?" I wondered. In a natural reaction I lifted my body and moved the three steps to the man kneeling behind me. "Seven."

He grabbed my arm. "What the hell are we doing a head count for?" he asked.

I shrugged my shoulders in the dark, said "I don't know," and then returned to my place, thoughts of quitting gone for the moment. The count came forward again, and it took only a couple of minutes for the next word to come back. "We're bypassing the stream. The RI says it's too cold to cross."

That was my lowest ebb in the entire course. I had made up my mind that I was not going to do it, no matter what, yet almost as soon as I was relieved of that worry I halfway missed the challenge of being forced to do it. I would have again tested my breaking point, and I don't think I could have quit. Though I thought about quitting almost constantly, that was the closest I came to drawing a line in the sand.

The Ranger God had intervened on my behalf and that of who knows how many others that night. We walked around the creek and drove on. I was rejuvenated. I thought, "God does want me to be a Ranger."

Flight of Fancy

Within the squad each member earned the trust of the others through hard work and action. We knew that as a squad we had each other's best interest at heart. Ranger Barry, a private first class from the 2nd Ranger Battalion, was an integral part of our team. For six weeks leading up to the event he excitedly talked about nothing but flying out to Dugway Proving Grounds, Utah. "Yeah, my buddy was in the same Ranger class a year ago, and he had a commercial flight out to Dugway. They had civilian stewardesses, all the Cokes and Sprites they could drink, and all the peanuts and pretzels they could eat. He said it was awesome."

We wanted to beat the hell out of him because in our half-starved state, the last thing we wanted to hear about was food, and that was all he talked about.

This civilian plane flight turned into one of the little prizes we focused on as an intermediate goal, and Barry's continuing enthusiasm made us dream about it more. The day arrived, and though none of us expressed our excitement as much as Ranger Barry, we were all looking forward to the aerial vacation.

At the Fort Benning airfield, my class sat in squad-sized groups throughout the hangar, filling the concrete floor with a camouflaged underbrush of people and equipment. My squad, made up mostly of second lieutenants and Ranger Battalion soldiers, was toward the front near the wide opening of the hangar. The congregation of field gear and dirty Rangers produced a musty smell that filled the hangar and mingled with the smell of our oil-covered hands as we cleaned our weapons and chatted among ourselves. Spirits were high for our last phase, our last challenge, and you could tell the mood by the bursts of loud laughter that escaped frequently from the groups around the building. Barry lifted his head from his rifle and said, "The planes are coming in."

This was Barry's moment of truth, the final seconds before the bell rings on the last day before summer break, his much awaited civilian airliner. We heard the distant roar and soon we saw them, C-141s coming in for a landing. I know he was disappointed, but in true Ranger persistence and rationalization, he stood his ground. "Nah, we're not jumping. It's too cold."

His whole premise was that it was too cold to jump. If it was below freezing we couldn't jump, because by regulations during a jump we couldn't wear gloves, and without gloves our hands would freeze. He had used that logic to keep us going for six weeks. Barry got a by on the fact that we were going by C-141 instead of a civilian airliner because he promised us we weren't going to jump. "At least we'll get to rest and not worry about getting hurt in a jump," we thought. Then we loaded the planes, and the RIs gave us parachutes.

"They're just fucking with us. We can't jump. It's too cold," he still insisted and continued to persist even as we started the midflight rigging process.

I wanted to believe him, even as I sat there in my parachute: "It is cold out there," I thought. "Maybe they *are* messing with us." I was comfortable, head back and eyes closed, feeling the roll of the plane. "We'll see."

Next came the order to stand up and hook up. It was all very routine for the RIs and most of the other students who weren't fighting a conflicting vision in their heads. Barry still refused to succumb to the obvious. "They're fucking with us. It's too cold. I heard the weather report," he said, and stood there next to me with a weak grin on his face.

The green light flashed on, putting the final sword into the heart of Barry's dream. Rangers started disappearing out of the door to our front, and those of us who had been hooked by Barry's vision were looking at him with fire in our eyes. Our looks were more playful than anything—like giving a team member a couple of solid punches in the arm, not a pummeling.

We all thought that Private Barry would have made a super platoon leader. He was a motivated individual, full of fire and vinegar, and he always gave 100 percent. The positive part of getting caught up in Barry's world was that he provided us the dream that got us to the next level even though *his* flight was a flight of fancy.

Play It Again

We always had a motivator to keep us looking forward to the next level. It was the blueberry pancakes in Dahlonega that got us through the Darby phase. Then it was the boodle helicopter flights in Florida, and it was flying the civilian aircraft down to Dugway. These pictures were the things that kept us looking forward, beyond the current day, as bad as it was.

One night in Florida, we needed something to look forward to more than usual. Our squad was the cast in a painful comedy of errors from which we received bruises, not roses. We were the weapons platoon carrying the heavy loads of the M60 machine guns and ammo. We had moved down the river in Zodiac boats and debarked at the shoreline into pure mud. The water level was extremely low, so it was not a swamp. It was knee-deep mud. There was no way to go around, so every step was into the heavy, sticky mess that kept us off balance. Finding the leverage to pull our trail foot out of the mud meant we put more pressure on our lead foot, sending it deeper into the mud. We had to grab onto trees and branches to gain some kind of advantage.

As in every situation, some people had it harder than others. As usual, my Ranger buddy and I had the M60 machine gun, tripod, and ammo. I couldn't manage all the ammo alone, so a squad mate volunteered to assist with one box of ammo. Somehow, in the course of patrolling, his ammo box had broken apart. The handle and top had come off, so he was carrying it like a football. Going through the mud in that manner was like bobbing for apples. He couldn't take his arms from around the box or risk losing the ammo, so each labored step found him on his knees for support and pushing against trees with his shoulders to move forward. It was a slow-motion running play up the middle on a muddy field with trees as the defenders.

I could hear him ask, "Where's Bagley? Where's Bagley?" as if I could have helped him even if I were there. We were all in the same awful situation. I couldn't carry any more. No one could. All I could do was shake my head and smile.

I thought, "What's he going to do? Give it to me on top of the M60?"

Eric and I laughed as we heard an RI telling him, "You'd better be quiet, Ranger."

Soon we heard the ammo can clank as he fell again. "Bagley!" he moaned. "Where's Bagley?"

It's hard to explain how difficult it was to struggle in that situation for hours without end. We totally surrendered our time and comfort to whatever Ranger School demanded. "I'm in Ranger School all day," was a common quote, or was the response to some threatened punishment, "What are they going to do to me? Shave my head and send me to Ranger School?" It just didn't get any worse.

Like so many situations, my friend with the ammo managed his burden and made it to the objective with the rest of us.

Once at the objective, we did the raid, shooting up as much as we could with our dirty weapons and ammo. It was the usual mad minute of gunfire, grenade simulators, and smoke that from a distance might look like a malfunctioning strobe light in the forest. After assembling and moving back to the rally point, we took a head count before moving the next many kilometers to the patrol base.

The count went back, each Ranger adding one to the total and passing it back to the next man in the column. Then the total came forward one short. This scenario was repeated too many times in Ranger School. One man was missing, sitting in the middle of the woods, alone, separated from the larger group, probably asleep.

"Who the fuck is missing? Do the head count again," the RI commanded.

Again the head count went back and then forward. "Shit," I thought. "Same count. Whose dumb ass are we missing?"

"You Rangers are worthless. Break in contact, one man left behind. Glad I'm not your buddy," was the RI's response. "Figure out who's missing or you all are no-gos."

We mumbled to ourselves until all were accounted for except a Ranger in our squad. Our first instinct was to hide his identity to protect him, but in the middle of the night, exhausted as we were, he was crashed and wouldn't awake on his own for hours. We had to call for him. We began to scream, "Ranger Locklear! Wake your ass up!" Over and over we summoned our slumbering comrade.

"How did we leave him up there, and how the hell did he sleep through all of the machine gun fire, simulator explosions, and grenade flashes all around him during the raid?" I wondered.

About five minutes later Ranger Locklear came sprinting down the hill, stopping at our position, winded, apologetic, and embarrassed. There was nothing to be said in that situation, either to the patrol or to Locklear. Now that he was with us we had to move out. No time to placate feelings or discuss issues. He fell in, and we marched forward into the night. For the next three hours the blackness was broken by nothing more than a nearby cat eye, and I probably imagined that. It wasn't until we were almost on top of the patrol base that we saw the glow of a small fire. The RI had radioed ahead to have one ready for our back brief.

The RI was furious as he recounted the fiasco of the mission, and we took his wrath unemotionally with blank stares and gaunt faces. We played the role of Ranger students perfectly. We stood around the fire, all of us staring into the flames in a trance as the RI talked. I don't know what time it was, somewhere in the usual 0200 or 0300 range, and as sure as unplugging a lamp turns off the light, setting Rangers in front of a fire puts them to sleep. One of the guys sitting down nearly fell off his rucksack.

The RI yelled, "If one of you guys falls asleep again, we are going to do this mission over!"

Just as the RI finished we heard the crash of a body and equipment on the ground, marking the start of our second run-through of the mission. The guy, standing up with his pack on, succumbed to sleep and fell over. It was like standing a sledgehammer up on its handle and watching it topple. The RI screamed, "Load up, men! We're doing it again!"

We went back up the hill and repeated the whole sequence.

The philosophy of not rewarding weakness was perfectly executed by the RI. The point wasn't so much that we did the raid better the second time—we didn't. It was the lesson we took away from events like that which counted. We could go so much farther than the farthest we could imagine. We all stood there cold, bone tired, hungry, and expecting a couple hours of rest before the next mission. What we got went against every principle of motivation except self-motivation. What I mean is that Ranger School wasn't training us to be better Ranger students. It was training us to be better Rangers and better leaders once we left the school. In our future units we would use our self-motivation and self-knowledge to take men and units to levels they thought unreachable, simply because it had been proven to us through the painful experiences of Ranger School that those limits, and more, *were* reachable.

I learned that there is always something left. When I got to the point where reason said I couldn't continue, there was always something left. Whether it was a friend who picked me up or a twist of good luck, I could always reach down and find a reason to move forward. I always picked up my ruck and walked on. It was amazing to learn how far I could push myself, how far down I could go and still function, and what teamwork meant. To me, that was the essence of Ranger School. I learned how a team helps you as an individual succeed and how you as an individual help the team succeed. I thought all of the guys in my squad were good leaders whenever they took the ground because they worked and the team worked.

Although we had to learn a painful lesson that night, and Ranger Locklear was a major reason why, he was still an integral part of the team, and we had a few good laughs after the pain. It was always a full team effort. We truly had 10 individuals who pulled their own weight and gave 100 percent, whether they were the patrol leader or squad leader or on a quiet walk in the woods.

Put It on the Line

One lesson I learned from Ranger School is that if you were show-boating, people could see through you. On the same note, the people who were real team players and who supported you were very evident also. There was one kid out of our entire squad whom no one particularly liked because he was a spotlighter. If he was the patrol leader, he would be screaming, "You better stay awake, Ranger!" But when he was not on the spot, he was always the one who was asleep. Our spotlight Ranger had already been peered (received the lowest peer ratings within his squad) three times earlier. We peered him as well. In fact, he joined us in the mountains and we ended up peering him in Dugway. He had been through every phase twice except Florida. You end up working harder when you try to weasel out of work.

At Ranger School we learned in practical terms that you had to lead from the front. You had to experience it. You had to sweat and share the pain together with your soldiers. People would support you if they knew you were honest and you pulled your fair share of the weight. The basic principles of leadership aren't difficult, but when practiced, they have to come from the heart with sincerity from being who you are, whether you are a platoon leader in the Army or working in the civilian world.

I've seen many examples of coworkers in the civilian world whose falsity I knew one day would catch up with them, and, by God, it did. You have spotlighters in civilian life the same way you do in Ranger School, and eventually they get peered. If you are not sincere, people will see through you in the end.

Living in sync with your values and beliefs makes life easier to live. At the end of the day, you have to live with yourself, and if you are not living true to who you are, then in the long run you won't succeed. That night in the woods when everyone was falling asleep there were no other options. What did I have to lose? The slogan I live by is "Who dares, wins." It is the British Special Air Service (SAS) motto. It means you sometimes have to put it on the line, and that may require being true to yourself versus the ideals of the company. You can live a lie for only so long.

When I was struggling in sales, at some point I had to stand up and say, "I have to do it my way and be true to who I am, not be somebody else." If I was going to succeed in sales, it was going to be by my personality, my character, and looking somebody in the eye and saying, "Doctor, this is what I am going to do for you," and then delivering on that. In the long run I was not going to win by bringing in the lunches and telling funny jokes.

My strategy began to work, and soon I converted a huge account from my competition. Things were great for three or four months until the account called me and said, "I had a very strong relationship with the sales rep from your competitor, and he is back in the territory. I think I owe him my loyalty, and I think I am going to give him back my business."

I said, "Doctor, I can respect that, but you gave me a chance four months ago, and I have delivered on everything I said I would."

He agreed.

I said, "Why don't you show me the same loyalty for exceeding your expectations? Because of my background of having gone to West Point, loyalty means everything, so I can respect your loyalty to him, but you have given me your trust, and I have delivered on it. Give me the same loyalty."

He stayed with me. It was the handshake, the look in the eye, and the frank talk that kept his business. It goes back to that night in the woods. Seizing the moment and delivering the goods was what it was all about. Tex Turner always used to say, "You don't have to like it. You've got to love it." You have to love what you do to succeed.

Limits

I've used Ranger School experiences as a measure to put the rest of my life into perspective. I have been able to use Ranger School as a frame of reference to help me through the tough times in life. Every time I have a bad day, I look back to that and say, "I've had worse days. I've been hungrier. I've been colder. I've been more tired. I've been pushed to a further limit." Anytime I've reached a breaking point in business, there has always been a worse day. "I've been here, and I've survived and pushed through in worse situations. If I fail, I know I have the strength to pick myself up and start over."

Ranger Bagley's Walk.

There is no doubt that what is suggested in this book is a major adjustment for most of you. Lance Bagley's point is that first you must be honest with yourself before you can truly lead others. The more closely you are living to your principles or your true motivations and passions in life, the less personal conflict and stress you will have and the more success because of it. If you are sitting in a work environment with the basic framework of boss, direction, and responsibilities, and you lose energy just entering through the door in the morning, you had better make some changes. I'm not talking about the strain of accomplishment. This whole book is about understanding the strain inherent in worthwhile accomplishment. I'm saying that if your company is going east and you feel a passion for going west, go west or make your company go west. Just don't let me see you going east again when it gets hard going west.

At some point you have to ask yourself, "What do I have to lose?" You will have to have the testicular fortitude to turn on all of the flashlights and yell at the top of your lungs, "You are going to succeed on your own or I'm going to kick you in the ass until you do!" You can say that to yourself or to your team, whomever the situation calls for. To extend this, even if you feel you are living a life in tune with your own principles, as a leader you will have to recognize when you have someone on your team who is working against their natural grain and help them make the hard adjustment.

One of the great illustrations of Ranger Bagley's story is how buddy teams can make sure people do not mistake accomplishment tension with integrity tension. The motivating power of a close friend or teammate who is on the same achievement path as you is a great leadership secret. Take a look at where you can incorporate this truth in your team. You'll hear many times in this book that it is the opinion and support of his buddy that keeps the soldier in place when the bullets start flying.

Not only does a close relationship provide automatic accountability, it can also keep individuals going well beyond their known limits. In the end, we are attempting to inculcate your organization with the No Excuse and Know Yourself philosophies by doing more than slapping a motivational poster on the wall. Buddies and camaraderie go a long way toward making those tenets a reality.

Ranger Bagley's buddy was Eric Werner, and you are fortunate to have his story next. He deepens the conversation of accountability through his experiences and provides yet another unique perspective on how you can be a better leader.

RANGERS

are

SELFLESS

ERIC WERNER

It is said that all politics is local. The same holds true for suffering. All suffering is individual. No matter how widespread the disaster or how many others suffer from the same or worse ailments, it is our own suffering that concerns us. It is within the confines of our own skin that we find the horrors that mean the most to us. Our focus can be yanked out to an external situation only temporarily since the home of our thoughts is within us.

Eric Werner learned that Ranger School demanded his ascent above his own suffering in order for him and his team to succeed. Leaders learn to set aside their personal distractions to overcome human nature and focus outside of themselves. The interdependence of each Ranger on the others forced an unselfish perspective that trained them to look out for the team first. Selflessness is a required trait of a quality leader. Consider a selfish one and you'll understand.

Are you sacrificing to build your team, or are they sacrificing to build you?

What Does It Mean?

I was branched infantry, so along with the Infantry Officer Basic Course (IOBC), Ranger School was marked on my orders, joined like ham and eggs. I wanted to do it anyway, but I was not given a real choice. Going into the Army from West Point, I wanted to learn all of the things that Ranger School could teach me, the practical field knowledge to balance the book knowledge from school—and besides, I would get a Ranger tab out of the deal. The Ranger tab is the mark of an exclusive club. You see a Ranger tab and you automatically feel that the wearer has been through a challenge and knows something that puts him into an elite group.

A good example of what the Ranger tab means is illustrated by my Air Assault School experience about six months after I graduated from Ranger School. Air Assault School seemed kind of bland after Ranger School, but one challenging event of the course was a 12-mile road march with rucksacks that was more of a run than a walk. Three privates chased behind me the whole way as I ran 50 yards, walked 50 yards, ran 50 yards, and walked 50 yards for the entire march. I kept looking back and seeing these three kids. I was not trying to lose them. I was trying to finish the event, and I found it strange that they were right there no matter what I did as if they were attached by an invisible dummy cord.

At the finish line I moved out of the way and dropped my ruck with a thump onto the ground. I bent over and put my hands on my knees to catch my breath. I was standing there when one of the kids came up to me and said, "Sir, I want to thank you. I got through because of you." He had the flushed face and red cheeks of a guy just out of high school and the definite pride in his eyes that reflected a big accomplishment.

"Man, give me a second to get my wind back before we talk," I thought. I was dumbfounded at his comment and finally said, "What are you talking about? I never even talked to you on the march."

He explained, "No, I saw that you were a Ranger, so I figured you knew what you were doing. You gave me the motivation to keep going."

I didn't want to tell him, "Heck, I just made that stuff up. The mix of running and walking was me just trying to conserve a little energy. It was not a secret, Ranger road march technique." When he said I was a Ranger I understood and replied, "Oh, yeah. Yeah, that's right. Right on, friend."

I understood what the Ranger tab means to people, including myself. It stands for knowledge, strength, and endurance. It is an intangible that lends credibility to the actions of the wearer, and that alone can motivate people to do above-average things. Perhaps the kid was right. It wasn't so much that the technique was special, but the fact that as a Ranger I knew I was going to make the march no matter what. Whatever technique I used was one these guys could count on to help them succeed. The young man was happy to have thanked his convenient mentor and trotted off to his friends again. I was happy that I had reinforced what "Ranger" meant.

Relax

At IOBC we heard all of the horror stories about going through Ranger School, especially in the winter, so I began to prepare as my date approached. I got a couple of must-have lists. One was supposedly from Rangers who had been through Ranger School, and another was one that Ranger Rick's, the supply store, had put together of all the things you needed while there to survive. In order to be ultimately prepared, I bought about $800 worth of stuff from Ranger Rick's.

I bought clothing made from materials that sounded exotic, like Polypropylene and Thinsulate, which were supposed to magically carry wetness away from the skin's surface to keep you dry and warm. Though they cost more, they were going to be worth it! I bought things like an adapter for my flashlight so I could signal to someone wearing night optical devices (NODs) without the light being seen by an unaided eye. "I really need this," I thought. It took about a month to gather most of my "necessary" gear, but there was always one more thing I needed.

There were five of us lieutenants living in one house in Columbus, Georgia, all on our way to Ranger School and all being good little squirrels, packing away for the winter. Often one of my housemates would come in with something new, and I would ask, "What's that thing?"

He'd say, "Man, you'd better get this. This thing is going to keep you warm." And I would think, "Damn, I've got to get one of those."

When I actually went to the course I took only about half of the junk I had bought, and once in the course I realized I did not need any of it. Having the equipment did, however, make me feel better. I thought I was being proactive and somehow mitigating the suffering of Ranger School, so in some sense the expense was worth it. It was like preparing myself to go to West Point. I knew there was going to be hazing, and though I really couldn't do anything about it, probably buying earplugs would have made me feel better.

Unfair Fight

David and Goliath Part II began to play out immediately after I reported, and damn if I wasn't Goliath. I'm six foot five, and at the time I was solidly built, whereas David, the RI, must have been five foot three and 110 pounds soaking wet. He picked me out right from the very beginning and told me straight out, and I quote, "I don't like you, and I'm going to make you fail."

I didn't ask why.

He would find me just to screw with me. He'd come up and say, "You're unmotivated" or "You've got a stupid look on your face," and then make me do donkey kicks or leg lifts designed to wear me out. He was the one who put me into major minus problems right off the bat. Within the first week I already had two major minuses and two minor minuses, solely from this guy and his buddy, another little guy. People liked having me around because I was a magnet for this kind of hazing. In one case I had my web gear unbuckled, a small thing, and he came up to me and said, "That's not sat," and gave me a minor minus. There were people near me with much greater offenses, their weapons broken down and being cleaned when those soldiers should have been at the ready.

I was in trouble. With three major minuses you have to recycle that phase, and I was at two major minuses and two minor minuses at the end of City Week. Soon I realized I was going to carry either the M60 machine gun, the radio, or the medicine chest to get positive spot reports for the rest of the time if I was going to get through the course.

Good Star

Carrying the radio had its positives and negatives. The last day of the Benning phase turned into a rainy night. We were doing squad operations, only 11 people per patrol, and our first task was to go through simulated friendly lines walking through a minefield on a mine-free lane marked with engineer tape and lined with barbed wire. I had volunteered to carry the radio, so after setting the squad frequency, I jammed it deep into my pack. Almost immediately after starting the movement challenges arose. The Ranger who was leading us could not find the entrance of the lane, so I had to get on the other unit's frequency to find out where we were supposed to be.

We were still using the Vietnam era radio, the PRC-77. The frequency numbers had tiny lights like those found on old digital watches. The lights on the damn knobs of the radio were worthless, like trying to light a theater with a match. It was raining and dark, and not being able to use any additional lights made it impossible to see the frequency. I sat there, still looking down into my ruck at the radio, trying my best, when the RI started yelling from way in front of the patrol, "Where's the goddamn radio?!"

The entire patrol was lying belly down on soggy leaves until I got the correct frequency and found out where to go. The radio was stuffed in my pack in a position that made it impossible to pull out without spilling many of the contents onto the ground. My knees were already soaked from the wet ground, and putting my other gear into that mess just to be able to see the frequency didn't seem reasonable. I imagined my gear spread out, radio next to my ruck while I made the call, and then the urgent move to the lane with no time to repack.

I pulled up on the short whip antenna trying to get it as close to the surface of my bag as possible. My hand slipped off with little progress made. I tried again with more success. I was hoping somehow my eyes saw what they needed to see. Unfortunately, the damn lights were so dim and the rain obscured the lenses so badly that it was no use. For many minutes I tried to adjust things to get a better view while my Ranger buddies soaked into the ground and the RI grew ever more restless.

"What the hell is taking you so long, Ranger?" the RI scowled. "What's your problem?"

"I'll have it in a second, Sergeant," I assured him. What in the world else was I going to say? I sat there nervous because I was almost out of the course with major minuses and I had told myself I was not going to recycle. I could feel the next major minus burning a hole in his pocket as I blindly clicked from our platoon frequency to the passing unit frequency. I took the only course I could. I knew what frequency I was currently on, I knew where I had to go, and I knew that each click was a single adjustment of five. The only question was whether I was clicking in the right direction. *Click, click, click.* I turned each knob the calculated number of times. I pressed the hand mike and prayed. "Romeo fife niner, this is quebec niner four, over." I released the switch and waited. The rain seemed louder, and I tried to concentrate on the squelch of the radio, attempting to pull an answer out with my willpower. Pessimism of certain failure surrounded me like the wet darkness.

The radio screeched, "Quebec niner four, this is romeo fife niner. Go ahead."

My heart jumped in disbelief, and I instantly categorized this event in the pile that proved I wasn't born under a bad star. Fortunately, the radio operator procedures were second nature to me, and the exchange of info was smooth. Any more delay would have sent the RI over the edge. I'd have been fired and handed a major minus—and in essence, my walking papers. Had I screwed up the radio call once in contact with the passing unit, I couldn't hope for leniency earned out of respect for my effort. It's impossible to look anything but incompetent while fishing feverishly for a frequency.

Keep Outside

I was way down, concerned about my future at Ranger School, burdened with four major minuses and a minor minus—nearly a recycle. I was hauling anything heavy to get even a minor plus. On this mission the night before my birthday, 27 January, I had the radio. We did a raid that was entertaining because so many people were falling asleep, but for some reason I was spot on. I was awake, coherent, and really clicking. As we moved out after the raid, on my own I radioed back to the RI manning the radio and called for artillery fire to destroy the objective. Afterward the RI came up to me and said, "Why did you do that, Ranger?"

I said, "Because I wanted to destroy the objective and clear it out."

He said, "That was stupendous! No one told you to do that. Way to think. You have a major plus."

It was now early on the morning of my birthday and I thought, "Wow, a major plus! Things are looking up." I was high, and I started planning to get out of my spot report hole. It was amazing how after midnight and a long string of patrols with the radio and machine gun I was ready to take on the world. The surprise reward turned my attitude positive, and I saw so many possibilities for the future. My adrenaline was pumping and my senses were sharp. I thought, "If I get a machine gun, maybe I can get a minor plus." I was not shooting to get into the honor grad ranks. I just wanted to get the hell through it. I said to my Ranger buddy, Lance Bagley, "Man, this is good. It's my birthday. What a present."

In the early evening of that day, we were moving on yet another patrol in yet another rainstorm. I was starting to get very tired just walking, and Bagley was in no better shape with the heavy load of the M60 machine gun and six or seven boxes of ammo hanging off him. He asked me to take some of the boxes to lighten his load, which I did, and put them on my ruck. The weight was negligible, like the difference between an altitude of 1,000 feet and 1,100. Who can tell the difference after a while? Coming upon a large stream, we had to construct a rope bridge. A Ranger swam across and set up the rope, and the patrol put the bridge together just as we had drilled it.

Though only minutes after taking the ammo from Lance, when we got up to the rope to cross over, I had forgotten about it. I hooked up to the rope and was walking across when the RI looked at me approaching and said, "What are you doing with that ammo in the water? You submerged that in the water!"

It was pouring down rain anyway, but I said, "Oh, shit, Sergeant. I forgot about it," expecting him to be reasonable and let me move on.

He said, "I'll tell you what. You go back across and cross properly, and that's a minor minus."

"Damn! Shit!" I thought. I went back to the other side to start over. I had tried very hard to keep my clothes dry by keeping my ruck out of the water but at this point I said, "Screw it. I don't care." I wanted to make sure this SOB saw me when I came over again. I wanted him to see that I was really sucking it back, sacrificing my ruck to get the ammo across "dry." Again I trudged into the water. My bag submerged as I carried the ammo like Excalibur across the stream. I didn't care about anything but my anger at this RI. I wanted him to see what absurd lengths he had pushed me to and force him to say "Good job" while thinking to himself what an idiot he was.

The rain slapped me on the face, splashed the water to my front, and dripped off the ammo over my head. At the deepest point of the stream my head submerged, but I thought, "These four boxes of ammo are going to stay dry." The bottom was solid so I strode a couple of steps to see air again and I never lowered the ammo. That bastard was going to realize his mistake and I was going to illustrate it to him by my suffering.

He did see me. "*What* are you doing?!" he yelled in an unbelieving tone.

I thought, "Fuck you. What are you talking about?" and stood there dumbfounded.

He said, "I told you put that in your pack to keep it dry."

I was about ready to go off on him but was smart enough to restrain myself. I said, "Sergeant, you told me to keep it dry."

He yelled back, "I told you to put it in your pack. Are you back talking me? That's a major minus!"

"I can crush you, punk," I thought, but moved on without responding. Coming out of the water I felt the waterlogged heaviness of my rucksack pull unrelentingly backward on my shoulders. That put me down to four major and two minor spot reports. One more minor minus and I was screwed. With five major minuses they recycled you all the way back to the beginning. At that point I had made up my mind to not recycle at all. I was not going to do it. No way.

I got out of the water, moved away from the RI, shoved the ammo cans into my ruck, and cussed under my breath. I got rucked up and started moving again, but it was not more than 10 feet before I was back down in a marsh and water. The roots and tree stumps intermingled with the mud, keeping us off balance and stumbling along. The patrol slowed and then stopped as we prepared to do yet another water crossing. I took a few steps onto a little island to wait, still up to my knees in muck.

With rain dripping from my ears and hat brim, in an unrecoverable spot report position, hungry, cold, and tired, I simply thought, "I'm quitting." I looked around at all the other people. I thought,

"My clothes are soaking wet. I'm soaking wet. I'm almost kicked out anyway. This sucks. I'm quitting."

I continued with that in my mind for many minutes, certain I was done but without the guts to do anything about it. Then lo and behold, there came my buddy Eric Titus. Eric was a classmate from West Point. I knew he was having a rough time with four major minuses also. He walked from the stream into the marshy area carrying the M60 and stumbling like the rest of us. I watched as his foot slipped from root to root and his ankles twisted too naturally to the contours of the ground. Without looking down he moved forward. Then, without warning, a root snapped under his foot and *whoosh*, his body, weapon, ruck, and all went under water. It was painful to see him in that position, but I focused on watching him climb out of his dirty bath, using roots and small trees to leverage himself up. He never said a word.

There was no way to tell where the deep water was, but on that day you did not want to follow Titus. No sooner had he regained his balance on semisolid ground when he again slipped and fell forward into a deep, swampy pool. He lay there, covered in muck on the soggy forest floor for the second time. He shoved the machine gun to the side and pushed himself to his knees before slowly standing and retrieving the weapon. No word was spoken, and I wondered what was going through his mind.

How beaten was his spirit? How much was he willing to take before lying in the mud crying and asking to go home? I was certain about one thing. I thought, "Damn, man. He's having it worse than me."

I seemed to focus on Titus with even greater intensity as he stepped from that pool right into another, falling like a drunk for a third time into the cold, dirty soup. I winced in sympathy for him. He stood up slowly like a man who didn't care who was waiting or watching, nothing light or easy about his load. His ruck was like a 100-pound tuba around his neck, and the machine gun acted like a giant fishhook in the roots. He got to his feet, straightened his back, and screamed at the top of his lungs, "FUUUCK!!"

I stood there suppressing my laughter.

Titus scanned around and gave a look that said, "Yeah!" and walked off to get into position.

The RIs ran back. "What's that? Who did that?"

We all looked the other way, playing dumb.

That was what I needed to see at that point. Perhaps it's sad to say, but I needed to see someone keep going who was hurting as bad as I was or worse. I couldn't draw on my own reserves any longer without outside instigation. It really put my situation back into perspective and gave me the motivation to go on. I thought, "Until I'm kicked out, I'm not quitting, and if I get to that hurdle, I'll worry about it then." I was able to see for a minute that even if they don't have four major minuses, everybody was in the same boat. I was able to look at someone else's misery and put mine into perspective and get out of my little individual shell and say, "Hell, there are a lot of things I can do to make my situation better. I can carry the radio again or something like that."

I was pitying myself, which was easy to do in that situation. I felt like I was not going to reach my goal. I had a task to perform, and I wanted to get it done, but the environmental conditions of rain and cold, the lack of food, and having to function on little sleep overrode that goal. What really broke me for that moment was the thought that I had three weeks to go and I had only one minor minus to play with. Combine that with rain coming down and standing in knee-deep mud waiting to cross a stream. All of those environmental factors wore down my resolve and I thought, "Screw it." Titus snapped me back, because in addition to sharing all of the environmental aspects, he was in a similar precarious grading situation.

In Ranger School, generally we were looking outside of ourselves. We were looking at our mission, at helping the other guy get a good grade because we wanted him to help us out later. But at that point I drew completely into myself, kind of crying. I got to the point of hopelessness without realizing that this misery was shared by everyone.

Promises

In winter classes it was always a hope that safety concerns about hypothermia would keep us out of a water environment. We hated getting wet because it meant a night of freezing in hasty foxholes somewhere. On most of the early days in the course, our fear was going into the knee-deep creeks we crossed in Darby and the mountains, but then we came to the day in Florida we learned how to do river crossings using a rope bridge.

We practiced first on dry ground with assurance from the RIs that we couldn't go into the water because the water temperature was below 50 degrees. We were excited since that meant we got to keep our clothes dry, and besides, I was having a ball with the dry land practice. I could do this all day long. It was an unexpected gift that lifted all our spirits and stole our memory of all the gifts previously retracted by the RIs.

It wasn't long before the next announcement was made: "Good news. The temperature has risen by a couple of degrees, so we are going to go in."

It was late afternoon, and I thought. "This is bullshit. It hasn't upped a couple of degrees." Motivation dropped like a chicken trying to fly, and it took a few minutes to get focused again.

Into the water we went, one after the other, in the process of building and crossing on the rope bridge. Actually, it should be called a submergible rope guide because there was nothing bridgelike about it. We were all up to our necks in the stream as we crossed, and the heavy guys like me stretched the rope enough to allow our heads to go under also.

My gear was attached to the bridge by a short rope and D ring to keep it from floating down the river. I pulled on the D ring, dragging my ruck behind, and slowly dragged myself across with numb, glove-clad hands to the other side. I watched the waterline on my ruck get higher and higher as my dry clothes and gear soaked up more and more of the stream.

I knew that my careful packing job and use of waterproof and plastic bags weren't working, but I didn't know why. It turned out that my army-issue waterproof bag had a hole in it, and my smaller plastic bags containing my socks and uniforms were just plain ratty. After many weeks of use and wear, the plastic and rubber were permeable in many places. At best they were water resistant, but in no way waterproof. I dragged my heavy ruck up onto the other side knowing it was going to be a long, miserable night with no chance of rescue. I had nowhere to turn for dry clothes and nowhere to hide from the cold. I was at the point where I thought, "Oh shit. I'm really going to have to suck it down here," but the RIs had the foresight to build warming fires at our patrol base that night. The compassion turned out to be real this time, and we were allowed to spend some quality time around the fire.

Somehow through the experience of Ranger School I lost any

sense of shame, and while at the fire I thought, "Screw it," and pulled all of my gear out of my rucksack and stripped stark naked. No boots, no socks, nothing. I sat on my rucksack completely buck-naked. This wasn't a real magazine-type shot. I was dirty and hairy and pale. I sat there dreamily looking at the fire, thinking about nothing in particular, allowing time to pass, just drifting off when all of a sudden I looked around at the red glow on the other faces at the edge of the fire and did not recognize any of them. "Who the hell are you guys?" I asked.

"Second squad, third platoon," one guy answered.

"Where the hell is second platoon!?" I shot out.

"Over there," he pointed.

I looked over to see a guy hiking up his rucksack and marching off. "Oh, shit!" I spit out, and moved like greased lightning. I had clothes on, boots on, and bag packed—relatively decent job, too, not just stuff thrown in—in under three minutes. I caught up with that guy and nobody ever noticed that I was missing. I was in such a mode that I was able to move that quickly and get everything put together, accounted for, and functioning properly without conscious thought. As I moved I realized that yet again the RIs had been able to recant on a promise.

Semihappiness

Our senses became numb to repeated sensations. Our nerves stopped transmitting pain signals the way our eyes and ears may stop telling our brains about a constant sound or sight, allowing us to sleep in the back of a moving deuce-and-half truck. While on Zodiac missions our minds became used to the pain of awkward body positions aided by the numbing effects of ice-cold water.

Ten of us paddled our leaking, half-inflated assault boat across the strait, five straddling each side, and an RI in the rest position without a paddle in the center back. My leg to the outside of the boat was submerged in the dark water from the midthigh down. I'd have bent it more to at least get my foot out of the water, but the pain in my knee made it easier to just let it hang and coast along. My other leg was extended awkwardly on top of the gear filling the middle of the boat. At first this position was painful, but with each stroke of the paddle my mind adjusted.

We were the fourth boat to shove off from shore and with the equivalent of a flat tire. Soon we were in the lead of the attack due to a combination of our constant paddling and the other boats being screwed up. Our RI told us to slow down, then to relax.

The boat continued to move forward a bit from momentum but was quickly at a stop. The RI gulped the last swallow of coffee, emptying the silver thermos cup that he had been sipping on during the trip, and then started digging in his rucksack. It was common to see an RI with some evidence of civilization like his thermos. In my mind an item like that was instantly linked with other normal things like a wife, a refrigerator, a convenience store. Sometimes it was some kind of food they had, and it always initiated thoughts of life outside of Ranger School. In this case I could see the early-morning kitchen countertop illuminated by the moon through the window as he stumbled to the wall and flicked on the light. I could hear the gurgling of the coffee maker spitting out the last few drops of a day's worth of coffee, and I could see him listening for the sound of a full thermos as he poured the coffee into the small opening. All these thoughts happened in a split second, and the one that stuck with me was the taste. I could taste the coffee. Then it was gone and I felt the icy cold on my leg.

The man behind me tapped me on the shoulder. I looked around to see the RI's beautiful silver cup, steam escaping freely out of the top! In such stark, thankless conditions this was unbelievable. Conscious of rationing, I took only the drink meant for me. The cup had to last all the way around to the last man. Unimaginable joy accompanied the taste and warmth of my swig. I actually felt the warmth heat my body as it went down and spread. Not a word was spoken as the cup went around the boat, Ranger to Ranger, but the gesture was a handshake and a hearty thank-you to us for putting out such a great effort. In that unexpected reward the RI showed us some appreciation, and though we didn't work for him, we each gained motivation to keep charging ahead for him.

Landing the boat started a whole new challenge. As I pulled my rucksack, loaded with the radio again, out of the boat, I could feel the concrete in my knees and hips strain against the movement. They soon warmed, though, and moved more easily under the weight of my load.

The one big plus about carrying the radio was that I was allowed to do the rucksack flop. Everyone else had their 100 pounds on, and I had my 126 pounds on, but they had to get down on one knee and then lie down while I could just flop down backward in a perfect rest position.

We pulled into a staging area prior to the attack. With a little time on my hands, I did a bit of investigating to find the best place to sit for a few minutes. Ideally, I wanted to leave my ruck on my back and put it against some elevated ground so I could lean back without going too far. Even in the dark I found what I was looking for, a perfect sand dune right in the middle of the base. I turned around. Then like an old man squatting on the toilet, I slowly bent over and fell backward, letting my ruck slam into the dune.

I wasn't really tired. I was simply sitting there, cold, but happy to let my legs rest. Soon after the sensation of relaxation spread through my body, my legs began to tingle, then itch. What was wrong with my legs? Why were they itching?' Instantly my mind screamed, "Ahhhhhh, shit." I jumped up and with my pack still on whipped down my pants, and started slapping at my butt. I had sat down right over a red ant hole. It must have looked like some grotesque peep show act as I danced around, but I did kill all of the ants that had invaded my clothes.

There was no permanent damage caused by the ants, just a reinforcement of the idea that I could never get too comfortable. The coffee, the rucksack flop, and my relative awareness put me on the verge of contentment in this usually hostile world. Fortunately, the repeated sensation of letdown after expecting comfort had numbed my senses to continued letdown, and I was able to pull up my pants and find another place to sit, all without feeling too sorry for myself.

Adventures and Obstacles

We never knew what to expect at Ranger School, so we became very good at adapting. Now I have the feeling that I can go into someplace new and get on top of the situation very easily. When I was younger I made plans and thought, "Hey, this is what is going to happen," and expected that it would turn out as I had seen it in my head. The adjustments to my plans required by real life frustrated me. All sorts of extenuating circumstances and unplanned events are going to come into play, and whether they are environmental factors or oversights, they will trip you up and make you adjust your plan. I now expect it, so I handle adversity well and can keep my head while those around me are losing theirs. I have a stoicism about things, and I take adversity and problems in stride.

Another great secret to overcoming obstacles is persistence. Ranger School taught me to drive on and on, to keep going until I'm done, and not to quit too early. The other side of persistence is planning. I always plan ahead and treat each situation as I would if it were a long shot, continually looking at contingencies.

These types of lessons will be lost on someone without a desire to step into the unknown and face those obstacles. I believe some people have an innate sense of adventure that drives them to accomplishment, and they learn to deal with obstacles. Once the self-confidence is built through experience and success, you can go into an unknown situation with the knowledge that whatever presents itself you can overcome and you can do well.

I taught English in Japan from 1994 to 1997. When that opportunity presented itself, I had to weigh everything. I had never taught before. I'd never been to Japan. I didn't speak the language, and the town I was going to was in the middle of nowhere, and I said, "I'm going to do it. It sounds great." A lot of my decision making is colored by my spirit of adventure and confidence in myself, much of which was developed in Ranger School. Even if I was offered a job teaching for a year in Mongolia, I'd ask, "Is the pay decent enough where I won't have to worry about eating yak every day?" If so, I'd say, "Yeah."

Nine-Week Reality

In so many ways, stepping into Ranger School was like stepping into a different dimension, an altered reality, a demented *Alice in Wonderland* existence. You had to stay focused even though there were things going on around you that might not be normal. If we saw a six-legged dog, we'd just look up and nonchalantly say, "Oh, there's a six-legged dog," and walk on. I don't remember ever having an erection or a sexual thought while there. You talk about unnatural. That's unnatural, but when you get in that situation, it's natural. All I thought about was, "Man, I hope I get my favorite ham and chicken loaf, and I hope I get the new ones that have the M&Ms and Tabasco sauce."

One day we were all drawing chow, and Bagley and I each drew our three MREs. We ripped them open to find that he had pulled two of the new MREs and I had none. "Hey, come on, give me one," I begged.

He replied, "Ranger buddy or not, I'm not giving you one."

I sat there looking at him, seriously thinking, "I don't know you." All his positives aside, I really hated him for a day.

I sat in the middle of a patrol base on a warmer day in Florida with the other squad leaders getting briefed on the mission when I looked beyond the group of us. A couple of car lengths beyond the guy across from me was the cat hole, the trench we went poop into. I looked up and there was a guy facing me, squatting over this cat hole. I thought, "Man, that's a huge turd," and went right back to work. It did not even faze me. Now, if I was here at my mother's house and someone was out in the yard popping a squat, I'd have to say something, but in that kind of situation, all the stuff that would catch your attention elsewhere, you just kind of shelve it with, "Oh, that's interesting. Will I ever see that again?"

Expect the Unexpected

If you are going to go to Ranger School, get as well prepared beforehand as possible. Get your equipment in order, and stay in great shape. Do not place too much trust in perceived expectations, as something extra might be demanded. In City Week the RIs will play with your mind. When they say you are going to run five miles, don't automatically prepare yourself mentally for a five-mile run.

Our run turned into a beast of a run. My legs and lungs were burning, and I couldn't wait to see the end point. I gave a little extra effort to get to the finish, but the RI didn't stop. He kept going, and we had to follow. I had a major revelation as we passed the finish. I realized nothing was as it seemed, and I had to stay mentally flexible if I wanted to survive. Instantly, I did the decision-making process that Ranger School forced us to develop, looking at two possible outcomes: quit or keep running. Before my foot hit the ground past the missed stop point, I had decided to stay and then had to work even harder to keep up. I saw people fall out right there, and before we got back to the barracks they were simply gone. I never saw them again. Be flexible and get mentally tough because no matter where you are in the school, you've got two options. Once in the patrolling phase, the end of the mission might not be followed by time to smoke and joke; it might be followed immediately by another mission.

Always expect more than the perceived requirements will be called for. If you do that and you do get a break, then it is a real reward. Look at situations, and never expect that they are what they appear to be. There are going to be all sorts of contingencies involved and things that are out of your control. You might be keyed and ready to lead the patrol but it turns into an unlucky pop, and 50 percent of the people are dragging butt because they haven't slept in two days, and you have to figure out how to work around that obstacle. Try to prepare for the contingencies, but be aware that sometimes you are going to have to react more than plan.

An example is when everyone sat around on pins and needles when the RIs called out the new patrol leader. They nailed one kid when he was, by chance, having a really bad day. As a squad leader for the patrol, I sat underneath a poncho with him and the other leaders getting briefed. He had his map and flashlight out and was saying, "Come on, guys. I really want you to do well. I've been helping you out."

We said, "Yeah, yeah, we want you to get a go."

He flipped on the light and bowed his head to focus on the map. We four squad leaders sat quietly waiting for him to speak. Pretty soon we figured out that he was asleep. "Someone slap him," I said.

Because we were keyed up, we made sure that he wasn't dragging his butt. We didn't carry him, but we brought him back to reality. We kept him moving and reminded him that this was his patrol. "If you want us to slap you every five minutes, we'll do it," we said.

In terms of leadership, when you are dragging butt, sometimes you need to be responsible enough to look at somebody and say, "Hey, man, I need your assistance. I trust you enough, and I don't think you want to see me fail. I'm dragging butt here. How about helping me out? If you see me dozing off, how about giving me a slap upside the head or something?" You have to be responsible enough to set pride aside in deference to the mission. You must stay coherent for the mission to succeed, but pride might encourage you to go it alone and count on your own discipline even though you know it is not equal to the task. Trust your team and use your teammates to help the whole organization succeed.

One time I was actually so bad that I saw *Captain Kangaroo*. I hadn't seen that show for years, so I don't know what psychic door the lack of sleep and food and walking around all night had opened up, but I saw that dancing bear everywhere I looked. That would have been a bad night for me to get tapped to be the platoon leader. It would be like drawing a Ford Pinto for a demolition derby.

Extreme fatigue created many fantasy worlds. I saw many things—from guys putting quarters in trees expecting a Coke to an interesting briefing given by an exhausted leader. He was going around the circle of soldiers briefing them and asking for questions when he came to the "guy" next to me. He briefed him, then asked if he had any questions. I said, "That's a bush, man. It's a bush."

A real leader, even as a subordinate, will help the current leader by being self-motivated and going beyond the realm of his own responsibility. He displays positive initiative, not the kind that finds someplace to sack out for a while. When the leader gives you the radio, you say, "I'll take care of it. I'll call for fire. I'll get you squared away, bro." A real leader will develop that trust, which is essential in excellent teamwork.

Appearances Can Be Deceiving

One night I saw the eroding power Ranger School can have on a person's emotional strength when I saw an acquaintance from West Point cry. He had always been rather arrogant, and I thought that he was really going to fly through Ranger School. It was a simple thing that finally broke him. He was carrying the machine gun cleaning kit and running through the forest. In the dark we heard the *clang-clang-clang* that announced somebody had dropped something. Then we heard, "Damn it, I dropped the cleaning kit. I just can't take it," and he started crying.

We all said offhandedly, "Shut up."

I wanted to butt stroke the guy for being a pussy. I didn't like him anyway. He was a real pretty boy up at school, always squared away with everything. We really had nothing in common except the desire to graduate from West Point and Ranger School. I thought,

"Buddy, you want to talk about problems? You walk in my shoes." I tried to help him find his stuff, but it was with disdain. "Here's one of the rods, you little wimp," I thought.

There was always a helping hand for those Rangers who were putting out their best effort, even when they had hit the wall and were at the end of their energy and cognitive ability, like the platoon leader under the poncho.

Giving their best effort was one of the three ways people reacted to total exhaustion, and we all made the decision of how we would react at one point or another. Most guys kept their weakness to themselves, simply taking one step after the other until they recovered—like my day in the swamp—or were forced to quit. Some quit outright at the first sign of struggle. Then you had the third way, like our pretty boy, who wasn't going to quit but openly begged for pity and sympathy.

He wanted his mother to hold his head to her chest and stroke his hair. It wasn't that we all didn't relate. The fact is we all did, but because we each had similar temptations, we knew that crying out loud like that was the weaker path, and we couldn't have sympathy for that person. Somehow quiet weakness was stronger than overt weakness. It goes hand in hand with a person taking sole responsibility for his situation. Seeking pity is an out in this case. His crying was asking for help finding the cleaning kit or even for someone to take it from him instead of admitting to a buddy his position and seeking help from a teammate the way we constantly did anyway. Had I cried in the swamp I'd have received no pity, and that is as it should be.

One of the guys I judged wrongly from appearances was a young 19-year-old, Private First Class Barry, from the Ranger Battalion. He did not strike me as being a real wit at first. I figured since he was from the Ranger Bat he'd bust his butt to make it through, but he wouldn't shine at all. He turned out to be a real leader and he motivated me. He was really squared away tactically in addition to being a "never say die" type of person.

Barry displayed his leadership in many small ways, setting the example for the others around him. He even handled his exhaustion in a manner that set him apart.

Winter in Utah was freezing cold, and we found ourselves walking through ice and snow. However, even in those low temperatures, we wore light clothing to avoid overheating from the physical exertion involved in humping our heavy loads and patrolling. We pulled into a patrol base in what the RIs confirmed was going to be a long stay. "Get into position and put on your bear suits."

Bear suits were extremely thick wool jackets and pants in a dark brown color that made the name a natural. Most of the time their large size made them a nuisance, as we had to find a way to shove them into our rucksacks along with everything else. At times like this they paid for their ungainliness by holding in our body heat like nothing else could. We looked like little children overdressed in winter clothing, arms straight out to the side held up by the padding of our jackets. I was at a point of comfort when a sergeant ran up and yelled, "Pick up your stuff! We gotta move. We gotta move!"

We rucked up and moved out, with no time to change out of the heavy suits. We marched down the icy road in two ranks. I was burning up, but Barry was not only burning up, he was tired and hungry, and falling asleep as he marched.

His eyes were almost shut as he shuffled forward. He opened them in an automatic manner every minute or so just long enough to make sure he was still walking in the direction he was supposed to be going. He must have mapped out the next 100 meters of road in each open flash of his eyes to avoid the bad ice spots and make any turns or stops. I watched his left leg slip on a slick spot and dash to the rear. Immediately his right leg adjusted for the unbalance, caught his weight and buckled at the knee. His eyes popped open in a snap but closed again when his balance was regained. It struck me that I was watching a sleeping infant—poke him and he opens his eyes, and if he is tired enough, his eyelids go right back down.

He wove back and forth, slipped frequently, and continued to march. Finally, the conditions were right for gravity to take advantage of his precarious situation. It happened in slow motion, and there was nothing I could do. His weave to the right went a step too far. His right foot hit a small ice patch on the edge of the ditch and glided to the left. There was no way for his left foot to recover and simply followed to the left as his heavy rucksack plunged into the ditch to the right with him attached. He struggled up by himself without saying a negative word. All he'd say was, "I love this stuff. I love this stuff," and I believed him. It seemed that the biggest inconvenience for him was that he had to wake up to get up.

He motivated me. I thought, "I'm not going to complain about being hot. At least I'm awake."

In the end, contrary to appearances, one guy ended up being a whiny wimp while the other was voted by his squadmates as a nominee for best Ranger.

Ranger Werner's Walk

Ranger Werner came into Ranger School with an unusual tendency; he made the most the spectrum of his experience between success and failure to have fun. His experience is enlightening because for the first time he had to narrow his spectrum and eliminate failure as an option. He found that as a leader you have to keep your focus on others, not yourself. You already know this lesson, and Eric knew this before he went into the swamp that day; but what was made clear on that day of suffering was the amazing power of the mind and its perspective when you switch from selfish to selfless. Nothing changed except his attitude, and he went from failure to success in a flash across a synapse.

By definition, when you are issued a mission and a team, you have more than yourself to think about, and the better you concentrate on those outside concerns, the better your team will do. If you are still trying to figure this out, think about it while you drop and give me 50 elevated push-ups right now. Then have your mamma slap you when you're done.

Ranger Werner also showed us how success breeds success. You'll have a Ranger tab on your shoulder too as you gain a reputation for high standards and success. You'll have those soldiers following you just because you've managed to consume that intangible something that others want to emulate. The reputation for success creates a legacy to live up to, not only for you but also for your team. It is a residue of ownership that travels wherever you go and is taken up by team members old and new alike. This compounding of success is what makes the super achievements possible and why the first blocks of this foundation are so critical no matter how difficult.

Finally, there is the great example of using rewards as a sign of appreciation and their effect on motivation. One sip of warm coffee from a canteen cup was remembered as a distinct high point in Eric's entire experience. Though I am frequently amazed at the contributions of the people in my companies, I realize that I rarely take the time to sincerely reward and appreciate each contributor. It is a mistake on my part, and I'm sure it has cost these companies more than I could ever calculate. I must take time, and so must you, to keep your team excited about the next goal through rewards and appreciation.

You have to have satisfied employees because you never know when you will ask them to innovate and sacrifice the way that our next Ranger, W. John Hutt, did in his Ranger School experience.

RANGERS

are

CONFIDENT

W. John Hutt

RANGER

Short-term comfort or long-term success—you can have one but not both. Stretching yourself physically or mentally is not comfortable. It's out of the comfort zone, yet to achieve a worthy goal you have to stretch. No one ever quits Ranger School because the goal is not worthwhile; they quit because comfort now becomes more important than Ranger qualification in the future. Lieutenant John Hutt stretched beyond perceived failure and personal discomfort to succeed at Ranger School.

John accepted whatever situation he was in, long odds or frozen pants, and moved on from there to his objective. John realized it was useless to complain about the conditions he was in, whether they were created by himself, someone else, or nature. He had the long-term goal of Ranger qualification and the professional recognition and personal satisfaction that it would bring. Where do you find yourself now on your journey to your goals? Are you making excuses or plotting a course? No matter the odds, you can get there from here.

Be All That You Can Be

One of the reasons I went to West Point was because of the Army commercials on TV. For whatever reason, they hit home with me. "Be all that you can be," was a challenge I could relate to. I felt I had a huge potential coming out of high school, and I wanted to really prove myself and push myself to unbelievable limits.

I finished near the top of my high school, number 11, and at West Point I graduated at 130 out of about 900 cadets. My senior year I was a company commander for the first semester and the Sandhurst Sergeant for the second. Every year West Point conducts a competition called Sandhurst that tests basic soldier skills such as road marching; nuclear, biological, and chemical (NBC); and various shooting skills. Each of West Point's 36 companies fielded three teams of two people each, and I was in charge of recruiting and training the teams from my company, A-4. One of our teams ended up finishing second out of nine in the regiment. That type of competition excited me and forced me to master the basic skills of an infantry soldier.

Choosing infantry as a branch was the logical extension of my desire for challenge and my natural affinity for the skills of the branch. It seemed to be the toughest and the most basic, down-to-earth branch and where the rubber meets the road in the Army. For those going infantry, like myself, the first road trip after the Officers Basic Course (OBC) was Ranger School. Ranger School was the ultimate challenge, and being Ranger qualified meant credibility within the infantry branch. There really was no choice. I was going to a light infantry unit, so if I did not go to Ranger School before getting to my unit, I would be sent from there. It was hard to get out of the starting blocks in a line unit without a Ranger tab.

The people who were Ranger qualified always had my natural respect, and I wanted that for myself. I knew it was extremely difficult to graduate from Ranger School, so anybody with a Ranger tab had what my West Point tactical officer, Captain Pope, called "Instant credibility." The Ranger tab warrants respect; it symbolizes competence for the wearer that you can count on without knowing anything else about the person. Somebody who has been through Ranger School carries with him the instant credibility of a professional in his field.

Leadership

Ranger School emphasized one of the leadership principles stressed at West Point: lead by example. That did not mean only when you were in a leadership position. A true leader always did the things he knew to be right, whether he was in charge or not. At West Point they called it doing your duty. At Ranger School he demonstrated leadership not by doing great things but by meeting a simple standard. He stayed awake when he was supposed to stay awake and did what he was supposed to do without someone telling him to do it. Not only was this leading by example, but it was showing compassion for the current leader by making his job easier and giving him a better chance for success.

To the End

My first graded patrol was conducted in virtually blinding winter conditions. The resident clouds above the mountains filled the air with heavy fog and blowing snow. Reading a map and navigating was difficult enough with plenty of time and full visibility, and for this patrol it was worse because I was also in a time crunch. I was responsible to deliver the squad to the proper place at the proper time, and it was very difficult to see even a couple of feet in front of me. There was tightness in my chest throughout the movement. I was hoping we were where I thought we were. I did not want to look incompetent by ending up lost.

I could hear the crunching of snow under the boots of our otherwise quiet patrol. I was alone with my worries as we moved forward. The frustration of blindness imposed by nature against which I was helpless was like trying to type while in a straitjacket. Somehow, through a combination of terrain orientation, matching the land to the map, and pace count (figuring distance moved by counting steps), we made it to the proper location. My anxiety lessened only slightly as we prepared for and conducted the mission. I thought I did a pretty good job with the mission considering the circumstances, and was happy to move to the base camp once it was done.

It was bitterly cold, and the RIs let us have a warming fire for a period of time and rotate people into it. The fire was an unwritten signal for admin rather than the tactical conduct expected of us on the rest of the patrol. I relaxed, happy to know that my first patrol was nearly over. I was somehow deluded into thinking that by allowing a fire the RIs were sensitive to our weary condition and would understand if we stood down a little. The difficult movement, the end of our first three-day patrol in the mountains, and the fire almost begged us to let down our guard.

Later, while still in the base camp, the leaders were called in to talk with the RI to get their after-action reviews, a go or a no-go. Mine was an RI who didn't yell and gave very little input during the whole mission, which gave me confidence in my success. Considering that a lot of the RIs yelled and were really on our case if we screwed up, I felt that if he was not saying much I was doing okay. Everything seemed to be going fine as he spoke about the movement and the mission. Then, like a surprise punch to the back of my head, he gave me a no-go. "You lost control in the patrol base. The base camp is still part of the mission," he said. "You are still behind enemy lines and vulnerable. You compromised your patrol's safety by letting your guard down too early."

I was devastated by my failure in the patrol. "I'm not going to pass this," I thought, "Gosh, I might get recycled out of here."

That was the only point in the course where I thought I might not make it. Even in the first two weeks when we were torn down physically, I never felt like I was going to get beaten. I was scared, humbled, and down. "I'm not going to get through this," I thought, while coping with the depressing feelings of being a failure.

We came back into friendly territory that night and out of the field. We ate at the mess hall and then got ready to go to sleep in the old mountain camp cabins. The cabins were a makeshift monument to all of the students of Ranger School. In marker and knife etchings on the inside walls of each cabin were recorded the squad rosters of the Rangers who had occupied the cabin in decades past. I knew that not all of the people listed had completed the course; that some of them, like me, suffered setbacks; and that many could not overcome their obstacles. I lay on my grimy, sheetless mattress and looked up at all of the names written on the walls and ceiling. I wondered, "Am I actually going to make it through here?" I felt like I had my back against the wall. I had given my best effort and it was not good enough. Even with 22 of us packed into this small room, it was very lonely realizing I had failed.

I could have quit right then and given in to that setback, but fortunately I hung on through the night. Early the next morning I was right back at it. Ranger School did not give me a choice but to keep going, focused on the next task in the very structured environment. We always had to keep moving, employed in some mission with no free time on our hands and little time to think. The tasks strung together to complete the day, and as I concentrated on one, then another, and then another, I regained my sense of desire and determination to succeed.

I also looked to my classmates from West Point for support, friendship, and a push. That day I still felt the sting of the failure, but I knew I couldn't let that be a permanent situation. My fear of not making it butted against my nature of not accepting failure. I certainly did not want to quit in front of my friends.

After that no-go I was more aggressive in checking security and making sure that nothing was left to chance. On my next patrol I received a go, which allowed me to put my nagging no-go behind me. I did not repeat the mistake of thinking that a patrol was over when it was not, and from that point on I passed all five of my remaining patrols.

Innovation

On patrol in the mountains at about 0200 we came upon a pretty large stream without a readily available bypass, which forced us to cross where we were at. At that early hour and already bone tired, we had to face one of the greatest demons of winter Ranger School—water. The possibility of getting wet was enormously disturbing. In so many trying times at Ranger School our only saving grace, and one that we hung our hat on to keep things in perspective, was, "At least it's not raining." To take that away from us was to leave us with no worse place to imagine to comfort our minds. We could go no lower. There was no relative pain we could imagine that could hurt more than having wet clothes in freezing temperatures overnight. Even if we stopped and were allowed to sleep, there would be no sleep, only shivering huddles of Ranger students. It was better to keep moving and keep warm even though in the meantime our soggy feet were paying a high price.

The air temperature was somewhere around the low 30s, and the water was near 40 degrees. The reality that we were going to have to get wet sat on each of our chests with the heaviness of extreme regret at our bad luck. The word came back, "Strip naked from the waist down and put on your rubber boots. We're going to cross, dry off, and redress on the other side."

I didn't ask whose idea it had been. I simply thought, "What the hell, I'll try anything once."

I dropped my rucksack and sat on it because I did not want to put my bare butt on the ground. I shoved my clothes into my ruck and stood up. Together with my squad we looked like a rubber-boot-clad chorus line ready for our swim. The air was cold even without the water, and as we waited, I could feel it sinking deeper into my skin.

Following the man in front of me, I started the slow movement toward the edge of the water and cautiously took my first step in. It was only a few inches deep, but I could feel the cold water press the rubber boot against my foot and the buoyancy of the air in my boot. My next step forward was into water that was deeper than my boot was high. The splash of the current into my boot, onto my bare foot and ankle, was painful. My goal now was to get to the other side as fast as possible.

Each progressive step forward brought the water higher and higher on my leg and inspired a new level of disbelief at what I was doing. The splash of icy water was like acid on my skin, burning deeply into my muscles and taking my breath away. At six feet two, it crested at my midthigh, and I felt sorry for those shorter than me. I bounded up onto the other side with a gasp and a chin quivering like a cold baby. I got out of the way of those following me and threw my rucksack down. I tried to dry myself with a towel, but with no sun or warm air to aid in the evaporation there was no way to completely dry off. I quickly put my pants, socks, and boots on and waited for what seemed an eternity to start walking again.

It took an hour after we started moving for my body temperature to get back to normal, but I was then comfortable and prepared for a long night without the fear of hypothermia or loss of precious sleep because of wet, freezing clothes.

That innovative move prioritized long-term success over short-term comfort. We got to the other side, dried off as best we could, put our clothes on, and we were fine. We traded that 30 to 40 seconds of discomfort for hours of comfort later. It seemed illogical at first but it was actually a very smart thing to do.

I take that lesson and relate it to problems I'm facing now. I try to look at different ways to solve problems that fall out of the normal way of thinking while keeping long-term success the highest priority.

Suicide

You lose a part of your life when you quit a worthwhile goal, one you know you should succeed at. Part of your self-esteem and confidence are laid to waste along with the discarded goal. People handle failure differently and with varying degrees of success. The two options on opposite ends of the spectrum are: one, accepting personal shortcomings and working to improve, and two, counting failures as permanent and never recovering.

In a sad turn of events, one of the students who quit committed suicide. The RIs gave him the menial task of guarding ammo while waiting for out-processing. He simply had to stay awake and walk back and forth with his M16 rifle at the entrance of the supply point. No one will argue that Ranger students are a stable lot, but no one expected him to pry open a box of ammunition, lock and load a round, and shoot himself, either. While at West Point a classmate of mine hung himself because of fear of failure. In stressful, high-achievement environments there will be people who quit, and of those there will be some who think they cannot live anymore.

It is exceptional that someone commits suicide after quitting, but the others who do quit must inflict incalculable damage to their self-image. Suicide is the extreme, but I wonder how many people hover in that end of the spectrum of negative self-worth.

Had I failed, I would have been devastated. It definitely would have shaken my confidence as a person, though it would have been incomprehensible for me to put a rifle muzzle into my mouth and pull the trigger. A suicide accomplishes nothing positive. Even in this case, finding out about his suicide did not have a really big impact on my unit; everybody just kept driving on, focused on their own lives and day-to-day struggles.

Many of us, like myself, had a significant amount of self-worth and credibility riding on our success, but I would not kill myself to avoid the embarrassment of showing up at my first unit without my tab. As a new second lieutenant I felt insignificant enough when I arrived at my first unit to meet my experience-hardened soldiers. You could have mistaken me for an ant if I had not earned my tab, especially looking at my platoon sergeant and two of my squad leaders who were Ranger qualified. But I would have done the job as platoon leader the best I could.

In-Flight Relief

For our airborne jump into the desert of Utah we started rigging up in Florida. It was a cool day in Florida as we rehearsed our parachute drills at the airfield. Jumping isn't a very difficult skill to learn, but the consequences of not having the techniques up front in your mind are serious enough to demand a review prior to every jump. We were tired, and the emergency actions required if our chute malfunctioned were not second nature for the vast majority of us, making the review necessary. We were happy to not be humping somewhere with our rucksacks on, so the day was already a plus.

Before boarding the plane, we drew our main and reserve parachutes and a case for our rifles. By the time we jumped, we would have our rucks and reserve chutes on our fronts, weapons on our sides, and parachutes on our backs. We'd be looking like pregnant turtles. Fortunately, there was no rush to get locked into all of that gear from the beginning. It was going to be a long flight. We boarded the C-141 carrying our rucksacks and rifle cases. My space on the outside row of the canvas bench was cramped and became smaller as all of the Rangers filed on and secured their own room. The tight conditions were welcome in one sense because the RIs couldn't easily traverse the aisle, and even if they could, there wasn't much they could make us do.

Like many situations in Ranger School we made the best of whatever conditions we found ourselves in, and in this case, it was an opportunity to sleep. Getting comfortable was like trying to stretch out in the back of an Italian sports car, but soon I accepted the cramps in my legs and the elbow in my side and went to sleep. The drone of the engines and vibration of the plane were like a rocking cradle to our tired bodies and minds, and I rested peacefully.

After some unknown amount of sleep, I was awakened, along with the rest of the planeload of students, to get completely rigged for the jump. That done, secure in my chute, rucksack, and weapon case, I collapsed backward into my space, and after a short adjustment was back to sleep. Then, after another timeless stretch, I woke up slightly to the pain in my bladder.

In the rapid decision-making process Rangers are known for, I weighed all of my options. I was encased like a mummy between my gear and the other students and still very tired. Even in my sleep I quickly saw that the amount of effort it would have taken to strip my gear, wade through and over all of the other sleeping Rangers to go to the latrine, and then return to regear was well beyond reasonable and would have cost a lot of good rack time. The decision was simple, though the consequence of a cold jump did cross my mind. I peed my pants and went back to sleep, for now my poly-pro underwear were warm.

The time between wake-up and hook-up was short. The RI opened the door to reveal a white sky and just as white ground—no horizon. The RI went through the jump commands, then "Go, go, go. . . ." I rushed to the door and stepped out—*white*. I was engulfed in the noise, wind, and jolt of the environment, then the relative quiet as I settled under my chute; unending white. I was already cold. I dropped my rucksack to the length of its tether and prepared to land. The two feet of snow surprised me as I did a horribly realistic parachute landing fall.

I noticed my pants were already frozen as I brushed myself off. I didn't consider my condition extraordinary. It was simply the situation I found myself in as I moved off to conduct the mission at hand. I shouldered my rucksack, and felt its weight slip familiarly into the slots in my back. My knees compressed and seemed as stiff as my pants as I creaked off to the rally point. Sleep time was over.

Decision Making

Graduating from Ranger School answered the question that drives so many people to accomplish difficult tasks: "Can I do it?" I learned that I could. While growing up, I never really doubted myself, and Ranger School gave me another reason not to as I entered adulthood and the responsibility for the lives of soldiers. It gave me a lot of confidence in my ability to do physically and mentally demanding jobs and take the challenge of very stressful situations. It gave me confidence to know that I would remain calm and cool if I ever found myself in combat or in other critical situations.

My experience has helped me make decisions in my civilian career with a cool head. Nothing in my civilian job is as time-stressed or critical as it was at Ranger School or in the Army. The decisions I have to make now are important, but usually the time factor is not as great as before. Sometimes I find myself in a time crunch, but for the most part I have some time to take a step back and take a look at the issues (maybe an hour or two or 24), whereas the Ranger School decisions had to be made on the fly.

I take the emotion out of my decision-making process and make decisions based on the best available evidence and where we want to go from here. "What is the right thing to do?" I try to make decisions that are sound, not just knee-jerk reactions. My Ranger School experience and learning how to operate under extreme pressure and scrutiny allows me to be cool under pressure now. The discomfort of reduced food and sleep added so much physical distraction to the already intense pressure on us that it makes it easy in the outside world to handle problems when those annoyances are absent.

Bad Odds

Not long after arriving at my unit in Hawaii I had to draw on the lesson learned from my first no-go in Ranger School. My unit was in a train-up period for an Expert Infantryman's Badge (EIB) competition. Three months were devoted to the train-up, and a whole week was set aside for the testing portion. There were 30 different tasks we had to perform, 28 without a mistake. In some units as many as 50 percent of the people get the badge, but in the 25th Infantry Division the standards were very high and the badge was difficult to earn; the success rate was more along the lines of 5 percent.

I'm not sure what happened, but after all that preparation I jumped right into the competition and got no-gos on my first two tasks. I retested and passed on, but I had used the only two first-time no-gos I was allowed. I had a daunting 28 straight tasks that I had to do without a no-go over the next four days. I wanted to stay in the competition as long as possible to set the example for my troops, and though some of the approaching tasks were easier than the first two, many others were harder, and I didn't know how long I would last.

As I completed each event, I looked expectantly into the face of the evaluator while waiting for his grade. My heart pounded, even on the ones I knew I had done properly. I continued through the first and second days without an additional misstep, though my troops joked, "Uh-oh, the lieutenant is going down."

As day three progressed successfully, my soldiers began to believe. Every day they expressed surprise and gained strength that I was still in it. "He might just do it" was their new tune.

The final tasks of day four came, and I felt like I was shooting a championship-winning free throw in front of a million people. My thirtieth and final task was completed successfully, and I once again showed myself that you can never quit. I did not give up. I did the last 28 tasks without a no-go and earned my EIB.

Of the 12 soldiers in the battalion who earned the badge, my platoon alone won five. I think a lot of that had to do with the example that I set. The perseverance I learned at Ranger School paid off in practical belief and motivation for my soldiers in the field. I always believe that there is a chance that I can come out on top no matter how bad the odds seem.

Camaraderie

When I first interviewed for a civilian job, the manager asked me about accomplishments I was proud of. One of the questions was, "What was your longest workday?"

I answered, "Basically, 23 hours for two weeks."

He repeated in surprise, "You mean 23 hours a day for two weeks?" Having not been to Ranger School, he was almost testing, as if to say, "Is that really true?" I know he was nonbelieving in a sense, thinking, "That has got to be fluff."

I said, "Yes. I got one to two hours of sleep a night during the Florida phase of Ranger School." Most people don't really believe at first that Ranger School is as you describe and is something in which you actually participated. Even after hearing the same story over and over again from different graduates, it is still hard to accept.

I was hired by a wonderful company and found a sizable group of other warriors on its rolls. A lot of people within the organization have been through extramilitary schooling, very tough military schooling. Within the company there are many people who went to Ranger School, Navy SEAL (sea, air, land) training, and the like, and there is a natural camaraderie among those of us who have gone through those types of challenges. We share an experience, even though different in many ways, that generates a lot of pride among us. We know that not everybody has been able to go through or succeed at that type of activity. There is also a kind of longing to be around people like that. Everybody who is out of the military for a period of time begins to miss the camaraderie of being in the trenches with the guy who has the same values as you do and that you could put it all on the line for. In that type of training, we had to put it all on the line. There was no holding back. That is why we identify with each other. We are each a piece of what the others are longing to be around.

Skills That Translate

I would expect that for the most part someone who has gone through Ranger School would succeed in the civilian sector. Ranger School graduates can succeed because of their will to succeed and the confidence that they can accomplish a mission, in an ethical way, no matter what it takes, whether it takes long hours, innovative thinking, or motivating people to do extraordinary things. That attitude translates to success regardless of what business you are in, and that is the type of person you want on your team.

Ranger Hutt's Walk

The self-esteem you develop for yourself as an individual is critical to your success as a leader. You will either accept less than success or you won't. You will either have the confidence in your ultimate victory or you won't. What you believe about yourself directly translates to everything you do and then to everyone you influence. Any doubt or anything less than complete conviction and confidence is multiplied in the individuals on your team. You are the leader; if you are shaken or weak you can expect your team to be trembling.

You can build solid self-esteem through the benefits perseverance will bring you, whether you succeed every time or not. After John failed his first patrol, 90 percent of the battle was just getting mentally back into the game. It is easy to keep going when you win every time; there is more opportunity for personal development when you have a setback and have to adjust to a new, less sterling reality, and then keep going.

Overcoming obstacles and disappointments can become easier as you face them more often, as do the innovative and difficult decisions you have to make on a day-to-day basis. Figuratively speaking, you may find that peeing in your pants is the only reasonable course of action. That's not necessarily innovative, but it certainly shows a willingness to do whatever is necessary to get the job done most efficiently. When you stretch yourself and your team you will be in unfamiliar territory, doing things and making decisions based on completely new and unfamiliar information. You must adopt a gotta-do-what-you-gotta-do attitude.

The idea of short-term sacrifice for long-term success deserves revisiting. You could take a whiteboard right now and on the left side list the short-term sacrifices and on the right side define the long-term success. This relationship between the two is part of nearly anything you and your team are attempting to accomplish. Just like John and his squad stripping to nothing to cross the freezing stream, the decision to sacrifice will probably be a no-brainer when you have defined success.

There is beauty in finding people with the proper attitude, the kind who will accept difficult challenges, dash into the unknown, and confidently attack whatever comes their way. If there is any aspect of leadership where you have to set the example, it is here. Before you ever develop a team of individuals like that, you need to lead them through challenges they thought were beyond their capabilities. You must provide an environment where they can develop self-esteem and a cohesive team.

It's time to dash into the lofty aspiration of duty as explained by Ranger Scott Sharp. Don't be surprised by his early experiences, ones motivated by convenience and tinged with insanity. A duty concept is sure to follow, and besides, you have to be a bit rabid to do this stuff in the first place!

RANGERS

are

DUTIFUL

SCOTT SHARP

RANGER

Lieutenant Scott Sharp had the opportunity to glance back into our historical past, or worse yet, into our future, to see the human nature that causes revolutions. People around the world are suffering—hungry, dirty, and without hope. So often in the past those conditions have led to mass chaos and clash. The circumstances at Ranger School were right to replicate one aspect of that trouble, and Lieutenant Sharp was on the periphery looking in. He witnessed mob violence, understood why it was happening, even in this disciplined group, and decided to rise above the rabble as a professional officer to stop it. A revolution of a different kind was happening internally for Lieutenant Sharp.

For Lieutenant Scott Sharp, Ranger School progressed from a destiny to a directive, but it wasn't until it took that final step to a desire that he also took ownership of being a professional officer. It was a revolution for him, a revolving of his values based on his experiences that brought around his new prospective. When the goal of completing Ranger School became a desire, Scott became much more emotionally involved. He began to take life and leadership lessons from his experiences instead of simply seeing them as another hard day in the Army. How emotionally involved are you in your pursuits? Are you making the right decisions regarding short-term problems, or are you taking the easy way out?

Destiny

My father was an instructor in the Florida phase of Ranger School when I was born, and as I grew up, he indoctrinated me with the stories of that assignment. Unfortunately he died as soon as I got out of high school, so there were not a lot of ways for me to compare myself to him as I started to become a man. I wanted to have some sort of kindred experience with my dad. When I figured out that I was going into the Army as an infantry officer, the handwriting was on the wall. Should you want to succeed in the infantry, Ranger School is your first stop after Airborne School. I never had a problem with the challenge, though I was always intimidated and sometimes downright terrified by it. The stories I remember my dad telling actually gave me comfort, because they were usually on the lighter moments, not the horrifying times. I was bright enough to understand that the Ranger School he was describing was from 22 years before, and that it had changed a lot by the time I showed up in 1988.

I went to college in Dahlonega, Georgia, the home of Camp Frank D. Merrill. I got to see all of the RIs hanging around town with their Ranger sweatshirts, black with a large gold RANGER across the front and a white name tag over that. When we did early-morning PT in the ROTC program, we could see the girls, wearing those same sweatshirts, slipping back into the dorm at six o'clock in the morning. There was a lot of mystique surrounding the school and the instructors.

Part of being drawn by the school may have been a personal destiny because somehow I always knew it was going to happen.

Prep

I went to the Infantry Officer Basic Course, and from there everyone went to Ranger School. I do not know if I was just too stupid to be really afraid or just such a mindless sheep that when they told me to go I said, "Okay, whatever. It doesn't matter to me." Probably a little bit of both of those apply. I do not want to say that they signed you up, but in OBC it was understood that the vast majority of us were going to Ranger School. Out of a 25-man platoon, 18 of us showed up the first day. The overall OBC program was geared toward getting us ready to go to a rifle company, which dovetailed nicely with preparing for Ranger School. We trained road marching, lots of PT, and individual platoon leader skill areas. We did not have a special program set aside simply for Ranger School the way the quartermaster guys did. Our regular PT was Ranger PT, and those of us not going to Ranger School were just going to get into great shape. Preparing for the school was so integrated into our routine that we even did the mandatory swim test as part of the basic course.

I did not do anything on my own. I was too busy drinking beer. I was getting a regular paycheck, so I was rich as far as I was concerned. A college guy with a steady income for the first time spelled high adventure.

I knew that without a Ranger tab it would be difficult to be assimilated into anything that resembled a high-speed infantry organization. My plan was to go to Korea for a year, come back, go to the Ranger Regiment, and be a hero. A couple of guys who were senior to me had already gone through the process and had been assigned to units at Fort Bragg, North Carolina. They always told me the story: "Four lieutenants walk into the S-1's office getting ready to see the battalion commander. The first thing the S-1 does is figure out who has a Ranger tab and who doesn't. Those who don't he sends back to brigade, or they meet the battalion commander on different terms." I had heard all of those scare stories, and I knew that positive things were not going to happen for me if I did not have a tab.

Weeding

There was total panic and fear the morning we reported. We graduated from the basic course on Friday and reported to Jump School the next morning. We graduated from Jump School Friday afternoon three weeks later and reported to Ranger School the morning after that. There was just enough activity over the prior couple of months that I did not have time to concentrate on Ranger School. Then on Friday afternoon it started to sink in, and it was now too late to do any further preparing.

A few friends, also on their way, and I had shaved our heads the night before. There was no need to look presentable for the next few weeks. Seeing the shapes of some people's heads is a great argument for hair, but pragmatism took over. Whatever worked was what we did, and because of hygiene issues in the field, hair was an unnecessary burden.

The next morning at Denny's four bald guys in jungle fatigues sat around the booth waiting to order. Finally, the realization of where I was hit me hard. The people in the other booths and at the bar had lives, and I was about to give mine up for 58 days. The guy in the dirty blue baseball cap and checkered shirt was going to have a warm meal tonight and sleep in a comfortable bed. The heavy lady smoking a cigarette with her two kids near the window was going to watch the special *Saturday Night Movie* and have a pot pie, and the cute college girl waiting to be seated would be at a dance club. I was scared. My stomach was having an involuntary reaction caused by nerves. I felt it tighten up and tip slightly off balance.

We all ordered the Grand Slam breakfast, and though most of us ate it, it did not taste or sit very well. Putting food into my already unbalanced stomach was like adding weight to one side of a tightrope walker's balancing staff—it completely turned. I excused myself at the same time another guy stood up to go to the bathroom. We were both in the bathroom, leaning over a toilet, throwing up. Future great infantry leaders, trained to kill, and scared to death.

We got in the car, drove down Casina Highway, and had a lot of fun, relieved to actually get it started and stop thinking about it. Once we started in-processing, I was very scared and intimidated, but that first day was not as bad as my imagination had made it out to be. I was well prepared for the first week, the running and PT, having done so much of it in the basic course.

We were billeted in wooden, World War II era structures. The infantry guys had already sewn cat eyes onto our patrol caps, so we watched as the others prepared their gear. We were the homeboys and as such had the home field advantage. The very first night I noticed an Air Defense Artillery (ADA) captain. This guy was tall and husky and carrying a little extra weight. It was midnight and they had fed us only one meal that day. He sat on his bunk fiercely trying to sew his Ranger eyes on with dental floss. He looked so completely out of his element. I recognized that emotionally he was barely hanging on. Looking around, I saw no one from my OBC in my squad, so I was in there with a bunch of strangers, but the captain was clearly the odd man out. It was obvious that he was not in the physical shape he needed to be in and was not emotionally ready to be treated poorly. I saw that in his eyes, and I thought, "He ain't going to be here."

Who knows what led him to attempt Ranger School. He had probably talked about it and pursued it for years and then in the months leading up to the course had been a bit of an oddity in his unit because he was "the guy going to Ranger School." His hopes for the Ranger tab may have been more real than mine since his was a personal choice to be there. He had prepared his family for a long separation and told them to expect a tired and emaciated shell of himself when he showed up at home nine weeks later. He sat there like an old woman in a large man's body, hands shaking, trying to sew a small, square reflective piece of tape to the back of his cap. I went over and told him, "All they can do is treat us poorly. They can't actually kill us." It was one of those poignant moments I saw someone who was really afraid. He did not make it through City Week.

Out of the guys from my IOBC company, I was very surprised by the ones who did not make it through City Week. One guy in particular, Harbone, was going to a light infantry unit, and had to have a tab to survive there. The second day of City Week I passed him on the road between the barracks. He said, "Oh, yeah, I've got a profile: my ankle."

I watched him as he walked away, straight up, no limp. "Yeah, whatever," I thought. That was where I came to the realization that Ranger School gave people a lot of legitimate reasons not to pass so they could save face. He was not the most squared-away guy in the basic course, but he was fairly competent and aggressive in his PT. He shot off his mouth more than he probably needed to, and I thought it was interesting that he was gone early.

At the end of the school we did the math; there were seven guys in my squad who graduated, but at one time or another there had been 16 people filter through. We had two ADA captains who came and went fast, one in City Week and one in the mountains. I could not even tell you their names.

Ow

I expect more out of people. It is not that I expect more out of Rangers as opposed to nonRangers, but the experience gave me an appreciation of what people are capable of doing. I saw strength in people that proved where the mind was willing, somehow the body functioned.

In City Week we did a grueling road march. It was still early in the course, and our bodies were adjusting to the work environment and the amount of effort that was expected of us. It was a warm day, and soon after starting we were all soaked with sweat, panting, wanting to get hit by a bus to end the exertion. I closed the gap with and then passed a guy who had started the march somewhere in front of me. He was now evidently testing his physical limits. During a fast march like that you spend much of your time in your head, looking down at the ground watching one foot go in front of the other, shuffling on like the ticking of a clock, thinking about the pain in your back, feet, and stomach alternately.

Head down as I passed, I looked at his green jungle boots. The fall of each foot on the pavement squeezed blood out of the eyelets. I looked up to see an absolute expression of pain on his face. He did not look at me. He just kept plodding ahead, though each step must have been like walking on broken glass. His body was failing him. His joints were surrendering and he started walking like Jerry Lewis, popping and snapping, and I thought, "That's what focus and determination can do." His body should have quit a long time ago, but he refused to let it. Somehow he cranked out whatever the last miles were. At the finish of the road march several of us were cheering him on, but it was at that time that his body absolutely quit. I was about 10 meters away watching as he veered to the shoulder of the road and fell. He had a buddy there holding his hand trying to pick him up. He was still moving.

Low Points

My low point in Ranger School was at Camp Darby. The adjustment to living the hard life was a shock to my system even though I had expected it. We were a new organization and had not built any cohesion. Everyone got along, but we were going through the process of establishing our competencies and capabilities as individuals and as part of the group. We were each concerned with how the others perceived us and also keeping tabs on how well our own bodies would adjust to the heavy physical toll of the field.

The Fort Benning training area was pretty tough country to navigate in. There were rolling hills, forests, and erosion ditches all over the terrain, and even though I knew the area and had been out there for parts of the light leaders course, it was a significant adjustment. The work was physically grinding but certainly no harder than the rest of the course. It was simply the first jolting shot of tequila before we became numb to the work.

Florida produced some low points also. We were fully adjusted and working well as a unit, but now the platoon had figured out that I was one of the guys who could navigate, and I kept getting asked to lead the way. I went from a leadership position into a compass man or point man and then back into a leadership position. I longed for a simple Joe Snuffy position where I did not have to think. It was not a difficult academic task to navigate, but to do so my brain had to be engaged at all times. There was tremendous rest value in not having to think. I felt like I had no oil in my engine, and the longer I ran it, the closer I got to seizing it up.

There were other low times that tested me and pushed me to question why I was there, but I kept going, partially because of the fear of shame. I would have been ashamed if I chose, in a time of weakness, to quit. My dad had been an instructor so I had some extra emotional baggage that acted as a motivator also. I could not come home without my Ranger tab. The thought of how I would think of myself if I failed, more than anything else, signed me up and was going to keep me from quitting. I was willing to get thrown out, but I was not going to quit.

Connections

Having gone to college in the town outside of the mountain Ranger camp, I found the terrain there painfully familiar. Land navigation was easy because I had been in that country before. I also knew what the deal was on an area that had been clear-cut by loggers. When the patrol leader said, "Okay, we're going to walk across this clear-cut," I was able to get him to think again by saying something like, "How about you go out there and break your ankles for a couple of hours and we'll stay here."

At one point we were north of Camp Merrill on the Appalachian Trail, and I could see the house that my girlfriend was staying in. It was the house I had spent my last year of college in. It was far in the distance, but I could pick it out. I looked at the area and silently pointed out different landmarks. "That's Camp Wahsega Road, and that's Master Sergeant Horton's home. My old girlfriend is over there, in my bed, in a house that I may still be paying rent on, and Master Sergeant Horton is an RI who is out here somewhere trying to kill me." Despite being so close to home, I was not homesick at all. We walked through a place just south of Degrasy Mountain by Flatrock Creek that I recognized. I said, "Just six months ago I was here. I camped right here!" I pointed: "That's where I left my jeep, and I left those beer cans!"

Apparently not wanting to be reminded that there was life outside of Ranger School, the other guys retorted, "Shut up! Shut the fuck up! We don't care. Just shut up."

In the mountains, Gerald the barber had set up his shop in a concrete building across the street from the line of barracks where we lived. The haircuts he gave were no better than the ones we gave ourselves before starting the school, but we had to take advantage of the service when we could. The less hair the better. Guys were lined up out the door waiting for their three minutes in his chair. I had gotten my hair cut and was ready to leave when Gerald said, "I have to get you some change out of the back."

At first I said, "No, I've got exact change."

He insisted, "No, I have to get you some change!" I was not the brightest guy on the planet.

He emerged from the back, handed me a brown paper bag, and said, "This is from your friend Gordon Quick." It was a bag filled from top to bottom with candy bars.

Gordon and I were good friends at North Georgia College, and both of us went into the Army. He was smart enough not to be in Ranger School. His wife was from Dahlonega so he was up there all the time. My dilemma was how to get from the barbershop across the street to the green huts without alerting the world that I had food. A Ranger with a brown grocery bag drew attention like a man giving away money in the projects. I took off my BDU top, covered the bag, and scurried across the open area into the hut. I swear to God, I took four steps into the hut and turned around and my entire squad was there. They had figured it out, and the guys who had been witnesses at the barbershop were there also, all with their hands out. "Fuck me," I thought. Everyone got a little bit, and I ended up with three candy bars from a full shopping bag. Fortunately, I still had Gordon as a source.

Gordon had buried a case of MREs at the Mount Zion Baptist Church, which is right outside the gate at Camp Merrill. The plan was that he would mark a tree with masking tape, step off five paces to the north, and bury it there. One night I sneaked out to get my treasure, entrenching tool and flashlight at the ready. We were not going to get much sleep that night and I would give up some to go on my trek. After lights out I had a couple of free hours, and I made my move. I anticipated the bounty of food I was about to receive. Not worrying about when I was going to get my next fruitcake or pork patty seemed to take some of the stress off of the experience of Ranger School.

I found the tree, marked out the paces to the north, and planted the first shovel stroke into the earth. It did not seem particularly soft; however, I was sure that Gordon had packed the ground down well and covered it with pine needles after he buried the food. One stroke quickly followed the other and the hole deepened toward my treasure. It was close now, and I knew any second I would hit the hard cardboard side of the MRE case. I was out there in the middle of the night with my red lens flashlight digging the hole furiously. Each shovelful was filled with high hopes.

The people camping nearby must have wondered, "What's that noise over there?"

I dug my ass off, thinking, "There's a ham slice in here somewhere for Scott." The deeper I dug, the surer I was that it was very near, until I had gone beyond a reasonable time and depth and began to have my doubts. I finally gave up the dream. I felt like a child lost in downtown New York City; I did not know which way to turn.

I wasted three hours of rack time looking for a case of MREs that I could not find. He must have buried it on the south side and I was looking on the north side. So, after three hours of fruitless effort, I plodded back to the barracks, just in time for my fire watch detail and then the start of another day—another bad day to be Scott.

Parachute Stir-Fry

I blew out a panel on my parachute during an Airborne School jump, which allowed me to do only a left turn all the way into the ground. I survived that, but in general I was not a very big airborne fan. I thought that it was a really bad way to get to work.

After exiting the plane on my Ranger School jump into Florida, I could not see the drop zone; all I saw were trees. So I prepared myself for my first tree landing. No matter how hard I looked for an opening in the trees, all I saw from the air was what looked like a soft green mattress of treetops. "Man, this is going to suck," I thought.

I was apprehensive at what I might hit when I broke through the concealment of the canopy. I knew the proper procedures to protect my body, but my fear stemmed from what I believe is a natural human fear—the fear of surprise. It's like the tense opening of a door in a horror movie: You anticipate the worst, even while bracing yourself for a scare.

I cranked my neck forward, looking down at my landing site, and it seemed as if I was moving exponentially faster. It took a long time to be able to make out the details of the trees, and as soon as I could, they were rushing by my face.

I landed in a bunch of 12-foot-tall saplings. Limbs snapped and leaves flew as I plummeted through the growth and collided with the ground. I went all the way through the trees and hit with the full force of my weight. I wasn't even lucky enough to land in trees tall enough to snag my chute and keep me from hitting the forest floor. My parachute did snag in the tops of the trees, however, forcing me to deal with disengaging it. I got the worst of both worlds. Of course, the positive side was that I didn't break any bones and could walk under my own power.

I was already tired, and now I was struggling to get my parachute out of the trees. Finally, I said to myself, "You ain't ever going to figure this thing out in the dark." I took out a parachute-remover-from-trees, that is, a knife. There was no way anyone could ever repair that parachute. I cut the shit out of it. It was the first time I had ever considered doing something like that, but as I got into it, I thought, "Oh, 5-50 cord, too!" *Whack*. Some guy came up and I asked, "Hey, do you want some 5-50 cord?" and he and I proceeded to butcher that poor parachute.

I gathered up the pieces in my arms and jogged to the turn-in point. We dropped the parachutes in the dark at a point marked simply by a chem light, so there was no good visibility to see what the pile of material really looked like. I continued stumbling across this drop zone to link up with my platoon. I woke up my Ranger buddy, Kenny Anderson, a non-airborne guy, who had been lying out there for about six hours waiting for the airborne jump. We talked briefly until we moved with the platoon into the Florida Ranger camp, Camp Rudder.

Just Lucky, I Guess

All of my airborne jumps in Ranger School were high adventure. I maximized the training opportunity in every one. The class jumped into Dugway Proving Grounds, Utah, which was jump number seven or eight for me, including the five in Airborne School. I was still a pure novice with no appreciable skill.

The airplane ride was horrible. We were all crammed in the plane, combat loaded, trying to do in-flight rigging, stepping on each other. It was like stuffing a telephone booth, then having the guy on top try to make a phone call.

I stepped out of the door in a classic night jump. I had my eyes closed. I figured, "Either I'll die or I'll feel the opening shock, but one of the two has to happen before I'll open my eyes." I felt something snap across my nose and thought, "This would be a pretty good time to open my eyes." There they were, parachute extension lines. It looked like I was going to get the opportunity to work through a high-altitude entanglement. I had a partial malfunction in Airborne School, then a tree landing, now I was continuing to push the airborne training envelope with a high-altitude entanglement. I was the upper jumper, looking down on the guy I was attached to. "Why the hell are you stuck in my parachute?" I yelled.

"Why the hell are you stuck in my parachute?" he yelled back.

We continued to argue while struggling to get free of each other. "What are we supposed to do?" I wondered to myself. We were instructed in cases like this that the lower jumper climbs up and the higher jumper climbs down. "Yeah, that ain't going to happen. A couple of Ranger students ain't going to make that operation work," I thought, and was proved right by the speed with which the ground was approaching. We stayed attached.

Being the lower jumper, he was able to lower his rucksack and prepare for the landing just like a normal landing. The desert came up quickly and I slammed into the ground, missing the other jumper by inches. I still had all of my gear strapped around me, rucksack in my crotch and weapon on my side. The landing broke my rucksack frame, and when the barrel of the rifle went into the ground, it ripped out the top end of my weapons bag. I lay on my side, aching and thinking, "This sucks! This is no way to start the last 20 days of Ranger School."

I was cussing as I heard footsteps approaching from behind me, and I heard a woman's voice ask, "Are you okay?"

Being diplomatic and still facing the other way, I said, "Fuck no, I'm not okay! I'm in goddamn Ranger School. It's day 38. This asshole fucked up my eighth jump. I'm in the middle of the fucking desert. I almost died, and you want to know if I'm fucking okay!? What kind of a stupid question is that?" About the time I finished my tirade, I rolled over onto my back and looked straight up at a female captain who was standing over me like an elementary school teacher. I finished my sentence, "Ma'am."

At that moment I would not have cared if they threw me out of Ranger School. "Bend my dog tags. Send me home. I don't care." I rolled back over, hoping she would go away. There was not much else I could do. I sat there trying to focus and figure out what was going on, when I heard more footsteps approaching from the same direction as the captain. I had not released anything yet. I hadn't even fully come to my senses. I just sat there in a daze, trying to recover and talking to the guy who was entangled with me. My rucksack with a broken frame was between my legs, the chute was still attached at my shoulders, and I was almost ready to roll over onto my back and start dicking around with my weapon and other gear. You could say I had a generally bad attitude.

Another voice from behind me, this time a man's, asked, "Aren't you supposed to put your weapon in operation?"

Without looking, I retorted, "Oh, a fucking critic here, just what I need now." I rolled over to look up and see who my latest conversation partner was—a two-star general. I thought, "Oh, this can only get better."

He was out there with his aide, the captain, dorking off watching the Ranger guys jump in.

I did not get any grief about that incident from the RIs, but I did not make any friends that day, either. Fortunately, there were no injuries besides the rucksack frame and bent rifle. I'm not sure of the intimidation value of a Ranger student on observers like that, but I think it is akin to running across a rabid dog—just leave the damn thing alone.

Where's the Truck?

We got off of the trucks and formed up on the side of the road as the trucks drove away. The sun was starting to set on what could be considered a pleasant day, which marked the beginning of the three-day swamp exercise in Florida. *Our* day was just about to start. We moved as the trail squad, following the others into the forest. We could hear the lead squad out in front thrashing around getting wet in the swamp and some RI dogging them hard in the darkness. I was thinking, "This is going to suck. This is going to extra-suck."

We were shuffling down the road in single file when the Ranger next to me turned to the RI and said, "I can't do it."

In the distance we heard two RIs screaming, "You guys can't figure nothing out! You all are going to drown!"

The Ranger repeated to the RI, "I can't do it."

We tried to encourage him: "You *can* do it! This is going to be a real miserable three days—big deal. You've been through that before. You can do it."

The RI, Captain Rose, said, "Okay, you want to LOM?"—referring to a lack of motivation statement.

He answered, "Yeah, I want one."

We were still trying to win him back: "No. Don't do it."

Captain Rose said, "Okay, just sling your weapon and stand out here with me."

The guy turned around and looked in the direction we had come from. He asked, "Sir, where are the trucks?"

"There ain't no trucks. Fall into the rear of the formation," came Captain Rose's reply.

The kid slugged it all the way through the swamps. It was bad, and I almost drowned, but this poor guy went through what he was trying to avoid and didn't receive the reward at the end.

That day we had to put up a one-rope bridge to cross a river. I was the radio operator, so I had a particularly heavy rucksack. As I stepped forward to give the guy my rucksack to hook onto the rope, I discovered that whatever I was standing on was not solid ground, mother earth. I went all the way under the water while still trying to hold my rucksack up. I maintained my posture as I went down—head under water, eyes closed, and the hand holding my rucksack the only thing dry. I felt someone fumbling around with my ruck trying to get it on the rope. I was not in a panic. I kept thinking, "I'm not going to drop my rucksack. I'm not going to drop my rucksack." Suddenly I felt a strong hand grab my shoulder—not my uniform, my shoulder—and pull me up. I gurgled, "Ahhhh, urrghhhhh."

I was looking into the face of Sergeant First Class Rubin. "Breathe, Ranger!" he screamed.

He had a face of worn leather with a hundred thousand miles on it if he had 50 feet, and a close-cropped haircut probably overdone even for Ranger School. He was as rough-speaking a human being as I have ever heard. His voice was so rough it was entertaining, and he found a way to put a curse word into every phrase. If he could figure out how to include profanity in a four-syllable word, he would do it. When you thought of the RI who was really out there, he was the guy you pictured. He was what an NCO was supposed to be. He hated everybody, but loved the Army. Every Ranger issue was his personal issue. In his mind, he *was* Ranger School. He held it that close to himself.

"Okay, take a fucking breath," he said, and then let go of me, dropping me back to the bottom.

Suddenly my rucksack was out of my hands, I bobbed back up to the surface, and the sergeant was yelling, "Go! Go! Go!"

For some reason I was not necessarily afraid at the time, though later I thought, "Holy shit, I could have drowned." Then I thought, "I would have gotten out of Ranger School. So what was the downside of that?"

We'll Be Here All Day

At Dugway Proving Grounds in the desert we were into the live fires, nearing the end of the course, and the cadre was almost treating us nicely. We were all sitting around a patrol base when an RI ran up and said, "See that hill out there. Get there now!" We looked to the high ground about 1,200 meters away. We all turned around and started to pack up our gear, and he yelled again, "*Now!* Run!"

I thought, "This ought to be entertaining. I wonder what this game is all about." I put my rucksack on and started toward the high ground. Running was out of the question. We had 70-pound rucksacks on, worn boots, tired legs, and a kilometer to travel. A fast walk was the most anyone did. They did not give us any more information on the reason for the movement, so to us there was no emergency. We were going to be in Ranger School all day whether we moved fast or slow. It was like rushing to be the first in line to get on a plane. You don't arrive at your destination any faster than the guy who read his paper and sipped his coffee while waiting for everyone else to board. The hill was going to be there when we got there. We did not move in any real formation, more of a gaggle, stepping over the rocky terrain and heading for our hill.

When we got there we were again relaxing and catching our breath when the RI told us what had happened. Someone in one of the other companies, while digging a cat hole—a place to take a dump—found a chemical munition. Dugway Proving Grounds had been a testing area for chemical rounds, and there were still unexploded duds lying around. Like picking the right lotto number, it was dumb luck if you found one. They moved us out of the area and called the guys in the white space suits. From where we sat, we could see the van drive up and the guys get out. They were exactly what you would expect, four figures dressed from head to toe in white, looking at the ground. They started messing with the round. We lounged around enjoying some unsupervised time, as the RIs were off talking among themselves. Just about then someone asked, "Which way is the wind blowing?"

Like a bunch of pecking chickens looking up at the same time, we all got curious. Chemicals are carried by the wind and can be very potent even kilometers away from the blast of a chemical munition. Several people licked one of their fingers and stuck it in the air. One guy pointed toward the white van, "It's coming from that direction," he said.

"Shit." We had just moved downwind. The common sense it took to ask that question before our walk was somehow absent. The Army has great classes for unit nuclear, biological and chemical

(NBC) officers and NCOs, which cover the wind issue very well, but no one there had been to that school yet. So we started to walk again, but to us it did not matter how far—we were going to be in Ranger School all day.

Revolution

Until I got to Ranger School the tab was not that important to me except as far as I had to have it to get past "Go" in the infantry. When I was in the mountains or Florida was when it became a gut check, a credibility and character check for myself. As an infantry officer, having it expected of me created a situation where there was not as much motivation going into it as there might have been had it been my own decision. However, somewhere in the course it made a transition to being an internally driven event. I wanted to be a part of the small percentage who graduated, and I really started to take ownership of my goal. I was going to get through this because it was important to me. It was now my goal instead of somebody else's directive. Accepting ownership of the goal of earning a Ranger tab was coupled with accepting ownership of being a professional officer in the Army.

For two phases, beginning in the mountains, our platoon had had a chow thief. From the first incident it was serious, but it really became an issue in Florida. We were far enough into the course that people's bodies were starting to burn the reserves of their reserves. We didn't know what fuel really kept us going. We were protecting our food to the point of writing our roster number on every piece of our MRE, an outrageous sign of distrust.

The theft of food was bad for the obvious reason: deprivation of sustenance to someone who was in desperate need of fuel. It was wrong because stealing was wrong, but it went deeper than that. In the armed services we train to fight and survive in combat. Critical to our success is trust in our leadership, who is taking us into harm's way, and trust in our buddies, who are going to watch our backs. We trust our buddies to take personal chances with their safety to protect us in battle, to work as a team for the survival of everyone. In an organization where you have to trust your buddy with your life, it is devastating to the unit not to be able to trust him with something as small as food. It is a breakdown of the fabric that holds the unit together. The inherent selfishness of someone who maliciously and with full intent deprives you of something he knows you need is incompatible with success in combat.

It was early morning. The sun was coming up, and the RIs were away doing changeover operations, the time when the outgoing RI briefs the incoming RI. We sat in a 20-meter open area in a stand of small scrub pines, completely unsupervised. Free from evaluating eyes, guys were resting against their rucks, conducting personal hygiene, or fixing a cup of coffee. I was sitting there being eloquent, talking about hitting on chicks or something, when I heard a commotion. There was an argument on the other side of the relaxed crowd, and it continued to get louder and louder. Everyone in my squad turned around to see what was going on.

When I turned around I saw a mob. Cartoon fights are more orderly. There was nothing military or organized about it. Rather, it was an angry lynch mob who had hold of their man. They had caught the chow thief, and a couple of guys had started to beat on him. They were not just beating him up like in high school; they were beating him with the absolute intention of killing him. If it had gone on long enough, there was no doubt in anyone's military mind that they would have ended his life. The depth of hatred that a chow thief generated was well beyond a simple food issue. These guys were weeding out the guy who was going to get them killed on some future battlefield.

I saw five guys who were actually hitting him, and a relatively large group of others standing around stunned. I thought, "This is what happens when military organizations lose leadership and lose focus. This is a mob. This is what the country fears." It scared me and I felt a professional duty do to something.

There were some pretty big guys in my platoon. I chose two of them, football players from West Point and Norwich, to walk over there with me. With these guys to either side of me I was confident that what I was about to say would get some respect. "Hey!" I yelled. "Stop beating the shit out of this guy!" The punishers were in no mood to hear logical or moral reasons for why the beating should stop, but even with their adrenaline pumping they were not ready to face down an RI. "We need to wait for the RI, and let him take care of it," I instructed.

The thrashing stopped, and the thief crawled away like a wounded seal. With his bloody face and battered body, there was nothing that resembled cockiness left in him. His was the worst beating I had ever seen anyone take in person. We waited for the RI, who showed up a few minutes later and immediately dragged the thief away from the rabble, never to be seen again.

The guys who were laying fist on flesh had no intention of stopping until they were stopped. I thought, "This is why the Army needs competent leadership." There we were, a bunch of frigging students who knew we were not going to die. We would have been happy with some Snickers bars, a few Cokes, and no one to fuck with us for 45 minutes. That gave me pause. It was eye opening that this level of violence could happen here, now, in these relatively controlled conditions. It gave me an appreciation of what could happen in the world. If we could do this to ourselves, what could we do to someone we really hated? In the back of my mind, I hoped I had the dignity and moral courage *not* to be the guy in the mob, but rather to be the guy trying to control the mob. That incident reinforced the realization that I had to live up to my commission, that I needed to be better than the crowd. I don't need to be in with the mob. I need to be the smarter guy. That is why the Army has leadership. That is why the Army has professional officers and NCOs as a check and balance.

Food was obviously a serious issue at Ranger School, and that beating, surprisingly enough, allowed me to understand world history better. I thought about food a lot, just like everyone, but I also thought about the state of being hungry. I studied the feeling, like looking closely at a scene to try to see everything in it. I knew, of course, that in 24 hours I would get my meal and a half and that life would go on, but I thought, "This is what it is like to be hungry. This is why hungry people with guns is a bad idea." I finally understood all of the French Revolution shit I had studied for my history major. It made sense now. How many times in the world's history had hunger played a part in changing the course of a country and the world? Where does discontent start? I somehow had a connection with the revolutionaries of the past. Sharp's law of politics says, "If the people are hungry and then they arm themselves, you have a problem on your hands."

Self-Confidence

Leadership lessons never happened at one discrete moment for me. It was more of a process of stress and self-analysis that helped me learn the lessons that made me a better leader. Ranger School stripped a lot of my perception of personal weakness away. Through my high school and college years I was an average student, and through the comparisons I made between myself and the A and B students, I felt inferior. I always thought that someone else had a clue, that they knew what they were talking about and I did not. I could do the job at hand, but I was not confident in my ability to do things really well. In Ranger School I was forced to deal with my core person. There was no room to bullshit, and through what I learned I became empowered. I realized, "Hey, these guys ain't any smarter than Sharp, and in some cases, Sharp is actually smarter than some of them." I learned that I could meet the challenge, do the job, and do it right. My navigation skills drew people to seek me out; that really built my confidence and affected my belief in all of my abilities.

Overall, the leadership value of Ranger School to me came in the form of personal confidence. I built self-assurance and I lead with confidence now. Ranger School provided a great education, and the more I think about it, the more I think I learned from it. It gave me the confidence to be the quiet, competent guy instead of the guy who always has something to prove. I appreciate the school for what it was, a great learning experience, and it was the start of a personal journey that changed and focused my life. The school helped mold me into who I am now, through what it did to my mind as much as what it did to my body. I have added to that learning throughout the years that have passed since I graduated.

A lesson that Ranger School taught through constant application is attention to detail. My first direct-fire plan was satisfactory in my eyes, but Captain Rose, one of the RIs in the desert, sat there and made me go through where every rifle was shooting. I wanted to think myself competent in a simple direct-fire plan, something we did numerous times in IOBC, but I found out I was nowhere near the standard. After answering each of his questions, I was sure that I had gone into enough detail and was prepared for the end of my instruction, but Captain Rose kept probing deeper into my plan. "What is his sector?" He pointed to a position on the drawing. "Don't give me a finger wave and say, 'Here is the kill zone.' You come up with a plan. What are your engagement and disengagement criteria for the different weapon systems? How are you going to make all of this work together?" It was a mental exercise to see the battle unfold and determine where each person should focus. I had to develop the attention to detail to take apart every piece of a plan and figure out how it worked in the bigger picture, as opposed to the simplistic, "These guys will all fire into the kill zone. They'll lay down fire and stop when the enemy is dead."

As a leader it was important to determine down to the gnat's ass detail what I was looking for. At the time, I did not appreciate Captain Rose's guidance for what it was, a great education.

Five Senses

There were some great thinking opportunities in Ranger School. In the desert, because of the daytime heat, we began our movements as the sun set and finished them as the sun was coming up. Their modus operandi was, "Okay, see that objective? When the sun sets, we are going to start walking and you'll get there tomorrow morning and attack." We shouldered our gear and moved out for a cold all-night march to the objective. There was no need to use a circuitous route. It was the desert; there were no obstacles, so in a straight line we went into the darkness. For hours we walked with no change in scenery; then I began to sense that the sky was lightening up and the stars were disappearing. Almost as a surprise, I saw the top edge of the sun rise to my right side. I was absolutely floored by how beautiful it was. I saw that sunrise in the desert and it was almost like I had never seen one before.

It was a beautiful sunrise in the perfectly clear, blue sky. A number of reasons made it exceptional. It was the first non–green, brown, or black thing I saw after a long night of walking, and it filled the scene around me with shimmerings and gold reflections. All of a sudden there was activity for my brain to be involved in. The cold of the long night began to give way and as the sun crested I instantly experienced a sense of relief. I could almost feel each ultraviolet ray strike my face and body to add a little more heat, making me that much more appreciative of that moment. It also signaled that we were almost getting somewhere in our patrol if our navigation had not been too screwed up. The end of a patrol was nothing more than the start of another one, but it was a mental boost knowing it was one more patrol we would never have to do again. I was a part of that sunrise with all of my senses, making it very special.

Our olfactory senses were deadened to the smells of the pine forest, damp uniforms, and plastic canteen water, but supersensitive to any hint of something different. These smells were equal to constantly seeing gray, tan, and pastel green: nothing zestful about them. By the time we got to the mountains, if someone opened a peanut butter packet anywhere in the patrol base, everyone could smell it, almost taste it. Having that level of observation was odd. In the desert with the wind blowing, you could smell what the guy on the other side of the patrol base was eating. I imagine it is similar to the enhanced sense of smell for a blind person. The RIs were adept with their noses also, and that was why it was dangerous to eat while on patrol, even crackers. An open package could set off alarms.

I will most likely be too busy for the rest of my life to really see a tree the way I did in Florida. I had spent forever on perimeter security lying there next to that tree. I began to study and really see every aspect of it. I do not know if it was a mind game to stay awake, but I saw the detail of the bark, how the pine needles came out of it, and where the pinecones were on the tree. I saw the branches and the pine needles. I saw the colors of pine and how the roots disappeared under the ground and reemerged a little farther away. It was like I was stopped in a traffic jam on the highway, sitting on the blacktop and able to see the texture of the road, the tar patches, and where the asphalt met the grass of the median. How strange an insight to *really* see something I passed every day.

After the last patrol in Florida, we marched back to the billets to prepare for movement to the desert phase. We tramped over the soft sand the same way we had for the previous 12 days, getting ever closer to sleeping on a mattress. The building came into sight through the trees and everyone's spirits rose. The pace picked up a little and we moved into the area near the building.

Something felt weird, and as I walked I looked at my feet. "Something feels strange about my feet," I thought. Still looking down I realized I was standing on asphalt and my feet could actually feel the difference. I had walked for 99 percent of my life and never really thought about it, and now I was feeling the difference. The way my boots settled into the ground felt different. My feet expected the slight give from the sand but got none. Out of habit, my body continued to compensate for the give of the sand, which threw my balance off slightly and gave me the enhanced sensation of the walking surface.

I had gone to school out West for a while and I did not like the wind. It was aggravating when I lived in New Mexico, but in Dugway the constant gentle breeze was welcome. We had camouflage on our exposed skin, which was like adding another layer of clothes to our faces and hands, and which was particularly uncomfortable in the heat of the desert. The wind blew just enough to keep us cool. Like the heat of the sun in the early morning, the whips of the wind on our faces and hands were refreshing and invigorating.

Positioning

At graduation I had feelings of disbelief and euphoria that it was over. I had difficulty accepting that I had been successful—probably because I had seen it as a bar too high, so I could have emotionally justified it if I did not succeed. I thought, "Oh, shit, now what?" Ranger School was a kind of veil that shielded my vision from anything beyond its accomplishment. Once I was done, I had to get on with the rest of my life, continue to operate as an officer. A couple of weeks later, I left for a year in Korea. I did not set another goal right away. I just got on the plane and went to Korea, wanting to put Ranger School behind me for a while and see how I could apply my new skills.

I believe that the people who tend to go and put up with that experience are quality people to begin with; however, I know that my standards for personal performance and responsibility are now higher. The true Rangers sign up for the long haul—not just the tab, but a life in pursuit of higher achievement. Here is the question: "Is the guy squared away because he has a Ranger tab, or is he a squared-away guy who went and got a Ranger tab?" You cannot say that a person is topnotch because of the Ranger tab, even though it is a pretty sure bet; every person has to live it out by displaying the Ranger characteristics every day.

Having Ranger School under my belt significantly influenced a couple of my assignments within the infantry. There were places that were not hiring nonRangers: "Sorry, you don't have a Ranger tab. We don't have a position for you."

A Ranger School classmate of mine reported to his unit, a light infantry battalion in Korea. He walked into the S-1's office with two other second lieutenants to set up an appointment to see the commander. The S-1 was an infantry captain who looked severely out of place behind a desk. Like many infantry soldiers, he belonged behind a tree, not a stack of papers. The first thing the captain did was look to see which of them had a Ranger tab. He told the two tabbed guys, "You two grab a seat over there. I'll get you in to see the commander." He looked at the third (non–Ranger qualified) lieutenant and told him to stand fast.

He then went into the commander's office next door. A few minutes later he returned. "Okay, you two get back here in an hour." Then, without saying a word to the lieutenant standing in front of his desk, he picked up and dialed the phone. Speaking into the phone he said, "Captain Brown, this is Captain Layman. What's going on?" He paused. "Listen, there's been a mistake. I've got Lieutenant Peanut here for an assignment as a platoon leader, but he isn't tabbed out." After completing the conversation, the captain sent the lieutenant back to the brigade headquarters, where he was reassigned into a slot for nonRangers.

I believe institutional discrimination like that is unfair. I will admit that I am a Ranger by the grace of God. How I got through there, whether it was because of a guardian angel or my stars were in alignment, I do not know, but I will sign up for all that shit and acknowledge it wasn't all my effort. There was some luck and perhaps some supernatural help. I know there were some great guys who were denied opportunities because there is an overwhelming prejudice against nonRangers in the infantry.

From Korea I went to the Joint Readiness Training Center (JRTC), and being an Airborne Ranger got me into the opposing force (OPFOR) battalion. It was like going to the amusement park as a kid and having to stand against the pole to see if I was tall enough to ride the roller coaster. I always made it, but there were others who were not tall enough and were denied the experience. My assignment as a platoon leader there, probably more than Ranger School, gave me great experiences to apply in both my personal and military life. Had I been part of the normal JRTC cadre I would not have learned the leadership lessons to the same degree.

There was a unique set of circumstances in that unit. Organizations sometimes build and reach an operational plateau where they work with total efficiency. Our unit may not have been at its absolute peak, but it was pretty close. The commander, the people, the mission, the location, time, and climate all worked together to make it a phenomenal experience.

As a platoon leader in the OPFOR battalion I was given responsibilities above those of my contemporaries in other units. In a normal unit I was expected to simply control 40 infantrymen in the woods and leave all of the combined arms coordination and synchronization to the company commander. At the JRTC, I had an air defender, a mortar platoon section, and sometimes an electronic warfare section to support and utilize along with the infantry soldiers. I had the opportunity as a know-nothing platoon leader to organize and see how all of these elements worked together.

I had a little extra fun in that assignment because of one of the soldiers assigned to the unit. I was sitting at my desk at JRTC when a sergeant strolled into the office and asked, "Hey sir, do you know where the first sergeant's office is?" He had obviously just found the first open office door in the building and asked for directions instead of taking the time to check the signs on the doors.

I looked up at an E-5 in BDUs whose face held an expression of anticipation. There was a hint of familiarity in his voice and face, but it took me a minute to realize it was Bill Kearns. He was an specialist stationed in Alaska when he went through Ranger School, where we had been buddies.

I questioned, "Kearns? Bill Kearns?"

He responded, "Scott?" It was not "Lieutenant Sharp" or "Sir" but an instant flashback to our days in the field together.

We got caught up briefly, and I walked him down the hall. We walked into the first sergeant's office, where the very orthodox, strait-laced First Sergeant Stiles sat. "This is my Ranger buddy, Bill Kearns," I crowed to the first sergeant.

He gave me a strange look. "Is that right?"

Kearns said, "Yeah, Scott and I were Ranger buddies."

In a very dignified way, without being cold or callous, First Sergeant Stiles said, "Well, that's wonderful. You guys can go outside and drink a beer later." Then, looking at me, he said, "You are a lieutenant." Then he looked at Kearns. "And you're a Sergeant. Are there are any questions about that?"

Kearns ended up assigned to my platoon and was one of my squad leaders for about a year before he got to take over a platoon as a junior staff sergeant. We had a great relationship and fun in our time together. I would give an OPORD with an innovative plan and say, "It'll work," and look over to him and see him roll his eyes and say, "Okay, another brilliant idea." Kearns knew me before I was the great Lieutenant Sharp.

He helped me out a lot in those times when the battalion commander wanted me to put a squad somewhere difficult or under a time crunch; I had somebody I could turn to. I'd confidently tell the commander, "Sir, I know Kearns can do it."

"Oh, yeah?" the commander would question. "What makes you so sure?"

"Sir," I would respond, "he was my Ranger buddy. I've seen about every inch of this guy's body. I know how he thinks and how he works. He won't fail."

Ranger Sharp's Walk

Are you scared yet? Scott Sharp certainly was, as was the ADA captain sewing cat eyes at the beginning of the course. At the beginning of an obviously difficult journey, there is much to fear or imagine you fear. The last thing Scott was afraid of turned out to be the most unsettling of all, people's capacity for violence. He learned that this capacity has to be kept in check by conscientious, dutiful leaders.

The easy definition of duty is doing the right thing at the right time without being told to do it. A major part of the fear of leadership rests in the expectation that you will do your duty. Leaders are trailblazers. They are the ones responsible for cutting paths through the jungle and will be held accountable for every vine, tree, and flower they clear away in the process. They are the ones responsible for knowing what the right thing is, when to do it, and then doing it properly. That means that they will also be held accountable if the path leads them off a cliff. It's not just lonely at the top, it's lonely at the front; but that's where you want to be.

This pursuit demands crazy things of you and not everyone understands this willingness to leave your comfort zone. Take special note: People in your own profession won't understand this, even people who work at the next desk over. As you can see from the captain and general who approached Scott after his parachute entanglement, their perspective of Scott's reality was flawed. If you are doing the right things, people will look at you differently, and most likely with respect (if not respect, then jealousy and envy).

Is it possible to envy someone whose boots are squirting blood out of the sides with each step? Absolutely. For some of you this makes sense without further explanation. You are getting it! We should envy people who are in the fight, people who are testing themselves and overcoming pain and anguish to see success. We should envy people who are pushing past their physical and mental limits to achieve greatness. These are the people who fill history books and through their extra efforts have changed the way we live today. We can't help but envy and respect those people. Then in our capacity, exactly where we are today, we can decide to become one of those leaders.

As a leader, you will inspire people with your actions! When you are expecting more of yourself in your daily life, people will respond and begin to live up to the example you are setting. This isn't a leadership pill, but you will see results in less than a week.

In this great leadership battle, you have to go as far as you have to. How far is that? Until you're done. This is a fitting lesson for the final chapter, the story of Steve Adams.

 RANGERS

are

DETERMINED

STEVE ADAMS

Fortunately, the young man's mind protected him through abandonment before his body ceased to operate. Clinging to a mossy tree trunk, sitting in cold swamp water, alone in every way, his blood became too cold to pump. Through circumstances beyond his control he was put into survival conditions his body capitulated to. There were others in the swamp that night, like Second Lieutenant Steve Adams, who survived.

The drive to outlast difficult circumstances and reach your goal comes in different intensities. The struggle for life in the midst of death is the most intense level. The closer you can come to that level of intensity, the more certain you are to reach your goal. Most people relate to a life-and-death situation like they do to sixteenth-century Mongolian art—completely unfamiliar; however, Steve and 67 other students in his Ranger class found themselves in just such a situation in the wintry Florida swamp in 1995. Through his thoughts and actions as he struggled and lived you can become more familiar with true intensity and translate them to your struggle for life.

West Point to Ranger School

My mentality has always been that I wanted to do something that was a challenge, something that was harder than the norm. I have always wanted to be where the action is, to set myself apart. Looking to my career as an Army officer I sought those challenges that would set me apart in that profession. Ranger School was held in high esteem by the people I associated with at West Point, and the Ranger tab was something that people respected and talked about. Most of the cadences we called during runs or marches invoked Ranger themes, and many of our professors were Ranger qualified. Over those four years I learned that Ranger School was the challenge I was seeking. It was something I had to do, to prove to myself that I could.

One of my sophomore roommates, Rob Glover, had been enlisted in the Third Ranger Battalion. In our room, after turning out the lights, he talked about life in the Ranger Battalion and in Ranger School. I lay in my bunk getting mental pictures of his stories and I started to build my understanding of the days at Ranger School. I respected Rob, and he passed along a lot of good insight into the Rangers and their beliefs. He was a psychology major so he always twisted it at the end, challenging me: "Oh, it's really hard—you probably wouldn't want to do it." I lay there steaming that anyone would think I could not do something just because it was hard. Still, I had to wait three more years to prove myself, which was frustrating in itself. My desire germinated from that small beginning before snowballing into a huge desire by the time I graduated in 1994.

One of the things that excited me was that most people did not have a Ranger tab. I knew it was not a school that modified its standards to let everyone pass, so I always looked at someone with a Ranger tab with a much higher degree of initial respect. You don't know what the person is really like, but a Ranger tab tells you a little bit about him even if you don't know the details. It was a group of people I wanted to be a part of. In addition to what others would think of me, I wanted to set myself apart for myself. I wanted to do it so I could look myself in the mirror and be proud that I was a Ranger when most people were not.

Prep

At the Armor Officer Basic Course (AOBC) at Fort Knox, Kentucky, right after graduation from West Point, my first goal was to win a slot to Ranger School. Part of that process included participation in a special Ranger physical training program during the four-month course. We got up earlier and worked harder than the rest of the AOBC class performing regular PT.

Early mornings in Kentucky were peaceful as they are at most places, but when the first morning exercise was to wipe up the dew off of the grass with our backs, there were other places we would rather be. During the PT we busted our tails running and doing calisthenics, and once a week we would put on our rucksacks and do a road march. Once in a while the instructors would check our fitness levels by giving us the Ranger PT, swim, and five-mile run tests.

The strength and stamina part of our preparation was thorough, but despite my desires I did not get any light infantry training. We were so focused on the physical aspect that the basic tactics involved in leading a patrol were missed. West Point did a great job of teaching us some of the most basic of basic infantry skills like marksmanship and three- to five-second rushes. It also hit on the other end of the infantry spectrum with instruction on Napoleon's campaigns; however, despite that and some academic work in small unit tactics, the practical application piece was missing. The other weakness in my education was the lack of knowledge about what Ranger School was going to look like. Going into Ranger School I had a very weak concept of how it was run, how they graded, and what I had to do to be a success in each phase. Fortunately, I was ready and willing to learn.

Beyond the physical and academic aspect, I prepared myself mentally. I kept telling myself, "I'll give it my all. I'll do my best and I won't quit." I figured it was only 61 days; how bad could it be? I looked around and saw other people who had their Ranger tabs and thought, "Well, this guy can't be that much better than I am. If he can do it, I can do it." I knew I could go down there, stick it out for 61 days, be a success, and get on home.

Ask Forgiveness, Not Permission

I faced a political obstacle just before leaving for Ranger School that resulted in a tense reception at my first unit.

When I first got to my battalion after graduating from Ranger School, the S-1 gave me the attitude that I had wasted my time going to Ranger School. The S-1 position is a glorified secretary to the battalion commander, and this guy was a captain with an obvious lack of appreciation for how common platoon leader time was in comparison to the opportunity I had just taken advantage of. He sat across the desk from me in cocky authority and tried to impress me with his shiny bars. "We had a job for you here," he temperamentally stated. "We didn't even know you were going to Ranger School!"

I had kept my new battalion in the dark on purpose. A friend of mine, who was also going to Ranger School and then to Fort Carson, called to the battalion and said he was thinking about going to Airborne School. He got the reply, "Nope, we've got a job for you. We need you to get out here as soon as possible."

He passed this on to me: "They don't want us going to any schools."

I said, "Well, I guess I'm not going to call them, because I'm going to Ranger School. By the way, when you get out there, tell them where I'm at." And that was where I went.

PT Test

When I arrived at Ranger School I knew one of the first tests would be the PT test. The Ranger PT test had a standard a little higher than the normal Army standard, augmented by the uniquely Ranger way they administered it. At the push-up site each Ranger performs the exercise, watched over by an RI. The RI squats to his side to make sure he goes down far enough or to whatever point that RI deems is necessary to get credit for that repetition. I was very anxious about the test because they did not count our repetitions out loud. They counted to themselves and did not tell you if you had met the standard until you were done, sitting exhausted after two minutes of all-out push-ups or sit-ups.

I did not feel like I had good control over my success. I saw a lot of my friends, guys I knew were stellar PT performers, get pulled off to the side and removed from the course and recycled right off the bat. I knew the PT test was one of the filters the RIs used to pare down the class to a manageable size, and sometimes it did not matter how physically fit you were. I was getting stressed out because that could be me when my turn came. This was what Ranger School was all about, stepping up to be tested and giving it your best shot. I did step up and I did pass.

One of the next events we had to pass was the five-mile run test. We had to run five miles in 40 minutes, finishing in formation. The idea of finishing in formation was important because falling out in a Ranger School run is different from anywhere else. If you fell a step and a half behind the man in front of you, you were pulled out and recycled.

For a solid hour before we took the test, they had us doing exercises in the mud. We jumped around, rolled left, rolled right, low crawled, and did push-ups, sit-ups, and anything the RIs could think of in the soggy mud before we took the test. After finishing the warm-up, we stood in formation, completely drenched, covered with mud, and tired. We looked like melting fudge bars by the time we got done.

On the run was where we lost one of the three guys I came down there with from Fort Knox. He must have fallen back or been behind someone who fell back. Either way, by the time we made it back to the barracks, his stuff was already pulled out of the wall locker and he was gone.

We lost the second guy at the end of the first week when we did a 17-mile road march. We did an airborne jump into a drop zone, moved to our start point, and began the road march. It was at a screaming pace through the woods, lots of weight on our backs, and carrying our weapons: M16s, M60 machine guns, and squad automatic weapons (SAWs). We did not know where we were going or how long it would take. All we knew was that we were going on a road march, to follow the person in front of us, and if we fell back more than a couple of meters, they were going to pull us out. All of the weapons had to finish the march. So, as people started falling out, the rest of us had to take their machine guns and SAWs in addition to our own weapons.

A deuce-and-half truck followed along behind us, a bullhorn calling out the names of the people who fell out. I believe that the major purpose was to dishearten us, to see what we were made of, to see if we were going to quit because one of our friends quit. The bullhorn blurted, "Matt Branson just quit. He's comfortable now, riding in the back of the truck. His legs aren't burning and he has plenty of water to drink. He is on his way to see Momma at home, get some good cookin'. No one is going to give you a hard time if this isn't for you; it isn't for everyone."

Psychologically it starts working on your mind. "Well, he didn't make it and everybody knows he's a good guy, so it's okay if I don't make it. We can both go home together." The bullhorn would say, "You want to quit? Quit. No one is keeping you here." We had a lot of the RIs throughout asking people to quit, especially when it really sucked, when we were getting rained on and were down in the dumps.

In one case, an RI walked out of a warm building at Camp Darby. I could tell he was comfortable and dry, while I was shivering, soaked to the bone, and standing in the mud. He bellowed, "I've got jelly doughnuts, hot coffee. Jelly doughnuts and hot coffee—anybody want to quit? It's right in there." He motioned with a tilt of his head. "Help yourselves." I never saw anyone take RIs up on it when they did things like that, but it did remind us of where we were and that it was really not a good situation. They wanted to remind us of all the good things that we were missing and that were waiting for us when we got out.

The Worm Pit

In Ranger School's world of misery, it takes extreme torture to stand out as a memory; the worm pit qualified easily. The worm pit is a miniature obstacle course incorporating water of differing depths, but a common freezing temperature, at every station. The worm pit came for us on an extremely wintry November day. Underneath, the obstacle was filled with water and mud, and on that morning, there was a thin layer of ice over the top of it. We were thinking, "Oh my gosh, we've got to get out and crawl around in that stuff!?" Imagining how cold it was going to be, I had to get myself psyched up. I knew that I was going to have to take the plunge. It was going to be like stepping off the 15-meter diving platform, feeling my heart race to my throat as I fell, and then slamming into the pool; there was no going back.

I was trying to get myself prepared, as I was in one of the first groups to go. The march to the pit had started. The man in front of me dropped from the pull-up bar, took a step forward, and stood waiting for his turn to run into the pit. I jumped up and grabbed the freezing bar with my bare hands. I could see the people in front of me starting the water portion of the course. It was getting closer. I did my pull-ups, dropped to the ground, took a step forward, and waited. My heart raced because there was nothing but a short space of time between me and misery.

The moment of terror was approaching, and my mind was no easier about it. I continued to psych myself up and then they gave us the signal to start. I took off running, telling myself, "I am ready!" I dove underneath the wire, broke the remaining ice covering the water, and landed in the freezing water. It instantly took my breath away. "Oh shit, I can't breathe. Keep moving." It completely sucked the oxygen out of my lungs. It took me a good 15 feet of low crawling to start breathing again. My world had shrunk to the size of my freezing body. The thought that anyone else existed in the world was unfathomable. I came up out of the low crawl shivering from the cold water and air.

We went across the monkey bars, feet swinging above the water. It was only about three feet deep, but I did not want to get any more wet. Then on the other side I dropped, looking at a giant log ladder. My hands were already starting to get numb, and I did not have good flexibility in my fingers. There was no time to think. I prepared to climb up this huge ladder where logs were the rungs, and they got progressively further apart as it went higher.

So I found myself, soaking wet, without good control of my fingers and hands, climbing up this ladder. I stepped on one rung, grabbed the next one with both hands, got up on top of it and pulled myself up to the next. The logs were already slippery from the other Rangers who had gone before me. The rungs started at waist level, easy to roll onto, and increased in space to face level at the top, which required me to hang with my weight supported by freezing hands clinging to wet logs. It was times like this, 30 feet up, that I knew what I was doing was dangerous. If I slipped, I could kill myself. But I saw the other people making it, and I went ahead.

This was where I saw my first person become a cold-weather casualty. It happened out of the blue, in the midst of the obstacle course. Standing there, he lost control of his body. He was on the verge of hypothermia. A couple of RIs got him out of the cold and provided treatment while the others kept the pressure on us: "Get your face down!" There, in the first week, his Ranger School days ended.

I continued through the course, pushed on by the yelling of the RIs and an intense desire to get myself into the better physical conditions that awaited me in the barracks. It was scary that in a short five days I came to look at the barracks as a relatively nice place to be.

Water Training

During the winter, there was no escaping the cold. We were uncomfortable every step of the way. In the mountains, it snowed on us. In the desert, the wind and freezing temperatures kept us cold, and in Florida we were always wet. Throughout the course we had people getting minor cold-weather injuries. Then we got to Florida, where we had a major incident and four of my fellow students died of hypothermia.

In the initial portion of the Florida phase we stayed out of the swamps, supposedly to maintain a certain level of dryness while we learned to operate in a swamp environment. However, fate being what it was, it rained on us every day. One of those days we learned how to work with the Zodiacs, river boats similar to the craft used on white-water rafting trips. We did all of this practice on dry land next to the slough that would act as the host for our next level of drill. We practiced rowing techniques and how to turn the boat back over if it capsized. We also practiced doing river crossings by constructing one- and two-rope bridges. These were as simple as securing one rope to either side of the deep water about a foot above the surface. To move across, we hooked our gear onto the rope with a D ring and pulled both ourselves and our gear to the other side using the rope.

The ground dropped into the slough like the side of an in-ground pool. We feared the inevitable dunking we were all going to take into that dark but calm icy water. We knew that by regulation the water had to be 50 degrees for us to get into it. The RIs messed with us all day long. In the morning they were saying, "It's 48 degrees." As the day went on, they said the temperature was 49, then 49.5 degrees; and an hour before we were supposed to get into the water they yelled, "Forty-nine point nine." Our hopes remained silent as the day progressed and we continued the training. When the RIs' radio squawked, usually too low or the words too unintelligible for us to make out, all of us quieted down in hopes it was a message from that unknown Ranger boss, saying we would not have to go into the water. But the time did come, and as expected, "Fifty point zero zero," came the almost gleeful RI announcement. This whole morning was tailor-made for toying with the students, and the RIs had played the game perfectly.

We looked at each other somberly. Now the only question was "How soon do I get wet?"

I did not know what the temperature was; all I knew was that it was cold. I had a feeling that even if it was not 50 degrees we were still going to get into the water. That mentality was the standard in Ranger School. We would get into the water, train, get out, and everything would be fine—simply a little more suffering where we expected it. Indeed, it was cold; we did the training, suffered, and lived to go on to the swamp-patrolling portion of Florida.

Only Two Ways Out, and Neither Is Good

It had been raining every single day prior to our first day of the swamp portion, making the water level extremely high. It was early afternoon. We paddled down the river, 12 of us to a boat, five straddling each side, a coxswain in the back, and an air-guard up front. We were so packed in we looked like an oval flowerpot full of broccoli floating down the river. Our gear was in the center of the boat, soaking up the water from the bottom of the boat and getting heavier by the minute. My foot on the outside of the boat slipped into the cold water and soon became numb, and my butt went to sleep from lack of movement and blood. Navigating down the river was difficult. The only way we could tell the difference between the river and the rest of the swamp was by the distance between the trees. It was a flooded forest all around us.

As we neared our debarking site, the RI looked for a relatively shallow place to get off into the swamp. The first time we stopped, the RI dunked his six-foot walking stick over the edge and unsuccessfully tried to touch the bottom. We were thinking, "Crap, how are we going to do this?" Understanding the Ranger mentality, "Nothing sucks enough," we expected the worst, and everyone was dreading having to get into the water. We finally got word that if we went down the river further there should be a place where we could get off and continue our mission.

There were three companies, Alpha, Bravo, and Charlie, moving on the river that day. I was in Bravo. Alpha company went much farther down the river than we did and got off of their boats right onto dry land and continued their mission. They did not have any problems that day as opposed to Bravo and Charlie companies, which got off within a few hundred meters of each other.

When we first debarked, the water was only knee-deep. We tied the Zodiac to a tree and one by one jumped into the water. The cold almost buckled my knees when I slid out of the boat. I shouldered my pack, adjusted my gear, and prepared to wade away. We started to move into the swamp toward the elusive dry land we knew was on the far side. However, within a hundred meters the water was already up to my belly and then up to mid-chest. As the water slowly crept up my torso each inch higher meant a new level of discomfort.

Looking at the surface of the water from that low angle was not normal. It was like being in a swimming pool without being able to see the bottom. I am about six feet tall and the water was chest-deep on me, but there were others who were already struggling to keep their chins above water. I knew we were supposed to be in the swamp for 700 to 800 meters, so I wondered how deep it was going to get before we started to ascend.

Even as the water got deeper and I felt more and more miserable, I still thought that this was what everybody goes through. "It's no big deal. It's still early in the operation," I rationalized. Then we got to a place where the water level was well over our heads and it seemed we had hit another river. We stood there on the side, water about hip to mid-chest level, while the leadership of the patrol gathered and then determined that we had to construct a rope bridge in order to cross this portion.

Unfortunately, we were not planning on doing a river crossing and were not well prepared to do one. It had been briefed that we would move through the swamp, get no more than chest-deep, and then keep going on to dry land. Because of our expectations, people had packed their ropes and other necessary equipment lower in their rucksacks, making it difficult to find and pull out. It was like looking for the pair of black socks in the bottom of your stuffed suitcase without taking out any clothes. After that struggle, we got started building the bridge.

Before the bridge was constructed, we had our first casualty. It was a Marine Corps soldier who was standing not more that 10 feet away from me. One of the other students had noticed that he was looking disconnected and came over to him and asked, "Hey, man, are you all right?" He did not respond. The RI came over, began asking questions, and he still could not respond; he physically could not say anything. He had a blank stare on his face like he knew he was in trouble but he could not do anything about it. I saw a tear come out of his eye, but he could not speak.

Right then I knew that this might not be the norm. I thought, "Maybe this *is* as bad as I think it is." The RI called for a medevac. Medevac is short for medical evacuation. In our location it meant that a helicopter with a medic on board would come to extract the soldier and take him to the hospital. Meanwhile the rope bridge continued to be constructed.

Everyone was susceptible. None of us had eaten well or had much sleep, and we were probably a little bit dehydrated. It was in this weakened condition that we found ourselves all of a sudden stopped in frigid water for an extended period of time.

We could not work any faster than we were because building a rope bridge was a slow project by nature. It was not a matter of sprinting or talking faster. It was a job made methodical by the cold, the water, and our weariness; try running in a pool. Unfortunately, going forward was our only escape route. The boats that had brought us down had already been policed up and taken away.

It took a long time for the medevac to get there, and by the time it arrived, we already had the bridge constructed and at least a squad-sized element, seven men, across. While we worked and waited, there were four or five more hypothermia casualties. My Ranger buddy, a normally stoic person, started getting a thousand-yard stare in his eyes, which scared me because we had worked together quite a bit, and if it could happen to him, I knew I was in danger. His hands were numb, so I tied his knots for him and helped him across the rope bridge, like helping an old lady across the street. From then on we kept talking to each other to make sure the other was doing all right. I just made sure we had contact and kept moving. He was a concern early on, but once we got moving he never really hit the point where he was going to give up.

The use of a jungle penetrator made the rescue effort a slow one. The jungle penetrator allowed the helicopter to hover above the treetops and still pull people up from the ground. It was, in essence, a seat connected to a metal cable lowered by motor through the canopy of the trees to the ground. Once somebody was strapped into it, the seat was lifted to the side of the helicopter. They could bring up only one casualty at a time until the helicopter was full.

While the evacuation was going on, people continued to move across the rope bridge. Two different companies, about 70 people total, were in the same situation, and only one bird was flying to evacuate people from both of them. For each company it turned into a highway traffic jam caused by all the lanes being closed except one, the rope bridge.

Our concern and concentration on the real-world situation made the time fly by. We tried to treat the casualties, get them to a place to minimize the amount of water they were in, and keep them coherent so they did not collapse and fall under the water. Our patrol was completely administrative at that point. It became an issue of survival, no longer a tactical mission. Everybody realized that this was not normal. This was not just another hard day at Ranger School. This was a complete foul-up in the plan, and things were bad. Our focus became trying to get everyone out alive.

The RIs took control of the operation. Two or three stayed with the group being evacuated to help them, and the rest took groups of Rangers and went across the rope bridge and forward into the swamp.

Survival

Everyone was helping everyone else, trying to make sure we were all around for the next day. We were trying to keep people moving and continuing on toward dry land. We knew if someone was stationary he was much more prone to hypothermia. If someone became a casualty, we kept another person with him and tried to get him evacuated. The movement was very slow, and we soon would lose the benefit of daylight. In the winter the sun set early, and under the canopy of the forest it would get dark quickly once the sun went down.

By six o'clock we had been in the water for about four hours. It was getting dark, and we still had to get to dry land. We were swimming from tree to tree, at points literally sidestroking to the next tree. At each stop I held onto the tree, looked to my front, and looked to my rear to make sure I always had eyes on both people. Then I helped the guy behind me if I had to, pulling him from his swim up to my tree. To continue moving I plunged forward and reached out my hand for the guy in front to pull me up to his tree. We could not rest. We were going to make it or go to sleep at the wheel of a speeding car. The setting of the sun felt like the falling of a guillotine. Once it got dark, I was focused on the guy in front of and the guy behind me, to make sure they were continuing to move. Some of our hope sank with the sun, and I can only imagine what it was like for those pushed to the point of capitulation that night.

Some guys tried to stop, even though they knew they could die there. They got to a strong root on a tree where they could get out of the water up to their knees, held on to the tree, and would not move. Their bodies were shutting down, losing touch with reality. The coherent Rangers yelled and screamed at them, "Keep your ass moving! You will not stop here, Ranger!" We yelled every obscenity, punched, pulled, and desperately forced them to keep moving. Some of the students did mouth-to-mouth and buddy aid on the guys who had stopped breathing, trying to keep them alive long enough to get rescued. The people who stopped like that, even for a short time, were part of the accountability challenge that night.

Complete squad integrity was impossible as guys started going down. As they stopped, we could not keep our whole squad there with them without endangering the entire group. There were others who were taking care of these casualties, calling on the radio to get medevacs arranged. When someone in the middle of the column became completely exhausted, he was no good to the person behind him so he broke off from the squad and continued to move, only more slowly, teamed up with another person or on his own. This caused a lot of breaks in contact within the squads. Instead of one contiguous squad, we would now have two or more groups of guys going on their own.

Three of the four guys who died were waiting to be evacuated. I do not know their exact locations, but I know they were spread out at different points along the route to dry land. The lack of command and control was devastating to individual confidence, especially for us. We were not a well trained unit by any measure. In our situation people drew confidence and strength from each other. Whether the motivation was "I've got to be strong to help this other person" or "I can't quit and look like a loser in this guy's eyes," it worked, and it was available for those who had a buddy or two but not those who were alone.

We were in a lose-lose situation. The loss of accountability came about as a result of the RIs' decision to get as many people moving out of the swamp as soon as possible. However, if we had all stayed back trying to medevac people, we would have had a heck of a lot more casualties. It was the right decision to make. Unfortunately, splitting up the company severely reduced the command and control. When faced with a no-win situation, the RIs had to act. The lack of a decision would have had worse results. It is disgusting when you talk about a military operation becoming utterly disorganized, but that was what happened.

While it was happening, I did not think about a whole lot except getting out of there and surviving. I thought, "Hey, this is not my time. I've got too much to lose. I've got a wife and son at home. This is not the time for me, and I am going to make it out." Once I realized how bad the situation was, way back at the rope bridge, internally I got really fired up and scared at the same time. It was a matter of "Hey, let's pull together and get it going." I started getting excited—not happy, but excited. I got totally into the situation, focused on myself and the people around me, and making sure that everybody I could help would make it out.

My squad of eight guys made it to dry land first. I was relieved to see my confidence rewarded in reality. I did not doubt that I would make it, but nevertheless I was happy to be done. We walked up on top of the hill and dropped our gear. Our attention immediately turned to those still struggling.

We tried to signal by making a fire, using our flashlights, and banging our canteen cups together, to say, "Hey, we made it to dry land. This is the way to come." The RIs started shooting parachute flares every minute or so. Then, for hours and hours, we watched individuals and pairs of people come out of the swamp. It was not every man for himself, but there were many small groups of people moving at their own speed and direction trying to somehow get out of the swamp. Finally we stopped seeing anyone else emerge, and though we heard yelling in the far distance, we could not tell where it was coming from or what they were saying.

That day my situation was not as bad as what some of the others experienced. I wish I could have done more, but it was almost impossible. Under the cover of darkness, in our own critical condition, and with the lack of proper equipment, we were all in the same boat. When you were in the water, you hurt no matter who you were. Once we made it out of the water and started to warm back up, we wanted to go back in and somehow help, but that would have been a foolish thing for us to do, and it was fortunate that our RI was thinking more clearly than we were.

I do not know why I did not get hypothermia; maybe I did. I know I was affected by the extreme conditions, but I had an internal flame that would not let me lose focus once I saw how badly others were physically reacting. I knew someone had to lead them out. It was not until the next morning that we were informed that four men had died. That news and learning who they were crushed me emotionally. One guy had been in my squad, and I had gone to school with two of them. Three of the guys who died were from Bravo company, my company, and in whose shoes I could have very easily been.

Ranger School is the protector of a special mentality that says, "Nothing is too hard." That is part of what makes the school special and makes the graduates special. This was an unfortunate incident that came about because of a series of common decisions based on wrong assumptions. It goes back to the temperature decision. It was 50 degrees whether it was or not. The water in the swamp that day was not too deep because nothing was too deep. You have to have that mentality, but it must be tempered with prudence—"When am I being hard and when am I being stupid."

This tragedy on February 15, 1995, was the worst accident in the 44-year history of Ranger School. The soldiers who died that day were Captain Milton Palmer, 27, of Fishers, Indiana; Second Lieutenant Spencer Dodge, 25, of Stanley, New York; Second Lieutenant Curtis Sansoucie, 23, of Rochester, New Hampshire; and Sergeant Norman Tillman, 28, of Grenada, Mississippi. An article written about the incident said, "They would learn a lesson usually imparted to young warriors in combat: that they who in their youth and strength think themselves immortal are frail and mortal after all." (Philip Caputo, "The Black Badge of Courage," *Esquire*, September 1995, page 98.)

Drive and the Proper Example

That day I did not give the thought of quitting a chance to enter my mind. I was focused on survival and that alone. There was no room for fantasies. There could be no question in my mind of my imminent success; otherwise I would have quit. In that situation I was doing my best to pull people through, and I could not do that with a whimper. The biggest leadership lesson I learned was that it is crucial to set the example. It was hard to motivate people when things were so bad. If I was not motivated and I was not doing the things that needed to be done, there was absolutely no hope, not even a prayer, that the other people were going to be motivated. As a leader you have to be Johnny-on-the-spot, and if you are not, nobody else is going to be.

I learned about myself that I am mentally tough, that I am not a quitter, and that I can rise to the occasion. When things were at their worst was when I seemed to do better. I started off with pretty good peer evaluations, even though I did not have any close buddies in my squad. My ratings were not a result of friends squaring me away. With every passing phase my peer evaluations went higher and higher, and at the last phase they were well up in the 90th percentile. I attribute that to being able to excel in stressful situations.

I learned how important the mental aspect is to success; it controls everything. Everybody, as far as I know, goes down to Fort Benning in great shape. Within a very short amount of time nobody is in very good shape due to excessive exercise and the deprivation of food and sleep. Once the formal physical exercise of PT, hand-to-hand combat, and bayonet drills was over, the course was still physically demanding. However, there was nothing that they made us do that our bodies could not take if we were in average shape. Where the major disparity came into play was in a person's mental toughness.

People who were mentally tough did what they had to do. Not all of them succeeded, but they sure as hell did not quit or give up. For the most part, the people who stuck to their guns and said, "I can handle whatever they throw at me" were the ones who made it. These Rangers might not have performed the best, and they might not have been the biggest PT studs, but they were strong enough mentally to move on to the next day, doing what they were told to do, and making it through.

You could tell the mentally tough people only after watching them in action. You had to expose the real toughness by taking everything away from them to see what they were made of. We never train to that level of intensity in the regular peacetime Army. When we go out and train, we do not put soldiers in a situation where they have to be extremely mentally tough. We try to do it with continuous operations, and you do have to be tough to do something like that, but the average soldier, unless he has been in combat, is never tested to the point that we were tested at Ranger School. My experiences allowed me to get to know myself, and that knowledge affects how I am as a leader and a person.

I hold people to a higher standard as a result of going through Ranger School. I am definitely not someone to complain to if you are looking for sympathy. I usually do not have a whole lot of it. In the field, I expect people to be training for combat, and I want to ensure that they are mentally tough. I do not accept excuses. I know what I have been through, and if soldiers are complaining about the picnic or camping trip we call field training, how would they react if they were put in a really stressful situation? I do not want to give them sympathy. I want to push them hard, beyond their known limits, and try to increase their mental strength and self-knowledge.

Ranger Adams' Walk

You are about to get an "A=Apple" truth of leadership, and a "nanny-nanny-boo-boo" of success. Both are simple but essential concepts.

The first is, you do not have to ask permission to succeed. Steve Adams does things because he can, or at least because he can try. Once you accept this statement, it is a great liberator. You don't have to ask permission to succeed! Sadly, this is novel thinking today. Everyone is waiting around, listening to the radio and TV hoping someone will tell them that it is okay to succeed. Then they are waiting for a simple road map to walk them through the steps. This is "A=Apple" most basic lesson. You have had permission to succeed all along, so now go do it.

The road map to success looks like the paths the Rangers took out of the swamp that horrible night. The trails zig and zag, stop and go; they cross each other and backtrack; and unfortunately, in some cases they stop short. From the time you disembark from your Zodiac, you have only one choice, and that is to move forward. Here comes the "nanny-nanny-boo-boo"—you have to keep going until you're done.

Everything we see and do is ultimately finite. One of the reasons that such a small minority achieves success is that few understand that the length and direction of the path to success is not measurable until after it's completed. Certainly success can be clearly defined, but the path can feel like a scramble through a dark swamp. Intermediate goals are the trees, and success is dry ground where we can build a fire. But nobody knows the route ahead of time and nobody knows how long it will take.

Recognizing this for yourself is one thing, but as a leader you are not alone. Your team needs to realize the innate ambiguity of the path and have permission to succeed and do whatever it takes to get the job done.

Conclusion

There are so many parts to our daily lives. We have our goals and we also have a generous helping of distractions, conflicting priorities, overlapping alliances, and emotions. Life is messy. It can be absolutely chaotic to be a leader. Why did I include stories about hamburgers, and peter ropes, and spooning? Because they were there! They are there in your situation, too, and they won't disappear when you start going 100 miles an hour toward your goal.

The Rangers of *No Excuse Leadership* took you on a unique journey to illuminate leadership lessons. Those lessons progressed from the prerequisite of perseverance to the liberating permission to succeed. The examples in between created a framework of solid leadership practices and principles that you can start using today.

Immediately you can begin evaluating your team's direction. We discussed directions and goals about as much as we talked about being hungry. My story discusses the importance of a worthwhile direction to increased motivation. Tex Turner involves his team in establishing the direction, Mark Chandler illustrates the importance of knowing what the end goal looks like, and Dave Stockwell tells us that to reach the end of a mission, you have to identify the details of your journey before you start. The central importance of a plan is undeniable. If carrying out the plan were as easy in real life as it is to put on paper there would be no need for leaders. You are the one who maintains focus and whips out flashlights in the middle of a tactical mission and gives a motivational ass-chewing.

Lance Bagley explained that a plan is all fine and good, but if it isn't in line with your personal integrity, you had better change it fast. Only when you have satisfied yourself on this point will you have the

265

ability to really achieve long-term success. Eric Werner reminded us that if you start with perseverance and a no excuse attitude, you have a better chance of instilling success habits in your team and keeping everyone on the same side. Against seemingly insurmountable odds, the momentum of your team will carry you past the obstacles in your way. This kind of growth in capabilities and confidence will make what once was hard easy. John Hutt makes the point that the trials are worthwhile because they develop the leader's confidence and expectations. In the end, exceptional achievement is available only to those with high self-esteem. And high self-esteem is available only to those who have persevered.

Scott Sharp not only persevered, he showed us the importance of conscientious, involved leadership. Once we're satisfied with the plan and we begin its execution, it is critical for leaders at any experience level to do their duty. To make our story complete, Steve Adams made it clear that you have to continue to do your duty until you are done.

Leadership is fascinating and tiring. It can be untidy and frenzied, and it can be rewarding like nothing you've ever done in your life. Not surprisingly, writing about leadership shares those same characteristics. The leadership rope is knotted in each story around the two leadership principles I highlighted at the beginning of our time together.

Seek responsibility and take it for your actions and know yourself and seek self-improvement.

These two leadership principles are the common threads of this book. They can be the common threads of your life, but you must act on your knowledge. When the movie director says, "Action!" everyone except one person moves; the exception is the dead body in the center of the room. He lies there waiting to be taken away and buried while everyone else moves on with life. Don't simply lie face down until it's your time to be taken away and buried. Take action now!

Colonel Turner summed up responsibility well. "You can't listen to those who tell you that you can't." Those are the people who can't. They are excuse makers. They think in terms of "Why can't I?" as opposed to "How do I?" The answer to "Why can't I?" comes in the form of an excuse. We just spent a whole book showing you examples of people who succeeded because they refused excuses. The outcomes would have been much different, and predictable, had any one of these soldiers given into the desire to quit. You must avoid excuses, both internally and externally generated. The only thing you can't do is listen to those who say you can't. No matter what decisions you make in life, you are responsible for them.

By definition, you are responsible for developing your own self-knowledge. No one else can do it for you. You've read this book and seen the personal growth that each person experienced and how it helped him later in life. None of them would be where they are today had they not moved beyond comfort to discomfort, where self-discovery happens. Have you thought about how you can grow? Have you thought about your weaknesses and how you can improve? Have you set a goal to do something that will stretch you the way I proposed you do at the beginning? If you haven't, you are following the common path of failure.

Have you wondered why some Ranger School graduates fail in life? Why, if they survived such a wonderful leadership experience, did they not succeed beyond the average? The reason is simple—they failed to take advantage of at least one of two opportunities provided by the school. They are the same opportunities you now have after reading this book. They either did not think about what there was to learn or didn't take action on the lessons they did learn. You have the power to succeed by knowing this truth. You can act on the same lessons that these graduates missed or failed to act on. You can make plans and move forward no matter where you are now!

Admittedly, part of the challenge of a book is that it is just a book. It is not a program or system that integrates into your day and helps you maintain the motivations you now feel. My ongoing mission is to help you connect the dots from concept to reality. In order to do that, you must determine that personal and organizational leadership development is something you want. I encourage you to look back to the Introduction, where I spoke about the importance of leadership philosophy, and decide to take that first critical step toward your future success.

I look forward to hearing about your triumphs.

Lead the way!

Terms, Acronyms, and Definitions

1LT First lieutenant/O-2. First promotion among the officer corps after second lieutenant. Primarily platoon leader or company/battalion staff officer.

2LT Second lieutenant/O-1. Initial rank upon commissioning into the Army. Primarily platoon leader.

5-50 Strong nylon cord with 1,001 uses in the field. It can be bought separately or cut from the risers of a parachute.

AAR After-action review. Formal or informal review of the previous operation—its strengths, weaknesses, and lessons learned.

ADA Air Defense Artillery. Branch of the Army responsible for protecting solders from attack from the air. They are equipped with different levels of ground-to-air weapons.

AG Assistant gunner. The AG position always seems to be the most thankless. You carry the tripod, which is very heavy, and in addition to that you carry the extra M60 ammo; yet the position does not receive the same recognition as the M60 gunner.

admin; going admin A low level of readiness that includes a bit of relaxation of standards, including dress, weapons, and security.

Airborne School Three-week course at Fort Benning, Georgia, designed to test students physically while preparing them technically and mentally to jump from a moving aircraft and land safely.

AIT Advanced Individual Training. Next step after basic training that teaches soldiers skills more specific to their specialties.

AK-47   Standard Soviet rifle. Very light and simple weapon, very effective under most conditions.

alice pack   *See* **rucksack.**

AOAC   Armor Officer Advanced Course. Course attended by armor officers after success as platoon leaders. Purpose is to prepare senior lieutenants and junior captains for company command.

AOBC   Armor Officer Basic Course. First course attended by new second lieutenants of the Armor Branch. Purpose is to prepare the officer for life as a platoon leader and as a member of the armed services.

APL   Assistant patrol leader.

azimuth   Direction as measured by a compass.

bat boy   Enlisted soldier from a Ranger Battalion.

BDU   Battle dress uniform. Camouflaged uniform with black, green, and brown pattern common among hunters. Primary uniform of the Army.

belay   A safety feature built into mountaineering, this person is able to stop an uncontrolled descent by a rappeller by pulling on and tightening the bottom end of the rope.

butt stroke   A favorite command in bayonet training. The rifle is lifted like a javelin, but held onto with both hands. The butt of the rifle faces your opponent and as you step toward your enemy, the butt of the rifle is thrust into his face.

C-130   Propeller-driven military aircraft used for many functions including airborne operations.

C-141   Larger jet version of propeller-driven C-130.

CAS³   Combined Arms and Services Staff School. Held at Fort Leavenworth, Kansas. The school is designed to break down and teach the military decision-making process to young officers. Part of the school focuses on proper military methods of briefing.

cat eyes   Two small strips of illumination tape sewn onto the back of a patrol cap. Used by Ranger students as guides to follow in the dark.

cellulitis   Infection of skin tissue. Can become dangerous.

chem light   Clear plastic cylinder about the size of a thick pencil containing two chemicals separated by a glass ampoule. When the ampoule is broken by bending the cylinder, the chemicals mix and create a neon light that can last for up to 12 hours.

City Week   Ranger assessment phase (RAP). The first five days of Ranger School at Fort Benning, Georgia. Testing phase designed to weed out those who are not physically prepared for the rigors of the remaining weeks of the course.

class As   Green semiformal uniform. Ribbons and nonsubdued rank are worn.

clear-cut   Refers to the waste left by loggers in the forest once they have taken out the trees. Consists of branches of all sizes strewn around like pick up sticks. They are murder to walk across because there is rarely level footing.

compass man   He is usually the second in line behind the point man in a patrol and guides the patrol on the proper azimuth as dictated by the patrol leader. The best navigators find themselves in this position often.

CPT   Captain/O-3. Second promotion among the officer corps after first lieutenant. Primarily company commander or battalion/brigade staff officer.

C ration   Precursor to the MRE. Instead of plastic bags the food came in boxes and metal cans. The metal cans required a can opener, and the cases included P-38 can openers.

CSS   Combat Service Support.

DA   Department of the Army.

Darby phase   Camp William O. Darby, Fort Benning, Georgia. Second part of Benning phase after City Week. Introduction to patrolling and stress of trying to operate while completely exhausted.

DAS-C   PreRanger course set up at Fort Knox for officers and soldiers preparing to go to Ranger School.

deadfall   *See* **clear-cut**.

desert phase   Dugway Proving Grounds, Utah, and Fort Bliss, Texas. Teaches patrolling in a desert environment. No longer a phase of Ranger School. Characterized by extremely long movements and cold nights both for summer and winter classes.

DMI   Department of Military Instruction at West Point.

droning   A semisleeping state of transformation, usually attained while walking for endless hours and with little sleep over the previous days. Symptoms include walking off into the woods by yourself, talking to trees, or trying to put quarters into a tree expecting a soda to fall out of the bottom.

DZ   Drop zone. Piece of earth designated as the landing site for soldiers during an airborne jump.

E-2   PVT, private. MOS/member of squad. Rifleman carrying an M16 rifle or assistant gunner carrying tripod and extra ammunition for M60 machine gun.

E-3   PFC, private first class. MOS/member of squad. Rifleman carrying an M16 rifle, SAW (squad automatic weapon), or M60 machine gun.

E-4   SPC, specialist. Assistant team leader.

E-5   SGT, sergeant. Team leader within a squad.

E-6   SSG, staff sergeant. Leader of squad made up of two teams.

E-7   SFC, sergeant first class. As a platoon sergeant, he is the highest ranking NCO within a platoon.

E-8   MSG/1SG, master sergeant/first sergeant. As a first sergeant, is the ranking NCO within a company; responsible for many administrative and leadership aspects of the company. As a master sergeant, works in a staff capacity at the battalion or higher.

E-9   SMG/CSM, sergeant major/command sergeant major. As a sergeant major, works in a staff capacity at the battalion or higher level. As a command sergeant major, is the ranking NCO within a battalion or higher unit. The commander's consultant on NCO affairs.

e-tool   Entrenching tool, a small, sharp-nosed shovel that folds neatly into thirds to about half the size of a laptop computer. It is used for digging holes, chopping trees, and ingeniously as a seat when utilizing a cat hole.

EIB   Expert infantryman's badge. A reward for passing a test, exclusively for infantry soldiers and officers, that demands high levels of proficiency in a series of infantry and basic soldier skills.

fart sack   Sleeping bag.

Florida phase   Camp James E. Rudder (Auxiliary Field #6), Eglin Air Force Base, Florida. Capstone phase where all of the previous learning comes into play to lead platoon-size patrols on more difficult raid missions. Characterized by long movements.

FSO   Fire support officer. Officer responsible to the battalion commander for detailed planning and consulting on the proper incorporation of artillery assets.

FTX   Field training exercise. Training conducted in a field, non-garrison environment. Anytime the students patrolled it was part of an FTX.

G-2   Intelligence officer at division level. Slang for "get intelligence."

grid coordinates   Pinpoints location on a military map using numbers to plot x- and y-axis locations.

Gulag   Two-story World War II building on the Ranger complex at Fort Benning that houses the students waiting to reenter the school.

gunnery   Firing range for tanks. Opportunity for armor commanders to see how well trained and maintained their crews and tanks are under live fire conditions with both stationary and moving targets.

humping   Walking on a march. Walking with a rucksack on.

hypothermia   Dropping of the core body temperature caused by prolonged exposure to the cold.

ID   Identification.

Ike Hall and South Aud   Nice auditoriums at West Point.

IOAC   Infantry Officer Advanced Course. Course attended by infantry officers after success as platoon leaders. Purpose is to prepare senior lieutenants and junior captains for company command.

IOBC   Infantry Officer Basic Course. First course attended by new second lieutenants of the Infantry Branch. Purpose is to prepare the officer for life as a platoon leader and as a member of the armed services.

Jump School   *See* **Airborne School.**

Kevlar   Standard protective headgear that replaced the World War II era steel pots.

LBE   Load bearing equipment. Suspenders connected to a wide green belt to which are attached canteens, ammo pouches, knives, first aid pouches, and flashlights, among other personal soldier choices. Worn at all times in the field over the BDU.

leaders recon   An opportunity for the leaders to move up close to the objective and get an idea of how they want to set up their unit to achieve success.

LOM   Lack of motivation statement. Provided to you upon your voluntary exit from Ranger School. A death blow to a successful career and an admission that you quit.

LP/OP   Listening post/observation post. Security element, at least two men, set to the front or sides of the main unit to provide early warning of an enemy's approach.

M14   Wooden stocked rifle used by the Army until the beginning of the Vietnam War, when the lighter M16 rifle replaced it.

M16 rifle   Standard U.S. Army individual weapon. Approximately 300 meter range.

M60 Machine Gun   Machine gun with approximately 1,000 meter range. Significantly heavier than M16 rifle.

mafia   A faceless group of officers and NCOs from the 82nd Airborne Division who practice nepotism in the form of continually selecting former 82nd Airborne Division soldiers for service there again, over equally qualified nonalumni.

medevac   Medical evacuation of casualty by either air or ground.

member of squad   Also called Joe, Joe Snuffy, or Schmedlap. The lowest level of responsibility you could hope to get in a patrol. His mission is to simply follow the man in front of him and not fall asleep.

minus and plus   RIs are able to reward extraordinary effort or failings with an administrative merit or demerit called pluses and minuses. There are two grades of each, majors and minors. The pluses and minuses cancel each other out at the equal level.

mountain phase   Camp Frank D. Merrill, Dahlonega, Georgia. Includes mountaineering training at Camp Merrill and Yonah Mountain. Characterized by strenuous movements over extremely rugged mountainous and wooded terrain.

MP   Military Police. The branch of the Army that enforces the law on military posts.

MRE   Meal ready to eat. One ration provided in a prepacked brown plastic container.

MSG   *See* **E-8.**

NCO   Noncommissioned officer. Encompasses the ranks of E-5/SGT through E9/SMG. Referred to as the backbone of the Army.

OCS   Officer Candidate School. Accepts qualified candidates from among enlisted soldiers and NCOs to produce officers.

OER   Officer evaluation report. Army system for rating and ranking officers. It is a series of checked boxes and remarks by an officer's chain of command at least on an annual basis that refers to the officer's performance over the previous rated period.

OPORD   Operations order. Military method of organizing information of complex missions for understandable dissemination.

ORP   Objective rally point.

P-38 can opener   A tiny little metal handle, not more than an inch and a half long, and a curved blade that hinges off of the handle.

PAO   Public affairs officer. Represents the unit with the media.

PCS   Permanent change of station.

peer evaluations; to peer; peered   Rating system performed at the end of each phase within each squad. Each person ranks the other members of his squad, using a number from highest to lowest. The person who receives the lowest peer ratings within his squad is removed from the squad, recycled from the class, or removed from the entire school. Present long before *Survivor.*

peer ratings   Ability of each Ranger student to rank each member of his squad in order from best to worst. Forced distribution. Those students with the lowest percentage rating are often recycled or dropped from the course. Other wise known as being peered.

PFC   *See* **E-3.**

Plus and minus   *See* **Minus and plus.**

pogie   Food/snacks.

point man   A security element designed to see the enemy first and warn the following patrol without giving himself away and allowing the rest of the patrol to react without being surprised by the enemy. He is the lead man in a patrol.

POW Prisoner of war. Also PW.

PSG Platoon sergeant. Ranking NCO within a platoon. Usually an E-7/SFC or E-6/SSG.

PT Physical training. Usually consists of calisthenics, push-ups, sit-ups, side straddle hops, and so on, and a run.

PVT *See* **E-2.**

Ranger Battalion Airborne organization designed for quick response and deployment to combat areas. Extremely fast mechanism for projection of American military force. Designed to hit hard and secure an area. All NCOs and above are required to be Ranger qualified.

Ranger eyes *See* **cat eyes.**

Ranger Regiment Coordinating headquarters over all of the Ranger Battalions.

RAP Ranger assessment phase. *See* **City Week.**

recycle The removal of a student from a class for any number of reasons and giving him the opportunity to repeat that phase before continuing on to finish the course. The repeating of a phase.

RHB *Ranger Handbook*. Ranger student bible. One-stop reference center for Ranger missions and information.

RI Ranger instructor. Cadre of Ranger School. Walks with and evaluates students on their patrols. Responsible for giving a go or no-go to the student.

RIP Ranger Indoctrination Program. Preparatory course for soldiers going to a Ranger Battalion.

ROTC Reserve Officers' Training Corps. Nationwide college program that prepares students for service as officers in the armed services.

RTO Radio telephone operator. A long way of saying he is the guy who carries the PRC-77 radio and extra batteries and constantly monitors the radio for traffic.

rucksack Dark green or camouflaged large backpack used for carrying all equipment needed for military operations in the field. Often contains all items necessary for several days without resupply. Frequently weighs 60 to 80 pounds or more. Also called an alice pack.

S-1 Adjutant. Staff member responsible for every crappy administrative action you can think of. At the battalion level the adjutant keeps the commander's calendar and is responsible for the Personnel Action Center (PAC).

S-2 Intelligence officer at battalion and brigade level.

S-3 A battalion-level staff position held by a major, also referred to as the operations officer. He is responsible for the planning of tactical operations and much of the coordination within the battalion staff.

sat Satisfactory.

SAW Squad automatic weapon.

SFC *See* **E-7.**

SGT *See* **E-5.**

shelter half Half of a small two-man tent. Your buddy has the other half. Made of heavy canvas.

sick call Opportunity for soldier to see medic in reference to a physical complaint/injury.

slug Slang name for punishment imposed at West Point meaning the cadet would walk the area.

SMG *See* **E-9.**

SPC *See* **E-4.**

SSG *See* **E-6.**

stand in the gap Many interpretations: Stand between freedom and its enemy. Fill the unholy space of the battlefield when no others will.

T-1 Wire-connected telephone. A step above two cans and a string.

TA 50 Military field equipment. Includes items like canteens, LBE, Kevlar, and e-tool.

TAC officer, OCS Tactical officers at OCS are responsible for one company of candidates and act not only as cadre, but also as a point of contact for administrative actions.

TAC officer, West Point Tactical officers at West Point are captains responsible for a company of cadets. They enforced discipline, pass information from the military chain of command, and act as an information source for the cadets.

TMC Troop Medical Clinic. Small treatment facility where most minor ailments are diagnosed and treated.

TRADOC U.S. Army Training and Doctrine Command.

TVD Tennessee Valley Divide. A portion of the Appalachian Mountains that Ranger School uses to test the students with an extremely steep climb while on patrol.

walk the area A contrived West Point punishment where cadets literally do walk the area. It is doled out in hours, usually four or eight, but can get much worse. Saturday, cadets are inspected and then set to walking back and forth in Central Area.

XO Executive officer. A battalion-level staff position held by a major. The XO is the senior staff officer in the battalion, responsible for coordinating the different functions in the battalion and acting as the second in command of the battalion.

Index

Corporate Leadership Training

Part of the objective of *No Excuse Leadership* is to create as much of a positive impact on your understanding of leadership as possible. With that worthwhile goal in mind, it makes sense to coach these principles and integrate them into the daily lives of people and companies who wish to be guided.

Every company has untapped leadership potential. It is that margin between today's performance and its potential that is the margin of victory in tomorrow's market. There is no opting out of the leadership decision. You either develop your leaders through purposeful, planned effort, or you choose an alternative. Unfortunately, the alternatives are expensive, frustrating, and time-consuming.

To reap the benefits of an enthusiastic leadership core that plays from the same sheet of music, I recommend corporate leadership training that is customized to your organization's needs. You want to raise your leadership quotient as close to possible to its potential—and keep it there.

As a business owner, I empathize with the need for constant leadership attention and development within an organization. I am currently the founder and owner of nine distinct businesses. Two businesses are multimillion-dollar enterprises, with two more right on their heels. They represent seven different industries, and at least six of the businesses are designed to operate nationally. Regardless of the details of their work, the leadership skills of my companies' management remain the most important component of our success.

I think that business math is pretty simple. There is a positive, exponential relationship between leadership capital and monetary capital. I believe that corporate leadership training develops the latent leadership potential in organizations and turns it into kinetic energy directed at innovating efficiencies, increasing profit, and strengthening their competitive position.

I have full contact information at www.NoExcuseLeadership.com.

—Brace Barber